# YBOR CITY

## POCKET GUIDE

**Second Edition**

Phil Sauerbrun

YBOR CITY POCKET GUIDE
by Phil Sauerbrun

Printed in USA by KDP and IngramSpark
ISBN: 9798986713243 (paperback, 2nd edition)
ISBN: 9798986713250 (ebook)
SECOND EDITION

Contributors: Joe King Carter, Tracy Midulla, Lucas Campoe, Arminda Mata, Marcolina Mercado-Perez
Proofreaders First Edition: Rosalie Simms, Sandra Alfieri
Cover Design and Formatting: Pique Publishing, Inc., Alejandro A. Martin
Additional Formatting: Alejandro A. Martin, Bloom Design Agency
Marketing: Mary Walewski, Buy the Book Marketing



Maps by Maptive
Comments and changes in information may be provided to yborcityguide@gmail.com.

COVER: The front entrance to the Columbia Restaurant in the middle of the 21st Street block of 7th Avenue. Its 52,000 square feet is testimony to not only it being the largest Spanish Restaurant but to its continued resurgence in the face of a neighborhood that was in serious decline for many decades following the Depression. The exterior is adorned with exquisitely designed tile from Spain.

"This offering is a comprehensive guide to Ybor City's rich history and community of businesses and sites. . . an invaluable resource for anyone interested in Ybor City's unique immigrant history or its current status as a vibrant destination."
*—Joe King Carter, artist, historian, civic leader*

"Delve into the legacy of Ybor City through the pages of this book. Start with the Ybor Visitor's Center, take one of the many historic walking tours, check out the Ybor City Museum. End your day with dinner at the historic Columbia Restaurant."
*—David Alvarez, Truist Bank*

*"The experience of exploring Ybor City validates the rich history of our diverse nation, that we all have a point of origin beyond these shores that can be acknowledged and valued."*
*—Phil Sauerbrun, author*

**Other books by Phil Sauerbrun:**

This Second Edition of the ***Ybor City Pocket Guide*** is the first in a series on Ybor City. The second book is ***YBOR CITY, Its Story in Pictures*** was released in 2024. A biography of Vicente Martinez Ybor will be released in 2026.

# How to Use This Guidebook

**1. Look over the Table of Contents briefly.** Best places to park, streetcar transportation, and accommodations can be reviewed in Section 1 if you need further information.

**2. Plan Your Time.** Start at the Ybor City Visitor Information Center. Watch the 7 minute video on Ybor City and browse the gift shop. The staff is there to assist you in planning your time in Ybor.

**3. Know About the Historical Figures.** Read the short biographies of the two key people of Ybor City history, Vicente Martinez Ybor and Jose Marti, either at the beginning or end of your day.

**4. Identify an Area to Explore.** Under *Ybor City at a Glance*, section 4, check out the list of what to see under the headings West Side, East Side, North Side to give you a brief look at Ybor City.

**5. Explore Ybor City's Street Scene.** Walk down Ybor City's famed 7th Avenue, read about the historical sights of the area(s) you have chosen to check out, of the West Side (p.117-130), or East Side (p.131-138), or North Side (p.139-143) as you encounter them.

**6. Explore the Cultural Dynamic of Ybor City.**
(a) Visit a Couple of the Museums. For starters check out the Ybor City Museum State Park and J. C. Newman Cigar Factory. (b) Read about one or more of the seven ethnic groups that came to live in Ybor City in section 6 and their contributions to the life, work and culture of Ybor City. (c) At Cigar Shops with baristas, enjoy a café con leche and see the intricate art of cigar rolling. (d) Section 8 is about how the roosters became an icon.

**7. Sign up for a Tour.** Choose one of the remarkable walking tours of Ybor in section 10. Several are mentioned covering the following subjects: Historical, Factory, Food, and Ghost. Same day registration is not always possible but check the websites of a tour that interests you. If time does not permit a scheduled tour consider a self-guided walking tour or car tour in section 13.

**8. Indulge in the Food.** You're going to need to eat while in Ybor if only to take a break. Historical restaurants include the Columbia Restaurant, Carmine's, Bernini. The eateries include Italian and Hispanic cuisine, Cafés, Coffee Houses, Pubs, Craft Beer Establishments, southern cuisine. A wide range of Latino food has become blended. Commit to experiencing the unique flavors of Ybor City: café con Leche, a Cuban sandwich and Devil Crab.

**9. Consider Places to Go and Things to Do with Children**, section 14.

**10. Experience the Arts and Culture Scene** including architecture, statuary, murals, Kress Contemporary (Ybor's arts center) which hosts the Florida Museum of Photographic Arts, rotating exhibits, galleries, and performances. In addition, check out the art scene at the Hillsborough College, Ybor City Campus Performing and Visual Arts.

**11. Take in local shopping at Saturday Market, Vintage Shopping**, and **Specialty Foods.**

# TABLE OF CONTENTS

## YBOR (IBOR): Derivation and Origin of Name

The Spanish spelling of the word Ybor was Ibor. Don Vicente Martinez Ybor changed the spelling from the Spanish Ibor to Ybor when he emigrated from Cuba, believing that it would facilitate pronunciation in the United States (US).

V. M. Ybor was born in Valencia on the Mediterranean coast of southeastern Spain. The name appears in village names and that of a river in southern Spain. Early in its history, the Ibor family is recorded as having fought the Moors for the survival of the Spanish kingdom.

Ibor is of Celtic-Asturian origin meaning "Yew tree." The range of Celtic civilization stretched from the northern coast of Spain (Asturias) to coastal France, to the British Isles including Wales, Ireland, and Scotland. The Yew tree has significance dating from ancient times. Its scientific name is *Taxus baccata*. It is a species of evergreen tree native to many parts of Europe especially southern Europe extending into Spain and North Africa and through Italy. It is an ornamental plant producing red berries and miniature cones, and most parts of the plant are poisonous. The Asturian word is *taxu* referring to its toxicity and *baccata* is Latin for "bearing berries." The tree can grow to significant size and can achieve 400 to 600 years, with some making it to 1,000 years. The oldest specimen in Spain is in Bermiego, Asturias.

In Asturian culture, the tree was linked to the province, its land and people, and the ancient Celtic religion. It was customary in early Christianity on All Saints' Day to bring a Yew limb to the tombs of those who had died in the past year. It can be found around churches, chapels, cemeteries, and in the main square of villages in southern Europe. Since ancient times the Yew tree has been a symbol of transcendence of death. They were planted because their long life was symbolic of eternity even though its poisonous nature reflected mortality. The tree symbolizes life through death. The Celts believed in the transmigration of the soul with the soul surviving death to move on and be reborn in a new life. In ancient times the Yew was an emblem of death. In Christianity, death was the precursor of life beyond the grave.

Hence Ybor City, a community that underwent its own death before living on in its new characterization and designation as a national historic landmark district, is preserving its life for the ages yet to come.

### SOURCE

Wikipedia, s.v. "Taxus baccata," last modified July 14, 2021, https://en.wikipedia.org/wiki/Taxus_baccata.

# INTRODUCTION

## A POCKET GUIDE

This pocket guide is published to promote the heritage of Ybor City in its numerous facets. Much of the information provided herein is disseminated on a regular basis at the Ybor City Chamber of Commerce Visitor Information Center and geared to the most frequently asked questions.

To provide information within a compact pocket edition, not all aspects of Ybor City, its heritage, and its many locations are included. This publication is intended as a starting point for more information, exploration, and learning about Ybor City. In some ways, this guide is a primer for understanding a unique story in the American experience based on the one overriding characteristic of our national history—immigration.

## AN IMMIGRANT COMMUNITY - A HISTORICAL OVERVIEW

The settlement of Tampa officially started with the establishment of Fort Brooke in the 1820s, and the town struggled for its first sixty years. When Don Vicente Martinez Ybor arrived from Key West in 1885 to check out Tampa, the population was only seven hundred. Tampa almost missed out on Mr. Ybor moving his cigar-making operation from Key West as he rejected an exorbitant sales price, but Tampa business leaders made up the difference as Ybor was preparing to leave town. In late 1885, following his initial purchase of 40 acres, he had the town laid out and cleared. The swampy areas were filled in and his first factory, a wooden structure was under construction.

Mr. Ybor had been attracted by the deep water port and the rail line that Henry Plant had just completed earlier in 1885 from Sanford, which stopped near the Hillsborough River but was later moved to Ybor City. By the end of the decade, Mr. Plant's large luxury hotel was nearing completion and Mr. Ybor's new brick cigar factory, the largest in the world at the time, was in operation. A massive fire in Key West, destroying many cigar factories, further motivated cigar workers to consider Tampa. The story of Tampa is: "If you build it, they will come." * Mr. Ybor invited many of his competitors to come and set up shop in Ybor City, and he built hundreds of homes for the cigar workers and sold them basically at his cost and offered no-interest loans.

By 1888, the population of Tampa was about 3,000, and by the 2010 census the population of the area had exceeded 3 million. The development of Tampa was jump-started by the cigar industry. In the first decade of the 20th century, Tampa became known as the "Cigar City," and in the following decade as the "Cigar Capital of the World." Millions of cigars were rolled each year. The town was constantly under construction for its first 20 years as factories appeared, along with community centers and retail businesses.

The Cubans, of Hispanic and African origin, and the Spanish arrived in Tampa first. They were followed by the Italians and Sicilians, the Germans,

Romanians, and others. Each group had its niche in the community's cigar economy. They worked and lived side by side, peaceably for the most part, in the primarily Latin Quarter of the growing Tampa. Ybor City is the epitome of a story that best characterizes America as a land of immigrants.

There were difficult times at the beginning. The environment—with its heat, mosquitoes, alligators, and snakes—was hostile. Labor disputes resulted in strikes. Embargoes and tariffs by both the US and Spanish-run Cuba impacted tobacco and cigars, which were used as a matter of foreign policy, placing the cigar industry at their mercy. The most difficult challenges were the Great Depression, the advent of cigarettes (a cheaper alternative to cigars), and the mechanization of cigar production. People cut back on cigar consumption as the world economy contracted, and Ybor City began a period of decline in the 1930s.

By the 1960s, urban renewal had begun with the destruction of abandoned buildings and the construction of major highways through the community. Without a funded rebuilding plan, the urban renewal initiative hastened the community's decline. Later in the 1980s, artists initiated the revitalization of Ybor City by establishing a community that occupied abandoned buildings at affordable rents. They moved in, renovated, and set up living quarters and studios. Bars and eateries followed. By the 1990s, Ybor City, the fourth ward of Tampa, achieved historical landmark designation, and the restoration began in earnest.

The flavor of different cultures, of different communities, of different cuisines, of different ways of life are all here to be explored and celebrated. To begin your Ybor City journey, you'll find the basics in this guide. Let's get started!

*Paraphrase of the quote from the 1989 US film, Field of Dreams, "If you build it, he will come."

# 1 PRACTICALITIES



## DIRECTIONS AND PARKING

If you are arriving in Ybor City for a day visit, parking and transportation is more than adequate to meet your needs.

### *Directions*

Located between I-4 and the Selmon Expressway in the City of Tampa, the two corridors leading to historic Ybor City are accessible by I-275 and I-75 from the north and south.

From the north

- on I-275, proceed east on I-4 to exit #1.
- on I-75, proceed west on I-4 to exit #1.

From the south

- on I-275, proceed east on Selmon Expressway to exit #9.
- on I-75, proceed west on Selmon Expressway to exit #9.

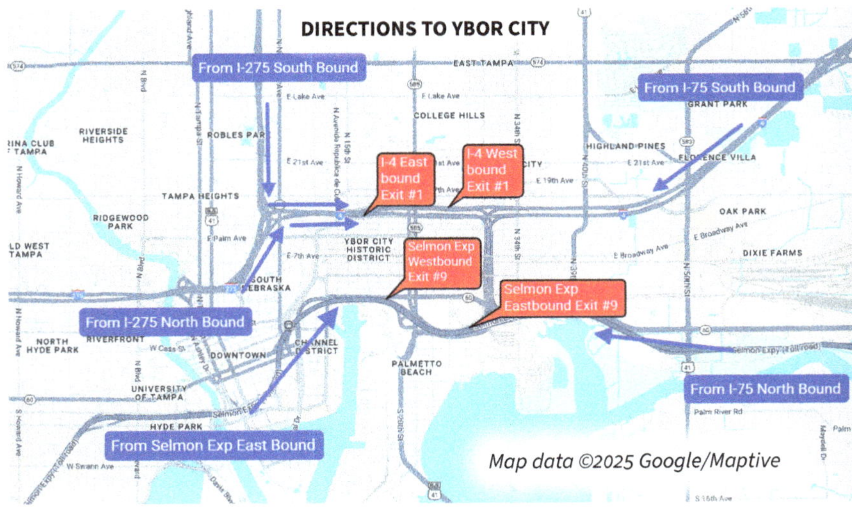


### *Parking*

Ybor City has three main parking **garages**, two on the west side of the historic district, the Fernando Noriega and Palm Avenue Garages, and one on the south side, Centro Ybor Garage.

The current rates in Ybor City Historic District for City of Tampa public parking:
**Garages** - first hour $1, every hour after $2, daily maximum $12. Next day charges start at 6am.
**Lots** - first two hours $0, every hour after $2, daily maximum $12.
**Street** - first hour $2, every hour after $2.

• City of Tampa Lots, street, and garage (deck) parking in the Centro Ybor garage is prepaid either through a nearby kiosk or the use of the app, parkmobile. For lots and street parking, the kiosk for prepaying is located within the lot or within the block if parking on the street.

• The information required for parking includes: plate number, the zone # of the space, the length of time parking is intended, and a credit card.

• In the Centro Ybor Garage and at the Noreiga and Palm Avenue Garages, the kiosks are located near elevators on each level. The deck must be exited after the parking period has expired unless parking is renewed through the parkmobile app or at the kiosk.

• Credit card required for payment at all parking locations. There is a short grace period in order to process payment upon arrival in the three parking garages.

**West Side (see map):**

- **Fernando Noriega Garage.** Use entrance at E. 8th Avenue near N. 13th Street, diagonally across from Friends of José Martí Park and the Cadrecha Streetcar Station (#4).
- **Palm Avenue Garage.** Access this garage from E. 9th Avenue between N. 13th Street and Nuccio Parkway.
- **Centro Ybor Garage.** Use entrance on N. 16th Street, or the entrance on N. 15th Street.

**East Side (see map):**

- **Fernando Noriega Garage.** This is adjacent to the Cadrecha Streetcar Station (#4) which can be taken to the East side by a 6-minute ride to Centennial Park Station (#1).
- Three public lots are south of Centennial Park's E. 8th Avenue location:
    - On the south side of E. 8th Avenue across from the park between N. 18th (Angel Oliva Senior) Street and N. 19th Street.
    - On E. 8th Avenue across from Centennial Park Station (#1) between N. 19th Street and N. 20th Street.
    - On E. 6th Avenue between N. 19th Street and N. 20th Street.
- **Columbia and Casa Santo Stefano Restaurants.** Parking in marked adjacent lots is free if dining there.
- **Hillsborough County Sheriff's Office in Ybor City.** Parking may be available in lots adjacent to the Sheriff's Office if conducting business or going to the Sheriff's Office History Center and are located off of 9th Avenue between 19th and 20th Streets. Parking is also available in lots across the street from Centennial Park along 8th Avenue.

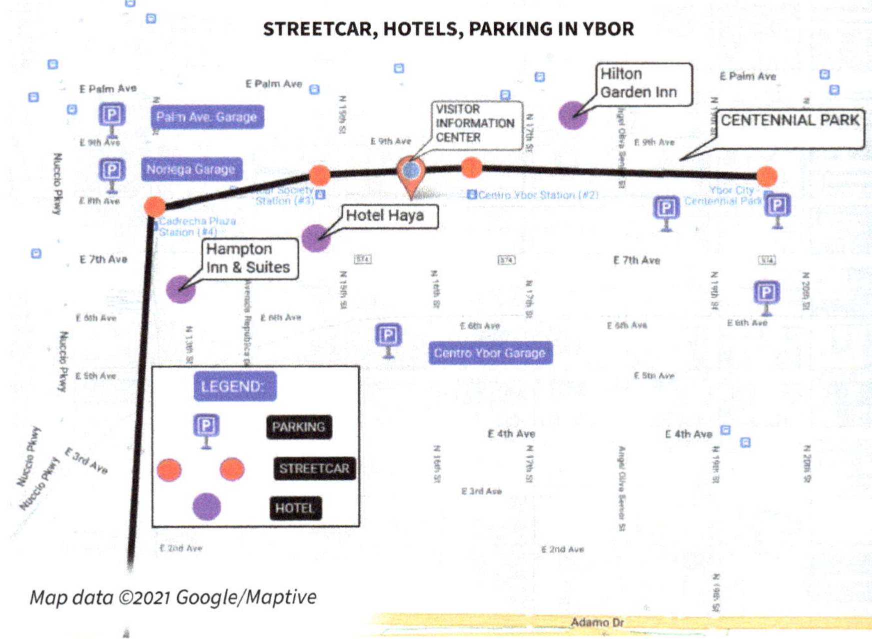


*Tourist Bus Parking*
This is available on E. 12th Avenue between N. 15th and 17th Streets.

## TRANSPORTATION

### *Streetcar*

The Tampa streetcar system, TECO, serves Ybor City with four stations and runs along 8th Avenue. Don't be confused by the single track, the streetcars go in both directions every 15 minutes, and they bypass one another on side tracks. The system continues beyond Ybor as it makes a sharp turn to the south into Tampa proper for 7 more stations, each providing visitors with points of interest. The streetcar is currently free, and no ticket is required. You just hop on and off at your pleasure at the various stations. Streetcar fares may be resumed in the near future.

Streetcar Hours of Operation
Monday – Thursday, 7am to 11pm
Friday, 7am to 2am
Saturday, 9am to 2am
Sunday, 8:30am to 11pm
The schedule is subject to change and can be confirmed at: www.tecolinestreetcar.org. For more information on hours of operation or other questions, call HART (Hillsborough Area Rapid Transit) information line at (813) 254-4278.

**Ybor Stations from East to West**

- **Centennial Park Station #1.** This station is near the Ybor City Museum State Park, the Tampa Baseball Museum at the Al Lopez House, Ybor City Saturday Market, the Columbia Restaurant, and other restaurants, cafés, pubs, and nightclubs.
- **Centro Ybor Station #2.** This station is near Centro Ybor Parking Garage, Centro Ybor businesses and shopping district, the Ybor City Visitor Information Center, the Hilton Garden Inn, Kress Contemporary Arts Center including the Florida Museum of Photographic Arts, and restaurants, cafés, pubs, and nightclubs.
- **Streetcar Society Station #3.** This station is near the Hillsborough College campus and Art Gallery, The Ybor Ritz event venue, and Hotel Haya.
- **Cadrecha Plaza Station #4.** This station at the West Side of Ybor is near such sights as the Noriega Garage, Rough Riders Park, the Friends of José Martí Park, the Vicente Martinez Ybor Factory complex (Ybor Square), El Pasaje (the Cherokee Club), and El Circulo Cubano (the Cuban Club)



**Additional Points of Interest Along the Streetcar Line into Tampa**

- **Port Tampa Bay Station #5.** Cruise Terminals
- **York Street Station #6** Cruise Terminals
- **The Florida Aquarium Station #7.** Florida Aquarium, Cruise Terminals, American Victory Ship Museum
- **Amalie Arena Station #8.** Sparkman Wharf, Tampa Bay History Center, Riverwalk, Amalie Arena, Tampa Water Taxi
- **HSBC Station #9.** Brooke Park, Amalie Arena, Marriott Hotels
- **Dick Greco Plaza Station #10.** Tampa Convention Center, Embassy Suites, Cross Bay Ferry, Pirate Water Taxi
- **Hattricks Station #11.** End of the line, Visit Tampa Bay (Visitors Center) (3 blocks north)

### *Streetcar Stations Map*

1. Centennial Park
2. Centro Ybor
3. Streetcar Society
4. Cadrecha Plaza
5. Port Tampa Bay
6. York Street
7. The Florida Aquarium
8. Amalie Arena
9. HSBC
10. Dick Greco Plaza
11. Hattricks

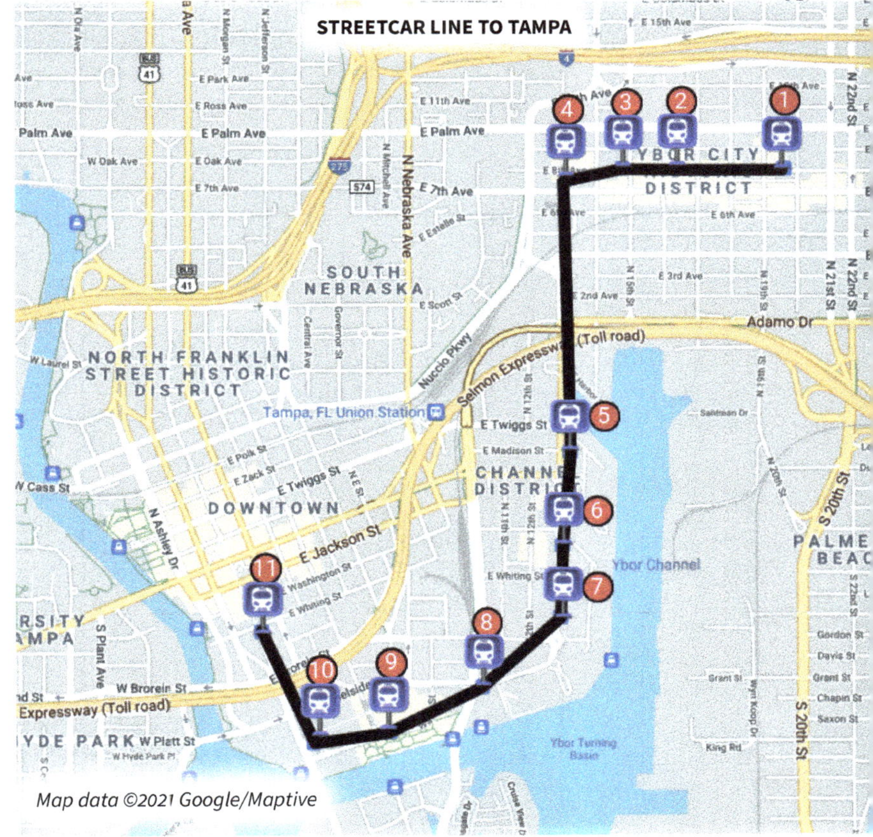


## ACCOMMODATIONS

Ybor City offers plentiful accommodations for those planning more than a day visit. Their accessibility to downtown Tampa makes them a convenient place to stay in the metro area. Reserve at least several weeks in advance. Check on rooming options through their websites. To get the best deals, book directly with the hotel by phone indicated below.

### In the Historic District

There are currently three hotels in the historic district. The rates for one night, single occupancy range from $180 to $220 per night. Different holiday and seasonal rates will apply. Rates fluctuate based on the following conditions: type of room, number of guests, number of nights, arrival and departure dates, special events in Tampa, special service requests (including cheapest room). All three hotels have room rate calculators on their websites. Make sure you are on the hotel website for Ybor City when viewing rates. Check the rates using the hotel's room rate calculator which will include taxes and other fees added to the room, then call to make reservations by phone as discounted rates are sometime applied to those posted rates on the website. Call back later to confirm room type, dates, and cost. If you cancel, please give as much notice as possible. Take advantage of free breakfasts which are usually great and a time saver if on a hectic business or sight seeing schedule. Each hotel comes with amenities some of which incur an additional cost.

The night rates in Ybor City are very competitive with hotels downtown. Parking rates are lower in Ybor City than many locations downtown. With limited parking downtown and free streetcar transportation, hotels in Ybor City are a great travel option.

**Hampton Inn**
1301 E. 7th Ave., Tampa, FL 33605
**Phone:** (813) 247-6700 (call to make reservations)
**Hotel class:** 3-star hotel
Located two blocks from both the Cadrecha Station and the Streetcar Society Station, this establishment is part of the Hilton chain and provides all the standard conveniences. For information and room rates: Google: Hampton Inn Ybor City room rates

**Hilton Garden Inn**
1700 E. 9th Ave., Tampa, FL 33605
**Phone:** (813) 769-9267 (call to make reservations)
**Hotel class:** 3-star hotel
The Inn provides almost all the amenities one would expect under the Hilton brand. It is located one block from Centennial Park, two museums, and the Centro Ybor Station is one block away. The hotel lies in the very center of the historic district. For information and room rates Google: Hilton Garden Inn Ybor City room rates

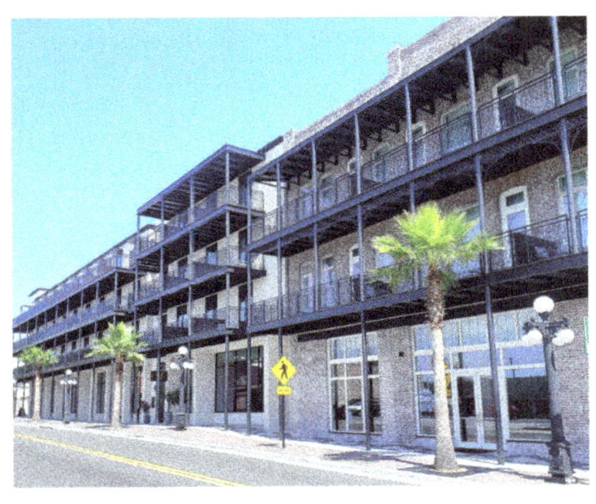

**Hotel Haya**
1412 E. 7th Ave., Tampa, FL 33605
**Phone:** (813) 568-1200 (call to make reservations)
**Hotel class:** 4-star hotel
Named after Ignacio Haya, a friend of Vicente Martinez Ybor who also bought property at the time Ybor did in 1885. Haya built his own factory, producing the first cigar in Ybor City. This boutique hotel opened mid-2020 and features many high-end services. It also

provides meeting services. It's a Top Ten Winner of best new hotels in the US in 2020, placing second. Accessible to and from Tampa by the Streetcar Society Station. For information and room rates: https://www.hotelhaya.com. Valet parking is available for guests staying at the hotel or dining there.

## *SAFETY*

As in most urban neighborhoods, crime does occur. Visitors to Ybor City should use common sense to avoid being victims of crime. This ward of Tampa is patrolled by the Tampa City Police and utilizes private security services. The streets are also patrolled by a group of **yellow shirt Ambassadors** who are the first level of assistance to visitors in the historic district. At night, it is advised that visitors park close to their destination and travel in groups. Pickpocket incidents do occur, so wallets and purses should be secure. Public displays of excessive drinking behavior can result in charges.

## *DRESS CODE*

While most establishments in Ybor City state there is no dress code, almost all require shoes, and some have restrictions for scant clothing. Restrictions can be confirmed by checking the websites of the various establishments. Appropriate dress will allow access to all venues.

# 2
# A STARTING POINT
## THE VISITOR INFORMATION CENTER



To get your bearings, plan on stopping by the **Ybor City Chamber of Commerce Visitor Information Center**.
1600 E. 8th Ave., Suite B104
(813) 241-8838
info@ybor.org
https://www.ybor.org/vic

The Visitor Information Center (VIC) makes a great first stop in Ybor City, helping you to get oriented on what to see, what to do, and where to eat in Ybor City and Tampa. It's staffed by tourist counselors that know their Ybor. It serves as a tourist center and a mini museum. It also offers:

- A 7-minute video on the history and background of this National Historic Landmark Town
- Museum exhibits, including clothing of the turn of the 20th century, an illustrated process of the hand rolling of cigars, the lithograph process utilized by the German printing businesses to make cigar labels and bands, and a large illuminated map of the historic district

*Mini theatre which shows orientation video.*

- The Gift Shop includes a variety of books and resources on Ybor City including cookbooks featuring the ethnic cuisines of the community. The Center carries more than 60 titles of books relating to the history and culture of Ybor City and Tampa. It also includes a selection of one-of-a-kind souvenirs, T-shirts, magnets, postcards, vintage cigar labels, decals, candles, and cigar boxes.

**Location.** The VIC is between the Centro Ybor Station (#2 stop) and the Streetcar Society Station (#3) on 8th Avenue next to Funny Bone, formerly the Improv Theatre. It is an annex at the rear of Centro Español.
**Parking.** Visitors can park in the Centro Ybor garage on 5th Avenue with entrances on 15th and 16th streets, two blocks south of the VIC, or on street parking. There is no parking in front of the VIC. The Noriega Garage is also available 3 blocks to the west, adjacent to the Cadrecha Plaza Station. And 15-minute free parking for the Visitor Center is provided across from The Castle nightclub on 9th Avenue.
**Hours.** The VIC is open every day of the year except Christmas and Thanksgiving unless otherwise posted as closed on its website or Facebook. Mon-Sat: 10am-4pm; Sun: 12pm-4pm.

*Front entrance to the Ybor City Chamber of Commerce Visitor Information Center.*

# 3
# THE HEART AND SOUL OF YBOR CITY



There are numerous prominent figures in the history of Ybor City but two are particularly preeminent who can be described as its heart and soul. First is the Ybor City's founder, **Don Vicente Martinez Ybor**, who was the heart of its creation and vision. He envisioned a community of workers who owned their homes, offering a quality of life for cigar workers better than anywhere else. He planned for a city's infrastructure that would serve his workers and all who would come. The soul of Ybor City can be said to belong to **José Martí**, the driving force behind the Cuban independence movement throughout the Americas. He espoused and promoted the principles of self-government and envisioned a republic for Cuba that would invoke human rights and have democratically elected, representative government with stable institutions.

Following are brief summarized bios of each man. A knowledge of their place in the history of Ybor City is helpful to understanding the nature and character of the historic Ybor Latin community.

*Vicente Martinez Ybor, circa 1890, Tampa History Center, P.D.- US.*

## *Birth in Spain, Life in Cuba*

Vicente Martinez Ybor was born in Valencia, Spain, in 1818 to a father who was an entrepreneur, the head of an upper middle class family. The name Ibor was attached to villages and a river in a region of southeast Spain, south of Valencia. Ybor later changed the spelling with the letter "Y" substituted for the letter "I," upon moving to Key West, believing it would make pronunciation easier for those in the US.[1]

Spain like much of Europe in the 19th century was involved in frequent wars. Following its involvement in the wars against Napoleon, the country was subject to internal conflict and war abroad to retain its colonies in America. The casualty rates from these wars were very high, and Ybor's family made arrangements to have him sent to Cuba in order to avoid conscription.

Ybor arrived in Cuba at age fourteen and began work as a store clerk before becoming a cigar broker where he purchased cigars from rollers, affixed labels, named them, and marketed the cigars. He later set up his own factory after learning the cigar business from the ground up. His early success enabled him to marry in 1853 to Dona Bernada who bore him four children before her untimely death in 1862. Four years later, Ybor married Mercedes Ravilla who gave birth to another six children and survived him.[2]

Before long, Ybor was able to open his own factory after marketing the cigars of several shops. He developed the brand name, "Prince of Wales," with a label that bore the supposed image of Queen Victoria's oldest son, Edward, Prince of Wales. The brand became wildly successful and was Ybor's most famous brand.[3]

As a colonial power, Spain was interested in extracting as much wealth from the Cuban colony as possible, which resulted in taxes being levied on cigar production at various stages in the process. The population's dedication to Spain ranged from separatists who wanted independence to loyalists who were satisfied with Spanish control. There were also reformers who wanted the colonial arrangement to allow for representation and some tax revenue to benefit Cuba.

Over time even some Spanish-born immigrants, like Ybor, were beginning to think that Cuban self-government would be more pro-business. The taxes significantly reduced revenue in the industry, which encouraged many cigar producers, including Ybor, to become sympathetic to the cause of a Cuba free from Spain; they were increasingly supportive of the movement for Cuban independence.

### *Refugee/Key West and New York*





As the Ten Year's War approached in 1868, Ybor got into trouble with Spanish authorities for supporting the independence movement. Learning of his imminent arrest by Spanish authorities, Ybor hid in a friend's residence while he tried to liquidate assets in case he would need to flee Cuba. While friends vouched for him with Spanish authorities, they had been tipped off by someone with inside information regarding Ybor's support for the separatists.

Ybor fled Cuba for Key West, Florida, in 1868, becoming a refugee with limited liquid assets. He was joined by many others. Both factory owners and tabaqueros (cigar workers) were seeking refuge from the conflict in Cuba and escape from political persecution for being separatists.[4]

It was the beginning of the Ten Years' War in Cuba when Cubans rebelled against colonial authority and fought for greater control and influence. It is considered the first war for independence. A son-in-law remained in Cuba to hold Ybor's business interests together and to supply his cigar business in Key West and later New York with the Cuban, light-colored tobacco (Clear Havana), which Ybor considered to make the best cigars.[5]

For the second time in his life, Vicente Martinez Ybor had to start over in a new place, this time to reestablish his cigar business as a refugee and new immigrant in the US. His experience and business acumen enabled him to reconstruct his cigar business on the tip of Florida, which he hoped would be less restricted than the business environment in Spanish-controlled Cuba.

While Ybor constructed a new factory in Key West, he was also aware that the city was off the beaten path and initially isolated from the cigar business world. As a result, he began exploring other locations to develop his business interests. After six years in Key West, he decided to branch out to New York City and that factory construction was completed in 1876.[6]

Using an NYC ad agency, Ybor's promotion of The Prince of Wales brand with its special Havana Clear brand of tobacco enabled production to take off almost immediately. However, labor was well organized in New York, and Don Vicente began to encounter the constant demands and challenges of dealing with organized labor that he had hoped to escape from in Key West. The issues in NYC were aggravated by poor living conditions for workers and depressed wages in the manufacturing community.[7] He came to realize that the city could not be the center of his business interests.

In 1878, the Ten Years' War ended in Cuba with the Spanish back in full control and having conceded very little to the Cuban people. Cuba continued to be a colony that would be economically exploited for the benefit of Spain. Ybor wanted to be closer to Cuba now that hostilities had ended from the war and the treaty ending the conflict allowed "Separatists" to return. From Key West, he went on to Cuba to check on his business interests there, having fled ten years before. His son-in-law Ignacio Casteñada had run Ybor's cigar business profitably, and Ybor had financial reserves with which to consider his next steps.[8]



### *Labor Strife Influences Move*

After Ybor's experience with unions in New York, the labor movement was taking hold in Key West in the late 1870s. The Union of Tabaqueros frequently sought union representation in the factory so that they could have some control over who was hired and who could be made foreman. Ybor was adamantly opposed to these demands, which he perceived as losing management authority over his workers. In the 1879 Key West strike, he closed his factory for four months, but Ybor was able to settle when the workers desperately needed to return to work. He thereby avoided the union presence in his factory.[9]

Ybor had dealt with unions in Cuba and New York and knew they would eventually organize in Key West. He could expect unions to follow him wherever he went, but he thought with the right conditions, he could operate a manufacturing environment where workers would be satisfied and would not turn to unions.

Again in 1885, the workers' union pressed for higher wages and for union representatives to be able to choose the factory foreman. The union was stronger now. In the four years since the last major dispute, the ranks of union members in Key West had grown significantly. The union was increasingly able to take on the factory owners and the local law enforcement, who acted in favor of the owners. While the wage increases were negotiable with the manufacturers, any element of union control of the workplace was abhorrent to the factory owners who were willing to compromise on wage issues.

By 1885, the manufacturers had formed their own organization and decided that a strike against one factory would result in all of the factories engaging in a shutdown. They hoped that this collective action would bring a quicker settlement, but the workers refused to be intimidated by this measure. As union funds for workers ran out, the Key West union appealed for support throughout the country, including in New York and New Orleans. The newspapers carried negative stories about conditions in the cigar industry in Key West as workers relocated from Key West, expecting the strike to continue indefinitely.[10]

With the factories closed and workers moving to other manufacturing sights, Key West entered a depression. A settlement was finally reached to allow for union representation in the factory but with the agreement that the union representative would "not interfere in the management of the factory."[11]

The damage to the cigar industry was extensive. Many workers had moved away, and Key West had lost markets to other manufacturing areas that it would now try to recover. The factory owners had to go to Cuba to recruit workers due to the labor shortage. Meanwhile, Ybor, somewhat disheartened by the downturn in labor relations in Key West, was looking further north for a relocation of his operations. His sights were set to make a new beginning in a work environment he believed he could create.[12]



## *Exploring Tampa*

Organized labor had always been an element in cigar manufacturing as the cigar rollers were skilled workers which gave them bargaining clout. They could not be workers hired off the street. They had to undergo a significant training and apprenticeship process in order to be employed in cigar factories. Ybor had encountered organized labor at the centers of cigar manufacturing in North America: Havana, Key West, and NYC; and strikes had regularly affected his factories' production. He came to believe if he could move his operation to a location where cigar manufacturing had not existed, he could affect a new beginning for his industry separated from the negative labor relations of the past. In 1885, as the Key West strike progressed and at the age of 68, he decided he would start over again in a new place. Of the various sites along the Gulf of Mexico he focused on the Tampa area, in part, because it was close to his tobacco supply.

A friend of Ybor's from New York, Gavino Gutierrez, had been to Florida earlier in the year 1884 with Bernardino Gargol to investigate an investment in guava growing. They had explored the Tampa area and on their return to New York, the two stopped to visit Ybor in Key West. Gutierrez and Gargol strongly recommended the Tampa Bay area to Ybor and Ignacio Haya, a fellow factory owner who was staying with Ybor at the time, as an ideal place to locate a cigar factory. The weather was conducive to the tobacco leaf process, a railroad was soon to be completed to Tampa in 1885, and the bay provided another transportation route to receive Cuban tobacco. Ybor and Haya set out the next day after their visit on a ship bound for Tampa. They were excited by this first visit.[13]

In September, Haya and Ybor returned to Tampa with the intention of negotiating a land purchase. They were accompanied by Eduardo Manrara, Ybor's factory manager. They saw a plot of land that interested them in the northeast corner of the struggling Tampa township, population 700. The seller's asking price for the initial acreage was $9,000, but Ybor was only willing to offer $5,000 given that the area was primarily marshland and would need to be drained and filled. As Ybor was preparing to leave Tampa, members of the Tampa Board of Trade informed him that they would reimburse him for the balance of the asking price. An agreement was struck on the spot.[14]

Almost immediately after coming to terms on the land purchase, Ybor had his engineer friend, Gutierrez, survey and mark off the area by establishing a town grid. Ybor began the logistical planning for the new community which came to be known in the coming months as Ybor City. By the beginning of 1886, both Ybor and Haya had constructed their first wooden factory structures. Ybor had also begun construction of his brick factory, which would be the largest in the world at that time. The railroad was then in operation as well. Henry B. Plant, the industrialist who saw the potential of Florida, had extended the line from Sanford, Florida, which made the uncomfortable coach ride from that town an obsolete form of transportation. The rail line ran through Ybor City on the way to Tampa, and Ybor later had it extended to the port.[15]



## *Fateful Turning Points*

Ybor's life was marked by fateful turning points. The first was his being shipped off to Cuba at age fourteen to avoid conscription in Spanish wars. Another was his flight to Key West to avoid arrest for supporting the Cuban independence movement. After seventeen years in Key West, Ybor was driven to consider leaving as labor sought more decision-making influence in the factory. He believed if he could start his own working community, he could avoid labor strife.

The Tampa Board of Trade had come through with the balance of the seller's asking price on the acreage that would be Ybor City. Otherwise, the transaction, instrumental in locating Ybor's cigar business in Tampa, would have failed. Another critical event was the decision by the only bank in Tampa, a branch of a banking firm in Jacksonville, to pull out of Tampa. There were not enough business interests in Tampa to justify the continued presence of a branch there. All the fixtures had been packaged for shipping, and the bank was no longer open when Ybor and Haya received news of its impending departure.

With Ybor City in the planning stages, the potential of a cigar business in the area was not yet appreciated. However, the plans of Ybor, Haya, and Gutierrez depended on a bank that could process a payroll, extend credit, and facilitate transactions for land. Without a bank, the task of implementing a community pledged to manufacture cigars would be impossible. Mr. Haya hurried over to the bank officials and told them of the plans for a cigar industry presence in Tampa. The officials were skeptical until Haya began projecting monthly payroll amounts and the other business that the bank would do. Tampa was saved from the loss of its bank when the officials, acting on Haya's information, unpacked the fixtures, reinstalled them, and resumed banking operations.[16]

As a community, Tampa had been hanging by a thread for decades, but things were about to change.

### *Largest Cigar Factory and Town Infrastructure*





Ybor dedicated himself to accomplishing three objectives to establish his cigar-producing enterprise in his namesake town. First, he would build the largest cigar factory in the world after initially building a wooden structure. Second, he was equally dedicated to developing the infrastructure to support the community. His primary objective following a devastating fire in Key West, which destroyed many cigar factories including his own, was to adjust the logistics for the arrival of more cigar workers and factory owners. Soon the brick buildings of the factory complex were under construction, while Ybor planned for a community where ample food would be shipped in or provided locally. Third, Ybor enticed factory owners with a free ten-year lease and the building of their cigar factory in exchange for a small percentage of the revenue from their cigar manufacturing operations.[17]

Ybor addressed the issue of housing, and an adequate and healthy water supply had to be provided. He began the construction of *casitas* (little houses) on a large scale and hired local contractors. The casitas were either single family one-story houses or a two-floor structures, providing for two families. They ranged in price from $500 to $900 to which Ybor added a small percentage to the construction cost. They were sold at just above cost and loans were provided at no interest. The casitas were an enticement for workers to come to Tampa with an opportunity for home ownership—something never provided before for cigar workers.[18] This action was also an indication of Ybor's intent to build a community of workers who were independent and happy in the life that they would find in Tampa. The houses were specially designed to help the dwellers survive the harsh conditions of frontier living in Florida.[19]

Ybor also became involved in the development of the streetcar line to Tampa. He founded other businesses to develop and improve the infrastructure of the town including an insurance company, street paving, gas stations, and Tampa's first brewery. He brought in doctors and allowed his first factory, constructed of wood, to be used for the town's first mutual aid society, El Centro Español de Tampa. Ybor's business interests led to the improvement and expansion of the Port of Tampa.[20]

### *Not a Traditional Company Town*

Ybor City was not to be a company town in the same way many northern US company towns were established. In many of those environments, it was not unusual for one company to own all of the major businesses. Workers were often exploited, only allowed to purchase needed food and supplies on credit from the company stores. With low wages, personal debt increased annually, and workers were unable to move away. They became bound to the system for their entire lives.

Ybor City would be different. Ybor invited his competitors to come to Ybor with lucrative options to help them purchase land and build factories. Both Ybor and Haya established real estate firms to facilitate the purchase of additional city property and to sell to incoming factory owners. His cigar workers would be well paid, and he frequently capitulated to most demands from labor that would improve the lives of the workers. Union activity would not become militant while he was alive.[21]

Ybor took an interest in his worker's lives, providing a meeting place in his first factory building and supporting the independence movement among his workers; he also continued providing concessions in labor negotiations. Yet his magnanimity did have limitations.[22] For incidents in which militant workers undermined the productivity of the workplace, Ybor teamed up with Tampa officials and the Tampa Board of Trade which had promised him complete support for his business. He was known to deal with the most intransigent workers by deporting them.[23]



## *"If You Build It, They Will Come"**

In an America ever-expanding in all directions in the 19th century, entrepreneurs could somewhat be assured of the American Dream, which had as a motto: "If you build it, they will come." This line reflects the story of Tampa and Ybor City. From a population of 700 in 1885, the town exceeded 3,000 three years later in 1888.[24] For Ybor, this growth was partly due to the great fire in Key West in April of 1886, which destroyed much of the cigar industry including Ybor's factory. It sent cigar workers who did not wish to return to Cuba, scurrying to steamships bound for Tampa.

Yet this larger-than-anticipated influx of workers presented another crisis for Ybor, placing a great strain on the logistical planning that could accommodate a modest rate of growth. Ybor City was forced to become a boom town. The industrialist Henry Plant was constructing a luxury hotel in Tampa in 1888, following completion of the railroad. Don Vicente had completed the largest cigar factory in the world at that time on 14th Street between 8th and 9th Avenues. Casita construction went into overdrive. From a population of 3,000 in 1888, 130 years later, the population of the metro area exceeded 3 million, and it was all jump-started by the cigar industry.[25]

## *Identification with the Independence Movement*

Having escaped incarceration in Cuba for supporting the independence movement of the Cuban people, Ybor was sympathetic to the plight of the Cuban people and their desire to live in a country where individual rights and freedoms necessary for a fruitful life were guaranteed. He supported the Cuban workers' desire to meet and discuss the issues of Spanish control of Cuba and allowed his original factory building to be used as a community center for that purpose. He permitted the revolutionary José Martí to come and speak to the cigar workers on numerous occasions and to raise money for the independence movement. The lectors, the readers in the factories, read from political publications that supported the independence movement of Cuba and a new Cuban government that would be democratically governed by elected officials.[26]

*Paraphrase of the quote from the 1989 US film, Field of Dreams, "If you build it, he will come."

Less than a year and a half following Ybor's death, Theodore Roosevelt and the Rough Riders would parade down La Septima in 1898 to cheering crowds from the Columbia Restaurant to the West Side of Ybor City before turning south to waiting ships in the bay. The flotilla of men and supplies would take them to Cuba for the Spanish-American War in which Cuba won its independence.[27]

## *A Final Pilgrimage*

On December 14, 1896, Vicente Martinez Ybor died at his home in Tampa following surgery from a liver ailment just a few weeks prior. The town of Tampa was approaching 15,000 inhabitants at the time of his death. The headline in the *Tampa Tribune* the following day read, "GREAT BENEFACTOR GONE."[28]

On the day of Ybor's funeral, the town was closed during his service. The procession from his home was over a mile long to the Oaklawn Cemetery. The newspaper recorded the nearly one hundred carriages conveying the leading personalities and dignitaries of the day and lists many by name. It only briefly referred to the large crowd of pedestrians who followed from the rear. The pedestrians gathered in large measure by their communities. There were groups of Spaniards. Near them were Hispanic and Afro Cubans, followed by Italians. Romanians, and others of eastern European descent including Jews, as well as Germans and immigrants of other nations. were just beginning to arrive. Those present were representing the multitudes who were yet to come. They had each made their pilgrimage to America. Now they were making the 1.5-mile walk to bury the man largely responsible for their being where they were.[29]

Each group had a niche in the cigar economy, had their own social and mutual assistance centers, and spoke different languages, but they lived and worked together in the same community. On that December day, they came together as one people out of mutual respect to pay homage to the man who had made it all possible for them to escape an intolerable past life for the possibility of a new one: Don Vicente Martinez Ybor, a refugee and immigrant himself. The phenomenon of his Latin community is the story of an America formed on the foundation of immigration, exemplifying the nation's immigrant story for the ages.

# *Endnotes*

1 Wallace Reyes, *Once Upon a Time in Tampa: The Rise and Fall of the Cigar Industry* (Scotts Valley, CA: Create Space Publishing, 2013), 352.

2 L. Glenn Westfall, *Don Vicente Martinez Ybor, The Man and His Empire* (New York: Garland Publishing, Inc., 1987), 19–20.

3 Westfall, *Don Vicente Martinez Ybor,* 18–19.

4 Westfall, *Don Vicente Martinez Ybor,* 21–22.

5 Westfall, *Don Vicente Martinez Ybor,* 24–25.

6 Westfall, *Don Vicente Martinez Ybor,* 28–30.

7 Westfall, *Don Vicente Martinez Ybor,* 31–33.

8 Reyes, *Once Upon a Time in Tampa,* 350.

9 Westfall, *Don Vicente Martinez Ybor,* 37–38.

10 Westfall, *Don Vicente Martinez Ybor,* 40–46.

11 Westfall, *Don Vicente Martinez Ybor,* 45, citing *Tobacco Leaf,* New York, September 12, 1885.

12 Westfall, *Don Vicente Martinez Ybor,* 46.

13 Westfall, *Don Vicente Martinez Ybor,* 57–60.

14 Frank T. *Lastra, Ybor City, The Making of a Landmark Town* (Tampa: University of Tampa Press, 2006), 12–13.

15 Lastra, *Ybor City, The Making of a Landmark Town,* 12–18.

16 Lastra, *Ybor City, The Making of a Landmark Town,* 14.

17 Westfall, *Don Vicente Martinez Ybor,* 66–75.

18 Westfall, *Don Vicente Martinez Ybor,* 66–69.

19 Westfall, *Don Vicente Martinez Ybor,* 66.

20 Westfall, *Don Vicente Martinez Ybor,* 66–74.

21 Westfall, *Don Vicente Martinez Ybor,* 82–85; 157–158; Reyes, *Once Upon a Time in Tampa*, 63–64.

22 Westfall, *Don Vicente Martinez Ybor,* 157.

23 Westfall, *Don Vicente Martinez Ybor,* 156.

24 Lastra, *Ybor City, The Making of a Landmark Town,* 378.

25 Reyes, *Once Upon a Time in Tampa,* 59–68.

26 Westfall, *Don Vicente Martinez Ybor,* 157–158.

27 Lastra, *Ybor City, The Making of a Landmark Town,* 44–48.

28 Reyes, *Once Upon a Time in Tampa,* 352.

29 Lastra, *Ybor City, The Making of a Landmark Town,* 38–40.

# THE SOUL...JOSÉ MARTÍ (1853–1895)

*José Martí, Wikimedia Commons, public domain US.*



## *The Man Who Guided a Revolution*

The statuary of José Martí in the Americas is the most numerous of any man who has lived in the Western Hemisphere. He was a man of many talents who used his literary skills across many genres, all in support Cuba's independence from Spain. His untimely death at forty-two was a martyrdom that galvanized a movement to fulfill his dream. As a symbol of patriotism, he was referred to as the "Apostle of Cuban Independence." He was spreading the "word" of the liberated Cuba that he and many others envisioned. Yet the focus on Martí in the 20th century has often eliminated the human side of his character to remember that which was most sublime about him.

At times Martí felt too much. He became so passionate in his persuasiveness of the cause of a free Cuba that he would take risks that endangered his life. He could be uncompromising in his courses of action, standing on principle rather than seeking common ground. Martí was also emotionally tempestuous in relationships. To the very end, his life was one of fits and starts. But it was filled with a singular purpose, passion, and commitment to which only a few great leaders are able to aspire.

Martí's intellect allowed him to make his way in the world successfully through various pursuits. He was a political thinker and analyst. His statesmanship transcended national boundaries. As a writer and journalist, he wrote essays, hundreds of articles for many publications in the Western Hemisphere on issues of his day. He published newspapers, journals, and other periodicals often political in nature. He wrote plays, poetry, novels, and children's books. Altogether his written works comprise twenty-five volumes.



Through it all, Martí's underlying goal was to make the world understand why human rights demanded the independence of Cuba from Spain. Through many literary genres, he espoused a total rejection of oppressive colonial rule; he disapproved of Spain's rejection of individual freedoms and wholeheartedly believed in Cuba's right to fulfill its own destiny. His empowering spirit inspired the movement for Cuban independence that imbued the Ybor City community with the fervor to see the goal through to the end even when he was no longer there to lead it. In this way, he embodied the soul of Ybor City, giving its people a higher calling beyond their individual lives.

## *The Making of a Revolutionary*

Martí was born January 28, 1853, in Havana, Cuba, the oldest child of eight children. All of his siblings were sisters. The man of both intense passion and intellect was not willing to ignore the suffering and injustice he observed in the world without doing something about it.[1]

As a young boy, Martí enjoyed horse riding in the countryside, but what he saw in the sugarcane fields of western Cuba alarmed him to the core. He witnessed Afro Cuban slaves brutally beaten with whips, a slave hanging by a rope from a tree, and slave ships unloading their human cargo in shackles. These incidents and others exposed him to the brutality of the Cuban social structure.[2]

Martí's mother, Leonor, realized that her son was highly intelligent and needed to pursue his education. He was enrolled in the distinguished Municipal High School for Boys in Havana in 1865 and came under the mentorship of its director, Rafael Mendive. The educator had an extensive library, which he made available to the young Martí. Mendive also invited Martí to his home to join academic discussions with Havana intellectuals regarding the social, political, and literary issues of the day. Martí blossomed in such a learning environment, and Mendive recognized genius in the young boy.[3] Through these experiences, Martí learned the principles of persuasive debate, understanding that strongly held beliefs became valuable when articulated and directed to the public at large.





### *Prelude to a Revolution*

The Cuban society was highly stratified. The Spanish-born segment of society represented less than 10% of the population, but almost all of the wealth. The laws favored those who were the wealthiest and who would be most obligated to be loyal to Spain. Next were the Spanish of Cuban birth, sometimes referred to as Creoles, an expression normally referring to a person of mixed racial birth. For those born in Cuba, there existed a similar aversion to the case of the North American colonies, "taxation without representation." Some Cubans wanted to stay in the Spanish empire but felt representation in Parliament and reforms were needed. However, efforts to seek reform in Madrid did not go anywhere. An increasing number of Cubans desired an independent nation. José Martí stressed that its evolution over 400 years meant that it was a country no longer Spanish in nature but one with a unique culture of its own.[4] Native peoples, along with freed Blacks and other immigrants, were a third tier, and at the very bottom were the Afro Cuban slaves who had no rights and were the property of their owners. José Martí opposed slavery and worked for the cause of human rights for Afro Cubans.

The causes of the three 19th century revolutionary outbreaks that took place for Cuban independence were all similar. With Spain's loss of all of its colonies in the Americas (except the islands of Cuba and Puerto Rico), Spain was even more dependent on extracting all the wealth that it could from the Cuban economy. Spain appointed governors, and there was no semblance of self-government in Cuba. The differences between those of extreme wealth and those who were very poor were always increasing.

A sugarcane plantation owner in the poorer eastern end of Cuba (in the vicinity of Yara), led a revolt in response to a burdensome tax increase in 1867, and to other oppressive measures of the colonial government. Addressing his slaves on the morning of an ordinary workday, Carlos Manuel de Cespedes informed them that they would hereafter be free men. He then urgently implored them to join him and his men who were going to fight for the independence of Cuba. The small group grew to thousands as the "Cry from Yara" became the rallying cry for all those who wanted to join the rebellion. It became the Cuban Declaration of Independence.[5]

While the conflict raged for ten years and became known as the Ten Years' War, the insurgents had few advantages. The Spanish threw a significant military force against them, and their tactics were brutal, terrorizing and destroying villages that supported the independence fighters. The wealthy sugarcane, slave-holding landowners in the west funded the campaign as the struggle became one of east versus west.



Martí became involved in an incident of the war, coinciding with the slaughter at the Villaneuva Theatre in Havana in early 1869. The theatre was attended by a large group of separatists who supported the newly developing insurrection. The separatists were fired upon by volunteers supporting Spanish forces, and many were killed before the Havana police could restore order. The incident initiated a crackdown by police in Havana, attempting to identify and arrest separatists. Rafael Mendive was arrested during the roundup and was exiled to Spain, much to the apprehension of the young Martí. He attempted to help fill in for the absent Mendive at the school, but a letter was found that he and his best friend, a fellow schoolmate, Fermin Valdez Dominguez, had authored and signed to another student, chastising that colleague for joining the Spanish volunteers. The unsent letter was found on a raid of the student's living quarters, and Valdez Dominguez and Martí were both arrested for treason. After a wait for trial of several months, both students claimed responsibility for the letter, but it was Martí who received a sentence of six years of hard labor at a rock quarry outside Havana.[6]

The young Martí was of slight build, standing five feet, six inches and the conditions brutalized him. He suffered injuries from beatings that resulted in a leg limp and hernia as well as permanent scars on his ankles from the chains bound to his feet. After several months, his family had used various channels to get him transferred to a prison on the Isle of Pine south of Cuba, which was administered by a family connection. There he stayed until six months of his commuted sentence was completed, but he was not allowed to return to Cuba. He was to be exiled to Spain to learn what it meant to be a Spaniard. His punishment only hardened his spirit for Cuba's independence, which he was convinced was a necessity. In January 1871, Martí said goodbye to his family and boarded a ship for Cadiz.[7]

### *Exile in Spain and Then to Mexico*

Arriving in Madrid as an exile at seventeen was a daunting experience. Martí lived in a boarding house and made friends with many Cuban expatriates who had either fled Cuba for safety or had been exiled there by Cuban authorities. The community of expatriates was his support group, and he received surgery in his boarding house room for an abdominal infection stemming from injuries while imprisoned.

He began writing for a journal published by an expatriate in whose home he met to discuss political and social issues of the day.

Seeking to educate the people of Spain on the atrocities of their rule over Cuba, Martí recounted his experience as a political prisoner in Cuba.[8] Earning money writing and tutoring, Martí enrolled in the University of Madrid to study law, an environment that nurtured him.

Spain was going through political turbulence of its own with one regime change after another in the nearly five years that José lived in Spain, but Martí's outspoken written narratives in Madrid forced him to move to Zaragoza where he completed a degree in law and philosophy. Feeling that the political upheavals in Spain distracted the country from considering or favoring Cuban independence, Martí decided to leave. Spanish authorities no longer wanted him there, but he could not return to Cuba.[9]

Martí rejoined his family who had moved to Mexico to escape the instability in Cuba. He moved in with his family in Mexico City in February 1875, and they were barely getting by financially after the move. Living in Mexico, he came to see similarities in the social inequalities occurring in Cuba, Spain, and Mexico which had been fostered by Spanish rule. In Mexico, workers were organizing to demand greater rights in the workplace, and Martí gladly joined the cause creating a publication called the *Boletin* (*the Bulletin*) to express his support. He wrote a play at the time, which became a big sensation in Mexico City and propelled him higher into society. This expanded his sphere of influence with civic leaders. He made contact with instrumental people he would rely on later as the leader of the revolutionary movement.

At the home of one of Mexico City's intellectuals and writers, he met Carmen Zayas-Bazan, the daughter of a sugarcane plantation owner in Cuba whose property had been destroyed in the Ten Years' War. They were drawn to each other. She admired the passion behind his beliefs, but she did not understand that the overriding obsession of his life would not be his relationship with her but ridding Cuba of Spanish control. In spite of their differing perceptions of the world, they fell in love and became engaged.[10]

Martí ran afoul of authorities in Mexico when he supported its president, Miguel Lerdo de Tejada. The president was ousted by a military coup led by a popular general, Portforto Diaz, instrumental in ending the unpopular rule of Emperor Maximilian. He would govern as a dictator and not allow dissent. For Martí, the coup was a major step backwards for Mexico, and he became an outspoken critic of the general. He was forced to leave Mexico for his own safety. The experience of the military overthrow confirmed in Martí's mind that the effort to free Cuba had to come under civilian control.[11]



### *A Statesman of Latin America*

In 1877, Martí headed for neighboring Guatemala where he met influential members of Guatemalan society that would be important contacts in the future. One such contact was José Maria Izaguirre, a fighter in the Ten Years' War who had settled in Guatemala and was director of an esteemed teacher's college. He hired Martí as an instructor to teach composition and European literature. A complaint was filed that both men were so obsessed with Cuban independence that it interfered with the main purpose of the school, to equip teachers. It was during this time that Martí returned to Mexico to marry his betrothed, Carmen, and he returned to Guatemala with her. The controversy at the school, fraught with political implications, led to both men leaving their positions.[12]

After the Ten Years' War ended, Martí and his wife were allowed to return to Cuba in 1878, and their son is born there. However, Martí could not refrain from voicing in print and in speech that the ultimate destiny of Cuba was independence. A failed insurrection took place in 1879 when farmers and slaves in Santiago attempted to rekindle the independence movement. It was quickly put down and Spanish soldiers began to hunt down sympathizers. Martí again was deported to Spain, but his wife of a little over a year would not go with him. Instead, she and their son Pepito would remain in Havana.[13]

After a short stay in Spain, Martí arrived in New York City in October 1879, which became his base of operations for the remainder of his life. He had made connections throughout Central and South America and Mexico through visits, articles, correspondence, a distinguished education, and his role as an appointed diplomat from time to time for several South American countries because of his vast knowledge of international relations.[14] A man without a country, Martí was becoming a statesman of all Latin America and its peoples.

### *Revolution Headquarters – New York City*

Martí's life before arriving in NYC had been a preparation for the final chapter to which his life had been dedicated. By espousing unpopular political positions, he had been forced to travel extensively, making contacts and persuading the Hispanic world why they needed to support the ongoing revolutionary movement to free Cuba. He then had arrived in a country whose Bill of Rights would protect his right to free speech, and would eliminate the threats to his personal security.



Yet in his first year in New York, the New York Cuban Revolutionary Committee to which Martí was attracted disbanded. Their leader, a stouthearted general from the Ten Years' War, Calixto García, had led an expedition of twenty-six men to Cuba to initiate another rebellion. After three months of fighting, they surrendered to Spanish troops on August 1, 1880; they had lost twenty men. The disappointment felt by the committee and those who supported the organization was extreme. They felt an opportunity had been lost and that future efforts had been damaged by the failure. Thus, the committee disbanded. Yet Martí saw the military failure as a temporary misstep on the journey to reaching independence.[15]

## *A Mastery of the Language*

Martí began a very productive phase in his literary career while waiting for an opportune time to reestablish an organization that would provide leadership for the independence movement. He spent time translating texts he believed his Cuban followers should read. He focused on identifying where the communities of Cuban Americans and other Latin Americans resided outside of Cuba, seeking those sympathetic to the independence movement. His attention turned to the many places he had lived and visited. In particular, he saw the cigar communities of Key West and the rapidly growing Ybor City in Florida as major sources of support. He maintained an extensive correspondence with his contacts in all of those communities.

Martí's understanding of language and phraseology was masterful, especially in communicating the reasons for Cuban independence. Some historical accounts of Martí primarily refer to him as a "Poet and Revolutionary." Indeed, poetry played a large role in conveying the passion of his life's mission for independence. It allowed him to express his great emotion for his Cuba, his "patria," a term that went beyond country to express something as personal as home, fatherland, and the sacrifices needed by individuals for their country if required. Poetry was also an autobiographical expression in which Martí expressed his love for his young son and his frustration over his marriage. After his wife returned permanently to Cuba with their son, following a visit to Martí in NYC, he expressed his love and devotion for the woman who ran the boardinghouse he lived in, Carmita Mantilla.[16]



Martí was a great admirer of Walt Whitman and Ralph Waldo Emerson and the Modernismo style of free verse in Spanish-American poetry, and he wrote extensively in the poetry genre. His best known works include a collection of poems entitled *Versos Sencillos* (*Simple Verses*), not published until 1891. He wrote of nature while convalescing from illness. In support of social justice, Martí wrote of Cuba, his opposition to slavery, and the oppression of the Cuban people. A second collection of poems was in free verse entitled *Versos Libres* (*Free Verses*). His most famous political poem was "Dos Patrias" ("Two Patrias") in which he described two countries, the existing Cuba and the one hoped for.[17] The passion of his poetry was effectively transferred to his prose and speech writing. A moving turn of a poetical phrase could bring tears to his audiences or rapturous joy that the dream of a free Cuba could be fulfilled. "Guantanamera" was a hugely popular patriotic Cuban song in the 1960s, which used lyrics from a poem written by José Martí.[18]

## *Relationship with Generals Maceo and Gomez*

As the year 1884 dawned, Martí knew it was time to consult with those who had provided military leadership for rebellions in the past to determine the timing of another revolution for independence. Two commanders of the Ten Years' War agreed to meet with Martí in New York—Generals Máximo Gómez and José Antonio Maceo.[19]

The three worked together for several months but became divided over who would control the movement. Both Gómez and Maceo believed in military control for an extended period of time to secure the successful overthrow of Spanish control of the island. Martí, however, was adamantly opposed to military control based on his experiences throughout Latin America. He believed that the replacement of one dictatorship with that of another was not in the best interests of the Cuban people. The progress made was stymied by the conflict, and the men temporarily parted ways. Subsequently, as Martí spoke at events in New York, he was sometimes booed by the audience as he was held responsible for the disunity. He was accused of trying to take exclusive control of the movement.[20]

After the split with the generals, Martí began a concerted effort through newspaper articles and journals to try to bring unity to the movement. There were many divisions besides Martí's insistence on civil control of the enterprise. Some conservative supporters wanted a complete disavowal of all socialist leanings. Some racists did not want the large contingent of Afro Cubans to share in leadership. Some believed that the intervention of the US was necessary.[21]





The power of persuasion through the pen and speech were innate in Martí's character. He was rallying a new group from a new generation to strengthen support for independence from which a new leadership body could be formed.

### *Anti-imperialism*

Martí also strenuously objected to a US policy that was increasingly turning toward imperialism in Latin America. Business and military leaders in the US had been clamoring for the annexation of Cuba throughout the 19th century, but it was reaching its climax in the last two decades of the century. For Martí, this was a reprehensible trend. The US would simply govern Cuba from the standpoint of what was in its best interests and the business interests of its companies.

His concerns were well founded and prophetic as Cuba's northern neighbor frequently intervened in the ensuing years into the affairs of the new Cuban nation and throughout Latin America, to the region's detriment.[22] Martí increasingly began to perform a greater role in three South American countries that utilized him on diplomatic matters because of his vast knowledge and understanding of international relations. He had become a statesman for all of Latin America. He published an article in January 1891, "Neustra America" ("Our America"), that identified his vision of a unified Latin American that could work together toward common purposes and solutions. For Cuba, he articulated the kind of nation he envisioned a liberated Cuba would be, a nation where all Cubans would be equal before the law. It would not be a duplicate of the US government but would have a constitution based on the unique character and traditions of the Cuban people and its culture which had evolved over 400 years.[23]

### *Martí in Ybor City*

On November 25, 1891, José Martí accepted an invitation to Tampa and arrived in Ybor City for the first of some twenty such visits to speak to the cigar workers and coordinate support. He was ushered into Vicente Martinez Ybor's huge 14th Street factory and brought to where the lector was reading to the workers. (Lectors were educated readers hired by the workers who read newspapers and classical literature to the cigar workers while they worked.) As Martí was introduced, the 800 cigar rollers rose to their feet in thunderous applause and cheering. After a short speech,

Martí was taken to meet Ybor before departing to West Tampa to visit a new factory and to later speak at the Cuban Lyceum. At that last event of the day, Martí held the crowd in the palm of his hand as the poetic style and cadence of his speech rallied attendees to think of their compatriots in Cuba. It is entitled "Con Todos, y para el Bien de Todos" ("All Together and for the Good of All"). Among his concluding remarks:



> Now let us form ranks...enough of mere words. From our torn insides let us lift up an inextinguishable love for our country... There she is, from there she calls us; one hears her moan; they raped her; they scoff her, and they cause her to have gangrene. Before our eyes, they corrupt us and they tear apart the mother of our heart. Well, let us rise once and for all, with one final charge from our heart...Let us rise on behalf of the real republic. Those of us with our love for what is right and with our dedication to work will know how to keep it alive. Let us rise to offer a place to die to the heroes whose spirit wanders through the world ashamed and alone. Let us rise so that someday our children may have a place to die. And let us place around the star in the new flag this formula for triumphant love—**with the people and for the people**.[24]

The speech is written down to be printed in the newspapers the next day so that his words would be read by lectors in cigar factories throughout America. While in Tampa and working with local leadership, Martí developed the "Resolutions Taken by the Cuban Emigrants of Tampa." He used these principles to develop the basis for a new organization in New York that would be called the Cuban Revolutionary Party (PRC).[25]

### *The Cuban Revolutionary Party Organized*

In the visits throughout Florida including Key West, West Tampa, Ybor City, and Ocala, the workers pledged a donation from their weekly pay in support of the revolutionary movement; this was instrumental in funding the next revolutionary campaign of 1895. The largest amount raised was from the residents of Ybor City.

The Cuban Revolutionary Party was formed in 1892, and its newspaper, *La Patria,* began publishing with Martí as its editor. Martí is made a "delegate" of the party, which amounted to its primary leadership position. Martí's public appearances to impassion his audiences in the cause, and to raise funds accelerated in the 1890s. On behalf of the new organization, in 1892 Martí sought out General Máximo Gómez in the Dominican Republic to lead the next attempt at independence. Martí also went to see General José Antonio Maceo in Costa Rica in 1893 to enlist his support. Both men had failed in the ensuing years to raise money on their own. They did not have Martí's persuasive powers, but they came to acknowledge, accept, and respect his instrumental role if Cuba's independence was to be secured.[26]



By 1893, the PRC was getting close to amassing enough treasury to finance another bid for Cuba, and other Cuban independence organizations were lining up behind the PRC. With the establishment of an effective independence organization, the generals came to accept civilian control of the impending enterprise. But there were to be several setbacks along the way.[27]

Martí's surveillance by Spanish agents markedly increased in the 1890s, and in late 1892 while visiting Ybor City, Martí was subjected to an assassination attempt by poisoning. The Afro Cuban community took control of his security and in his future stays in Ybor City, he resided in the homes of members of that community, notably the home of Ruperto and Paulina Pedroso whose boarding house was located on the property of the present day Friends of José Martí Park in Ybor City.[28]

In 1893, the US was entering an economic depression which struck all industries including the cigar industry, and the flow of contributions to the PRC slowed. In that same year, an insurrection unauthorized by the PRC took place in Purnio, Cuba, which was unsuccessful and was a setback to the party's planning.[29] In the summer of 1894, Martí traveled the Caribbean, Central America, and the US, meeting with exiles, raising funds, and coordinating efforts for the final independence push.[30]

In early 1895, the Fernandina Plan launched by the PRC failed in its execution. The ships meant to transport men and supplies to Cuba were to assemble in Fernandina in northeast Florida, but the plan was revealed, and US military authorities seized the ships. US policy was bound by treaty not to allow a hostile force to be assembled against another country outside of formal congressional action. The widely broadcasted failure of the Fernandina Plan, while initially a great disappointment, served to galvanize support as Cubans saw the new organization taking decisive steps to liberate Cuba. Money and volunteers once again began to pour in, revitalizing international attention to the movement. With economic conditions worsening in Cuba, a final plan was put in motion.[31]

## *The Third Attempt at Revolution*

In late January 1895, Martí arrives in the Dominican Republic and joins up with General Gómez in Montecristi to revise their military plans.[32] In February, an uprising occurred in Baire near Santiago, and the Spanish quickly attempted to put it down and round up the instigators as they believed that an outside force arriving was imminent.[33] Martí and Gómez issued a declaration on March 25, known as the Montecristi Manifesto, supporting the insurrection of Baire and outlining how the cause of revolution would be conducted. They would abide by the rules of civilized warfare. They would respect noncombatants and not oppress the population. They would respect private ownership of property, and their goal would be to set up a civilian government not beholden to foreign influence.[34]

## *Difficult Landings*

The same day the declaration was issued in the Dominican Republic, Maceo, his brother, and Flor Crombet, a veteran of the Ten Years' War, left Costa Rica on an American ship. They encountered Spanish ships and the captain of the boat, out of fear, dropped the group on a Bahamian island. An American ship then took them through a storm in which the ship was wrecked, beached on the coast on the eastern tip of Cuba near the town of Baracoa on March 30, 1895.[35] The advent of Maceo back in Cuba was a rallying cry for the people of eastern Cuba. Meanwhile, in the Dominican Republic, the Gómez-Martí group attempted to convince Martí to stay behind and perhaps return to NYC and work to support the revolution from there. But he refused. The need to prove himself after so many had died for Cuban independence was overwhelming. He wrote, "I was beginning to die of shame...at the thought that a nation might allow itself to be served...by one who preached the need of dying and then did not begin by risking his own life."[36]

Martí wrote a will leaving all his literary works to be safeguarded by a friend and his watch to be left to his son. The group made two attempts to leave the Dominican Republic by ship, but in both incidents the crew backed out. Finally on the third attempt at departure, a German ship bound for Haiti agreed to drop them off at the coast. The six men were required to disembark to a small rowboat in a storm three miles off the coast of Cuba. The rudder broke and after a harrowing night at sea, they managed to beach on the coast. Even though completely exhausted, they were relieved to have made it to Cuba in one piece on April 11, 1895.[37]

The group rode through the countryside with their numbers increasing in search of news of Maceo's location. Maceo had headed to the mountains upon his arrival, and he reported in a letter to his wife after being in Cuba for a couple of weeks that his numbers had swelled to 6,000 men who were well armed.[38]

Martí had adjusted well to the life of a soldier. He carried a backpack over fifty pounds of gear including medicines and maps. In early May, Martí and General Gómez linked up with General Maceo. Both generals tried to convince Martí to leave the fighting to them and consider returning to NYC, but again he refused. Biographer Alfred Lopez calculated that Martí persevered for 245 miles through rough terrain, one-third of which was made on foot in the five and half weeks he was with the troops.[39]

### *Martí Enters into Immortality*

While General Gómez's fighting strength was a few hundred, Maceo was popular among the Afro Cuban population and accumulated the much larger force. The two groups split again as Maceo went in search of contact with the enemy, and Gómez and Martí headed westward to the province of Granma to pick up more men. Camped on the banks of the Dos Rios River (where two rivers come together), the Gómez-Martí group greeted a contingent of rebels who then joined them. Gómez spoke to the group. When Martí did so, he was hailed as the "President of the Republic."

Gómez learned that he was being pursued by a Spanish force and decided he would lead their forces to make contact. Gómez instructed Martí to stay with the rear guard, and Martí initially obeyed. Upon hearing gunfire nearby a short time later, Martí mounted his horse, heading in the direction of the fighting. He ran into a squad of Spanish soldiers who opened fire, killing him. While the revolutionaries attempted to recover his body from the Spanish troops, they were unable to do so. The Spanish troops hastily buried him and upon learning who he was, dug up the body and reburied it in a cemetery in Santiago.[40]

Instead of being demoralized by his death, the revolutionary forces rededicated themselves to accomplishing what Martí had worked so hard to achieve. Their army of 50,000 soldiers was outnumbered by Spanish forces five to one, but their campaign was brilliant as Maceo and Gómez marched from one end of the island to the other. They inflicted heavy casualties on the enemy and wore down Spanish forces before Maceo was killed in a skirmish in December 1896, leaving Gómez as principal leader.[41]

History recorded the arrival of Theodore Roosevelt and the Rough Riders and the charge up San Juan Hill in 1898 but ignored that the revolutionary forces kept the fighting going for three more years after Martí was killed on the battlefield. In 1898, the explosion of the battleship *Maine*, sent by the US to protect American lives and property, occurred in Havana harbor. No evidence revealed the cause or who was responsible, but it is used as pretext for US intervention to support the revolution. With a declaration of war from Congress and the arrival of troops, Spanish morale collapses and the so called Spanish-American War (the Cuban Revolutionary War) ended three months later.[42]



### *A Dream Unrealized*

The US agreed to facilitate the creation of an independent government in Cuba in 1902, four years after the cessation of hostilities. In the interim, American business interests moved in to expand their holdings in the Cuban economy. The wealthy aristocratic segment of the population who had little regard for the revolution continued living undisturbed by the regime changes, whereas the poor who gave all for the revolution's success were not benefited.

The US granted independence to a Cuban government provided the Cuban legislature adopted the Platt Amendment passed by the US Congress as part of their Constitution. That provision allowed the US to intervene militarily in the affairs of Cuba whenever its interests or security warranted such action. Interventions occurred in 1906 and 1909 when Cuba was administered by a provisional governor appointed by the president of the US.[43] Martí had been quite prescient regarding the interference by the US in Cuban affairs.

Both the governments of the new republic and Castro's communist regime invoked the name of Martí and the principles he espoused in seeking a Cuba governed by Cubans. Governments under the republic changed hands frequently. Close elections were challenged as fraudulent, and some presidents chose to remain in office after their terms expired. The US backed dictators who pledged to protect American interests.[44]

While Martí lamented the oppression of the Cuban people by Spain, he also would have opposed the more oppressive communist government like that of the Castro regime. Martí was somewhat skeptical of socialism as well, having written the following:

> Socialist ideology, like so many others has two main dangers. One stems from confused and incomplete reading of foreign

> texts, and the other from arrogance and hidden rage of those who, in order to climb up in the world, pretend to be frantic defenders of the helpless so as to have shoulders on which to stand.[45]

Martí was a great admirer of the US Bill of Rights, so he would not have been supportive of a one party communist government in Cuba that did not allow dissent with a head of state ruling for life.

For most Cubans, Martí's dream of a democratically elected republic that supported human rights and freedoms remains unfulfilled. Cuba still is not free. As Martí feared, big brother to the north never allowed the development of institutions that would enable Cuba to join the ranks of democratically elected governments. Martí's death was a great tragedy in that his guidance and direction in the new republic was absent at critical times. Yet his life and the study of his immense literary contribution to political thought mean that the dream of *Cuba Libre* (a Free Cuba) will never die.

# *Endnotes*



1 Jon Sterngass, *José Martí* (New York: Chelsea House/infobase Publishing, 2007), 6–8.

2 Sterngass, *José Martí*, 8–9.

3 Alfred J. Lopez, *José Martí, A Revolutionary Life* (Austin: University of Texas Press, 2014), 26–37.

4 John M. Dunn, *José Martí: Cuba's Greatest Hero* (Sarasota, FL: Pineapple Press, 2015), 7–8.

5 Sterngass, *José Martí*, 15–17.

6 Lopez, *José Martí, A Revolutionary Life, 45*–59.

7 Lopez, *José Martí, A Revolutionary Life,* 59–65.

8 Lopez, *José Martí, A Revolutionary Life,* 71–82.

9 Lopez, *José Martí, A Revolutionary Life,* 82–92.

10 Lopez, *José Martí, A Revolutionary Life,* 101–124.

11 Lopez, *José Martí, A Revolutionary Life,* 124–135.

12 Dunn, *José Martí: Cuba's Greatest Hero,* 31–34.

13 Dunn, *José Martí: Cuba's Greatest Hero,* 35–37.

14 Dunn, *José Martí: Cuba's Greatest Hero,* 37–41.

15 Dunn, *José Martí: Cuba's Greatest Hero,* 38–39.

16 Sterngass, *José Martí,* 48–56.

17 Sterngass, *José Martí,* 55–58.

18 Sterngass, *José Martí,* 54.

19 Dunn, *José Martí: Cuba's Greatest Hero,* 41–43.

20 Dunn, *José Martí: Cuba's Greatest Hero,* 43–45.

21 Lopez, *José Martí, A Revolutionary Life,* 231–240.

22 Dunn, *José Martí: Cuba's Greatest Hero,* 49–53.

23 Dunn, *José Martí: Cuba's Greatest Hero,* 53–54.

24 Frank T. Lastra, *Ybor City, The Making of a Landmark Town* (Tampa: University of Tampa Press, 2006, 34, citing Jose Rivero Muniz, *The Ybor City Story 1883–1954*, trans. Eustasio Fernandez and Henry Beltran (Tampa: n.p., 1976), 52–53 and Jorge Manach, *Marti: Apostle of Freedom,* trans. Coley Taylor (New York: O'Toole, 1984).

25 Dunn, *José Martí: Cuba's Greatest Hero,* 55–57; Lastra, *Ybor City, The Making of a Landmark Town,* 32-35.

26 Lopez, *José Martí, A Revolutionary Life,* 260–264; Dunn, *José Martí: Cuba's Greatest Hero,* 60–63.

27 Dunn, *José Martí: Cuba's Greatest Hero,* 60–62.

28 Lopez, *José Martí, A Revolutionary Life,* 265–266.

29 Dunn, *José Martí: Cuba's Greatest Hero,* 63–65.

30 Lopez, *José Martí, A Revolutionary Life,* 276.

31 Lopez, *José Martí, A Revolutionary Life,* 277–281.

32 Dunn, *José Martí: Cuba's Greatest Hero,* 70.

33 Lopez, *José Martí, A Revolutionary Life,* 289; Sterngass,*José Martí,* 86.

34 Dunn, *José Martí: Cuba's Greatest Hero,* 70–71; Sterngass, *José Martí,* 86.



35 Dunn, *José Martí: Cuba's Greatest Hero,* 71–72; Sterngass, *José Martí,* 89.

36 Dunn, *José Martí: Cuba's Greatest Hero,* 73, quoting *José Martí Reader, Writings on the Americans*, eds. Deborah Shnookal and Mirta Muniz (New York: Ocean Press, 1999), 216–217.

37 Lopez, *José Martí, A Revolutionary Life,* 283–295; Dunn, *José Martí: Cuba's Greatest Hero,* 73–75.

38 Dunn, *José Martí: Cuba's Greatest Hero,* 72, from Philip S. Foner, *The Spanish-Cuban-American War and the Birth of American Imperialism, 1895–1902,* Volume 1: 1895–1898 (New York: Monthly Review Press, 1972), 8.

39 Lopez, *José Martí, A Revolutionary Life,* 296–300.

40 Dunn, *José Martí: Cuba's Greatest Hero,* 79–81; Lopez, *José Martí, A Revolutionary Life,* 319–320.

41 Dunn, *José Martí: Cuba's Greatest Hero,* 82–83.

42 Lastra, *Ybor City, The Making of a Landmark Town,* 44–50; Sterngass, *José Martí,* 98–101.

43 Sterngass, *José Martí,* 102–103.

44 Sterngass, *José Martí,* 103.

45 José Martí, *José Martí: Thoughts/Pensamientos: A Bilingual Anthology,* trans., Carlos Ripoll (New York: Eliseo Torres & Sons – Las Americas Publishing Co., 1980), 47.

# 4 YBOR CITY AT A GLANCE



## A NOTE ABOUT HISTORICAL SIGHTS

Many of Ybor City's historic buildings are now utilized by various organizations and companies, but feel free to wander in. The occupants who either own or lease the premises understand the historical nature of their site and welcome visitors.

You'll also find that many sights display historic markers. The buildings represent the many architectural styles of the countries from which Ybor immigrants came. These sights and others are dealt with more fully in subsequent sections.

The information below is an overview dividing Ybor City into three sectors: the West side, the East side, and the North side. Each sector includes multiple sights of interest which are grouped by their proximity to one another.
**"Must-see" places are indicated by ◆ ◆.**
**Sights "worth seeing" are indicated by ◆.**
**"Places of note" have no symbol.**

**WEST SIDE** (from Nebraska Avenue to 17th Street)

*Sights at the Gateway to the Latin Quarter*

- ◆ ◆ **Archway Entrance to Ybor City** is the freestanding steel structure on 7th Avenue marking the entrance to Ybor City from Tampa proper. Registered among the world's freestanding arches.
- ◆ **Hotel Haya**, a boutique hotel with its own unique style features a restaurant and café.
- **Rough Riders Park** memorializes the Spanish-American War veterans, and the Rough Riders participation specifically.
- **Afro Cuban Club, Sociedad La Union Martí-Maceo** is the community center for this group and was named after two heroes of the Afro Cuban community.

*Sights relating to Vicente Martinez Ybor and José Martí*

- ◆ ◆ **Friends of José Martí Park (1956)** is owned by Cuba and was established in recognition of Martí's tireless efforts for Cuban independence and the sacrifice of his life in that endeavor. He was a frequent resident of Ybor City as he rallied cigar workers' support for the independence movement.
- ◆ **Ybor Factory/Ybor Square (1886)** is Vicente Martinez Ybor's fully restored cigar factory complex that was one of the first brick buildings in Ybor City.

- **Ybor City Land Development Company (1886)** is across the street from the front of the factory building. Founded by Mr. Ybor and Henry Manrara, the building was completed in 1893 and served as the center for business and commercial development in its early days. It later became the Ybor Inn before transitioning to offices.
- **El Pasaje** (also known as the **Cherokee Club**) **(1886)** means "passageway." Across 9th Avenue from the factory, this building has an Italian Renaissance architectural style. It was built at the same time as the factory complex in 1886 to house the offices for Vicente Martinez Ybor's enterprises.
- ◆◆ **The Cuban Club, El Circulo Cubano de Tampa (1917)** was organized in 1902 and is the second building on the corner of Palm Avenue and 14th Street. While serving as the Cuban community assistance center, it was initially established for political purposes relating to the Cuban independence movement.

*Sights around the Visitor Information Center*

- **The Castle** (historically, **The Labor Temple**) **(1930)** was the meeting place for the various union organizations in the early 20th century. Today it's a popular nightclub and dancing venue.
- ◆◆ **The Ybor City Chamber of Commerce Visitor Information Center** provides key insights on everything Ybor City. In addition to being a visitor center, it also serves as a museum and gift shop.
- ◆◆ Bronze statues of Vicente M. Ybor and Roland Manteiga.
- ◆ **Centro Español de Tampa (1912)** is no longer an active club; the building is now utilized by restaurants.

**Cigar Shops** on and off 7th Avenue on the West side:

- King Corona Cigars, Bar & Café
- La Faraona Cigars
- Nicahabana Cigars
- Sterling Cigar Lounge and Bar
- Tabanero Cigars
- Tampa Sweethearts Cigar Co.

**Cuban Coffee places** – Tabanero Cigars, King Corona Cigars, Bar & Café, The Bricks, Hotel Haya's Café Quiquiriqui

**Cuban Sandwich places** – King Corona Cigars, Bar & Café, La Segunda Bakery, Tampa Bay Brewing Company, Hotel Haya's Café Quiquiriqui

**Nearby Eating** – See Restaurants, West Side, under Section 11, Eating. Also Funny Bone, previously Improv Theatre. See Cheeseology under Specialty Foods

**Shopping** – Visitor Information Center & Gift Shop, La France, Agora, Indie Flea Market at the Cuban Club



## EAST SIDE (From 17th Street to 23rd Street)

*Museums and Centennial Park area Sights*

- ◆ ◆ **Centennial Park/Saturday Market** is a place to relax and explore as it's surrounded by historical markers, statuary, and roosters. It commemorates the 100th anniversary of Ybor City, reached in 1986. Saturday Market occurs every Saturday.
- ◆ **Hillsborough County Sheriff History Center** documents the story of law enforcement from the early days.
- ◆ ◆ **The Tampa Baseball Museum at the Al Lopez House** documents through exhibits the history of baseball in the Tampa area in Al Lopez's house.
- ◆ ◆ **Ybor City Museum State Park** is located in the historic Italian Ferlita Bakery and documents the beginning of the cigar industry in Tampa through early photos, displays, and videos. An adjacent garden incorporates plants native to Florida.
- ◆ ◆ **Casita Tour** is a guided tour included in the admission to the Ybor City State Museum that conducts a walk through a staged "little house" Vicente Martinez Ybor and his manufacturing colleagues built for the cigar workers.

*Sights around the Italian Club*

- ◆ ◆ **The Italian Club, L'Unione Italiana (1917)** is a three-story Renaissance clubhouse that was founded in 1897 and has served as the community center for the Italian immigrant community.
- ◆ ◆ **Restaurant Central** refers to an area of 20+ eating places located within two blocks of the Italian Club (intersection of 7th Ave. and 18th St.). Restaurants are listed in the Eating (Section 11) of this guide.
- ◆ ◆ **Columbia Restaurant (1905)** is the oldest restaurant in Florida and the largest Spanish restaurant in the world. The building is a unique historical attraction in its own right with early 20th century Ybor decor.
- ◆ **Dysfunctional Grace Art Gallery** is a mainstay in Ybor, full of tokens and decor representing the oddities of life and macabre of death.
- ◆ ◆ **Viva Ybor Mural** is a dramatically colorful mural displaying many icons of Ybor's heritage.
- ◆ ◆ **The Kress Arts Building,** established in 2022, houses the Kress Contemporary group of artists, art organizations, and galleries as well as the Florida Museum of Photographic Arts (FMoPA).

**Cigar Shops** on and off 7th Avenue on the East Side:

- La Herencia De Ybor Cigars
- Long Ash Cigars
- Tampero Cigars
- Ybor Cigars Plus

**Cuban Coffee** – Blind Tiger Cafe, The Foundation Coffee Co. at The Bunker, 22nd Street Coffee
**Cuban Sandwich** – Gaspar's Grotto, Carmines, Columbia Restaurant
**Nearby Eating** – See Restaurants, East Side, under Section 11, Eating.
**Shopping** – Dysfunctional Grace, Columbia Restaurant Gift Shop, Saturday Market, Vintage Roost, Stained Market.



## NORTH SIDE

(accessible by car, beyond walking distance of 7th Avenue)

- ◆ **Centro Asturiano de Tampa (1914),** at 1913 N. Nebraska Avenue, was organized in 1907 by those immigrants who traced their heritage to the region of Asturias along the north coast of Spain. It's one of two Spanish clubs.
- **The German-American Club (1908),** at 2105 N Nebraska Avenue, was organized in 1901 as a community center that served the Jewish, German, and eastern European immigrant communities during its heyday. It's now utilized as an inclusive healthcare center.
- ◆ ◆ **La Segunda Central Bakery (1915),** at 2512 N. 15th Street, is the historic bakery of Ybor City and run by a fourth-generation Cuban family. It makes authentic Cuban bread for Tampa and beyond.
- ◆ ◆ **The J. C. Newman Factory (1910)** is the last remaining cigar factory in the United States. The iconic building celebrated its 110th anniversary and the company's 125th anniversary in the cigar business in 2020. It contains a store, museum, and provides a factory tour.
- ◆ **Hillsborough College Ybor City Visual and Performing Arts** on the north side of Palm Avenue has an active schedule of exhibitions in its Gallery 114 and performances which include concerts, plays, and dance in its two theatres.

**Nearby Eating** – Tampa Bay Brewing Co., La Segunda Bakery
**Cuban Coffee** – La Segunda Bakery
**Cuban Sandwich** – La Segunda Bakery
**Shopping** – Baked goods at La Segunda, Museum Store of J. C. Newman

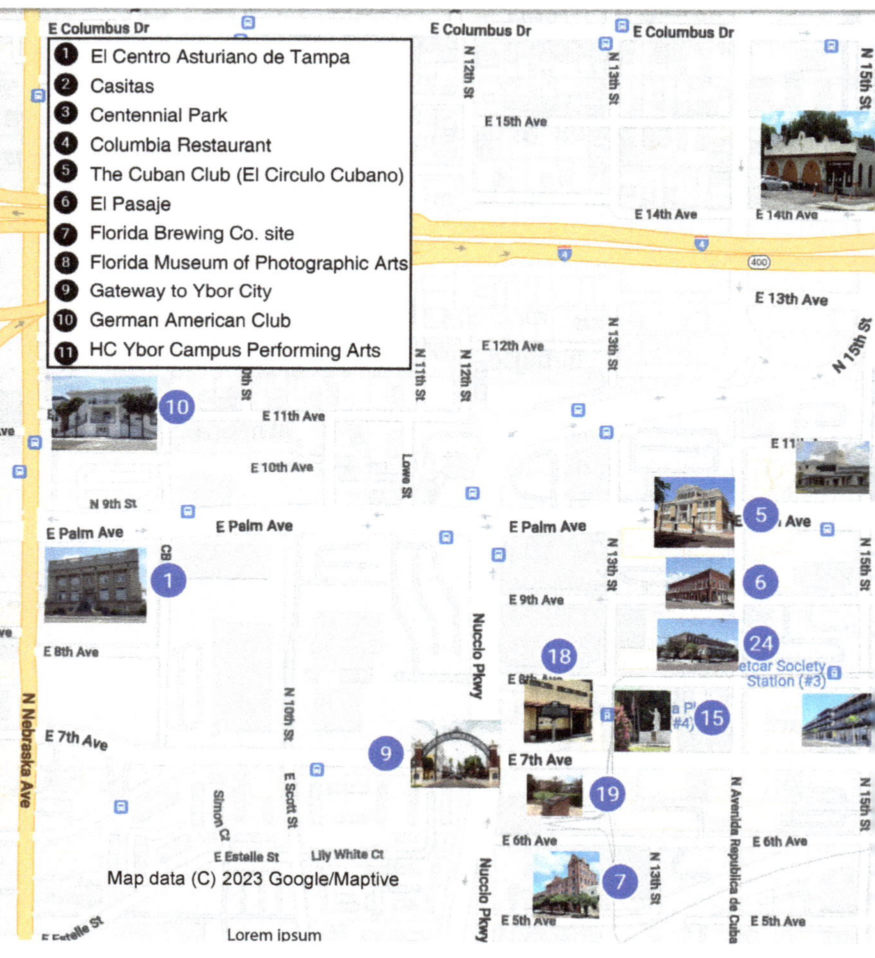

1 El Centro Asturiano de Tampa
2 Casitas
3 Centennial Park
4 Columbia Restaurant
5 The Cuban Club (El Circulo Cubano)
6 El Pasaje
7 Florida Brewing Co. site
8 Florida Museum of Photographic Arts
9 Gateway to Ybor City
10 German American Club
11 HC Ybor Campus Performing Arts
E Columbus Dr
N 12th St
N 13th St
N 15th St
E 15th Ave
E 14th Ave
E 13th Ave
E 12th Ave
N 11th St
E 11th Ave
E 10th Ave
N 9th St
E Palm Ave
Lowe St
E 9th Ave
E 8th Ave
E 7th Ave
E 6th Ave
E 5th Ave
N 10th St
E Scott St
Simon Ct
E Estelle St
Lily White Ct
Nuccio Pkwy
N Avenida Republica de Cuba
N Nebraska Ave
Map data (C) 2023 Google/Maptive
Lorem ipsum

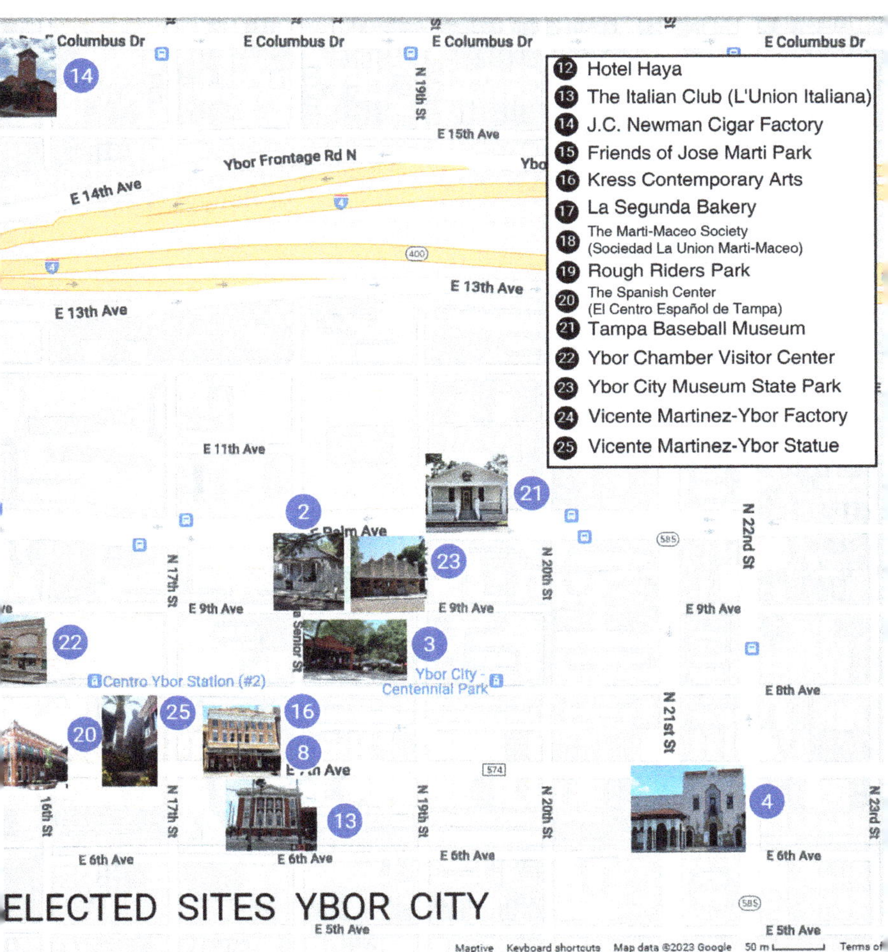


ELECTED SITES YBOR CITY

# 5

# MUSEUMS AND HISTORICAL EXHIBITS



This section covers the museums and locations with exhibits about Ybor City and its historical development.

▹ **Ybor City Museum State Park**
1818 E. 9th Ave.
*Location:* Across the street on the north side of Centennial Park.
*Phone:* (813) 247-6323
*Hours:* Wed-Sun, 9am-4pm; Closed Mon. and Tue. as well as Thanksgiving, Christmas, and New Year's Day
*Cost:* $4 per person, children 5 and under are free. Admission includes a tour of an adjacent cigar worker's casita on a first come, first served basis, according to the schedule posted on the state park website below or as posted in the museum.

*Websites:*
https://www.ybormuseum.org/ (Ybor City Museum)
http://www.floridastateparks.org/parks-and-trails/ybor-city-museum-state-park/ (Florida State parks site)

*Ybor City Museum*

The museum is a must-stop for all visitors to Ybor City. It's located in the historic **Ferlita Bakery,** which is described on a historic marker outside the yellow brick museum building. The museum features a film, vintage photos, and exhibits illustrating the development of Ybor City and the cigar industry. Included in the charge is a tour of a neighboring casita (little House) according to a posted schedule. Thousands were built for the cigar workers and specially designed to help residents survive in 19th century Florida. The casita contains period furniture and household items from the late 19th century. Between the museum and tour of the casita building is an enclosed garden park displaying a bust of Vicente Martinez Ybor, along with plants native to Florida.



An effective way to support the historic Ybor community is by contributing to the Ybor City Historical Society which operates the Tampa Baseball Museum, referred to next, and promotes the historic integrity of the Ybor City district.

▹ **Tampa Baseball Museum at the Al Lopez House**

2003 N. 19th St.

*Location:* On 19th St. across from the Ybor City Museum.

*Phone:* (813) 400-2353; Email: info@tampabaseballmuseum.org

*Hours:* Thu-Sat, 10am-4pm; Sun-Wed, closed; Closed Thanksgiving, Christmas Day, New Year's Day

*Website:* https://tampabaseballmuseum.org

*Cost:* $12 adults; $10 military, seniors (65 and over), first responders, educators, students 18 years and older with ID; $6 for children; free for children five years and younger. A second admission ticket for the Ybor City Museum is offered at a discount with the purchase of ticket to the Tampa Baseball Museum.

The Tampa Baseball Museum is located in the childhood home of Al Lopez, Tampa's first Major League player, manager and National Baseball Hall of Fame inductee. The Lopez house was moved from its original location and underwent a complete historical renovation so that it could be transformed into a museum. Exhibits represent the Major and Minor Leagues, spring training, early leagues beginning in 1887, Negro Leagues, and Tampa Bay's iconic baseball traditions. The museum serves as a place for inspiration, education, and the celebration of a game that became the fabric of an immigrant community—in a town that is known for developing a wealth of baseball talent at every level.

*Tampa Baseball Museum in the home of Al Lopez.*

▹ **J.C. Newman Cigar Factory**
2701 N. 16th St. at Columbus Dr.
*Phone:* (813) 248-2124
*Visiting Hours:* 9am-5:30pm

*J. C. Newman Cigar Factory.*

*Tours:* There are usually three tours scheduled per day, Monday through Friday. See website to register for an available tour on one of these days with occasional Saturdays offered. The tour involves significant walking as the cigar-making processes are observed through the multi-level factory. An elevator makes the tour accessible.
*Cost:* $15 adults and $12 seniors, students, veterans

This is a cigar manufacturing factory with a tour, store, museum, and online sales.

The J. C. Newman Factory is a workplace but also one large museum devoted to how cigars are made both by the hand rolling process, the age-old process of Ybor City, and by machine, which came into use close to the Depression. Take a walk through the lobby, gift shop, and museum. See the handrolling of cigars, but experience the most by signing up for the hour and 15 minute tour at https://www.jcnewman.com/. The last remaining cigar factory in the nation is a must see, just north of I-4 and best accessible by car. Parking is adjacent to the factory building. The factory, store, museum, and tour opened in the summer of 2020 after extensive building renovation to commemorate the company's 125th anniversary and the 110th anniversary of this iconic building with its landmark clock tower. The company has a legendary heritage of cigar making in Nicaragua, Cleveland, and Tampa.

*Map of Ybor City Historic District, Chamber Visitor Information Center.*

▹ **Ybor City Chamber of Commerce Visitor Information Center (the VIC)**
1600 E. 8th Ave., B-104.
*Phone:* (813) 241-8838
*Hours:* Mon-Sat, 10am-4pm; Sun, 12pm-4pm. Closed Thanksgiving and Christmas.
*Cost:* Free except for purchased items.
For further information, call, visit https://ybor.org/vic/ or inquire at info@ybor.org.

The VIC, located in Centro Ybor, is a great first stop. It includes museum exhibits, a gift shop, and a 7-minute video on the history and background of Ybor City that will place your visit in perspective. See Section 2 for further information.

▹ **Tampa Bay History Center**
801 Water St.
Phone: (813) 228-0097
*Location and Parking:* The Center is located in the Channelside District, south of Ybor City. Parking can be a challenge. It is a convenient ride from Ybor City by streetcar to Amalie Station (stop #8). If driving, the nearest parking is at Garrison Street Parking Lot to the east of the History Center at 615 Channelside Drive and East Cumberland Garage to the north at 1045 E. Cumberland Avenue.
*Hours:* Sun-Sat, 10am-5pm; Closed, Thanksgiving and Christmas and open until 3pm on Christmas Eve and New Year's Eve
*Cost:* Adults $16.95; Senior (60+) $14.95; Youth (7-17) $12.95; College Student $14.95; Child (6 and under) free; Members free. To obtain tickets, purchase online or at the door. https://www.tampabayhistorycenter.org/

The History Center is a must-see, world-class museum that offers many amenities, especially for those who join its society. Its exhibits are frequently changing but feature wonderful depictions of Ybor City and the development of the cigar industry in Tampa. These exhibits include a large model of a cigar factory building, highlighting the process from the entry of the tobacco leaves into the building to the emergence of the final cigar product. It has a full-size replica of a cigar shop as well.

The Center also recounts history in the Tampa Bay area with many artifacts from the Indigenous Americans, dating as far back as ten thousand years ago. It includes an art exhibit featuring wildlife and a floor devoted to pirate lore. In detail, it covers the history of this part of central Florida from the earliest inhabitants to the present and is documented by more than 40,000 artifacts. The **Columbia Restaurant** has a branch location off the History Center lobby on the second level.

▹ **Hillsborough County Sheriff's Office History Museum**
2001 N. 19th St.
*Location and Parking:* This museum is located next to the Tampa Baseball Museum at the corner of 9th Avenue and 19th Street. Parking is available in lots across the street from Centennial Station and Centennial Park accessible from 19th Street and 8th Avenue, and may be available in the adjacent Sheriff's Office lot as space allows for business with the department or to visit the museum.
*Phone:* (813) 297-0950
*Hours:* Thu-Fri, 9:30am-2:30pm; Sat, 8:30am-2pm
*Cost:* Admission is free and open to the public.
The museum contains artifacts and photos about the history of law enforcement in Hillsborough County from the earliest days of Tampa and Ybor City to the present.
https://hcsocharities.com/history-center

▹ **The Florida Museum of Photographic Arts (FMoPA)**, see section 15, Arts and Culture, page 160

# 6
# CULTURAL AND ETHNIC GROUPS

There were seven distinct cultural and ethnic groups that came together to make up the cigar economy of Ybor City. Each had one or more roles either directly involved in the industry or in supporting its community. Ybor City epitomizes the heritage of immigration in America, representing the coming together of many ethnic groups into one community. And amazingly enough, it happened in the Deep South.

In the late 19th century and early 20th century, America saw the greatest influx of people from Europe. Between 1880 and 1920, more than 20 million people came to the US from Europe. More than 80% of new arrivals came through the Port of New York, but ships also steamed into Boston, Philadelphia, Baltimore, and New Orleans. A second leg of the trip was often done either by rail or the boarding of a steam ship to points in the South or to Port Tampa.[1]

Port Tampa was the first port for Tampa and was created at the eastern side of the long peninsula on which Fort MacDill sits today, six miles south of Tampa and Ybor City. It was the location in Tampa Bay at which the harbor was the deepest, and a rail line connected it all the way to NYC. Port Tampa became the Ellis Island for Tampa with a processing center for new immigrants and was well established by 1900.[2]

**Immigration Routes to Tampa, Florida, late 19th to early 20th centuries:**[3]

- Afro Cubans by force from Africa to Cuba, 16th century through 1878
- Spanish from Spain primarily arriving in Cuba, then to Key West and Tampa
- Cubans from Cuba to Key West and to Tampa
- Sicilians arrived from Palermo and Naples to the Port of New York or to New Orleans, then to Tampa by rail or ship
- Italians from southern Italy arrived from Naples through the Port of New York (primarily), then made their way south to New Orleans or to Tampa by rail or ship
- Romanians and eastern Europeans principally from the port of Trieste through the Port of New York then southward by rail or ship.
- Germans from port Bremen and Hamburg through the Port of New York, then southward by rail or ship.
- Black line from NYC to Tampa common route by train or ship

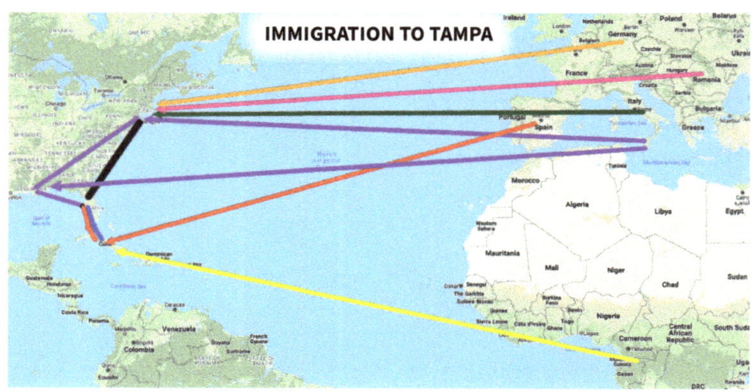


*Map data ©2021 Google/Maptive*

## SPANIARDS

The first three people to scout out the Tampa area for the cigar business were born in Spain. They included Vicente Martinez Ybor, Ignacio Haya, and Gavino Gutierrez. These men and others identified as Spaniards (a person from Spain) even though they had been in America many years since leaving Spain.

Their journey was similar to many Spaniards who came to the US through Cuba. Ybor moved to Cuba in 1832, then to Key West in 1869 as a refugee. Haya sailed to Cuba in 1860 before moving to NYC in 1868. Gutierrez came to NYC by way of Cuba in 1868. In 1885, they had been Americans for an aggregate of 95 years, but being born in Spain meant a great deal in the Hispanic community, so their Spanish origin remained their primary identification.

The connections of Spanish immigrants were with communities and relations in their Spanish homeland. A significant number came from the Asturian province of northern Spain and some from the southeastern Mediterranean coast, like Mr. Ybor. They came in large numbers to Cuba to seek better living conditions and, like Mr. Ybor, to escape the constant European wars, which had huge casualty rates. Most Spaniards emigrating from the Iberian Peninsula maintained a loyalty to Spain at least initially and tended to go to Cuba, one of last areas still controlled by the Spanish monarchy. They learned the cigar business from training programs in Cuba after they arrived and became an integral part of the industry.[4]

Many who came were well educated and became **lectors**. The lectors, who were readers to the cigar rollers as they worked, were introduced into the cigar factories in Cuba. The first occurrence was in Cuba in 1864 before they became an integral part of the factory environment in Key West, Tampa, and further into the US. They spoke the educated tongue of Castilian Spanish and read newspapers about local and international news. They also read European classics including novels, philosophy, works of literature, and political thought, which introduced the workers to the concept of democracy. This wide-ranging curriculum made cigar workers well educated.[5]



## HISPANIC CUBANS

Those of Hispanic heritage born in Cuba comprised a major component of the cigar factory workers. They developed a different perspective about being governed from Spain and felt oppressed by a colonial rule that was for the economic benefit of Spain rather than Cuba.

This population formed the core of the cigar industry. They were involved in the production of cigars from selecting the tobacco, to stripping the unusable parts, to blending the leaves in the cigar product, to working the tobacco into a well-formed, tapered, and skillfully made product. While Spain tended to tax the cigar industry for the benefit of the mother country, Spanish-born workers in Cuba also became disenchanted with Spanish rule and joined their Cuban colleagues in supporting independence movements not only in Cuba but also in the US from Key West to Tampa, and to cities in the Northeast including NYC where Vicente Martinez Ybor also had a factory for a period of time.[6]

The Cuban community centers that developed in Ybor and Tampa were initially focused on the politics of the day as their reason for being. As Spain became more oppressive in Cuba in attempts to hold on to their last American colony, Cubans were organizing to support their compatriots in Cuba who had been making numerous attempts to throw off Spanish rule as early as the 1860s.

The immigrants to Florida and Ybor City came for several reasons. For the Cubans, the emigration to the US and elsewhere in Latin America coincided with the Ten Years' War (1868–1878), which was the first Cuban War for Independence. During the outbreak of hostilities between the Spanish colonial government and those seeking independence, arrests were widespread for anyone supporting or sympathizing with the independence movement. The crackdown which ensued at the beginning of the war sent many Cuban cigar workers, including Vicente Martinez Ybor, to Key West, so they could escape charges of treason and imprisonment. The driving force for emigration to the US for most Hispanic Cubans was the political turmoil and the conflict that centered on independence from Spain. In Ybor City, the Cuban immigrants would come to focus more on community assistance, health, and support following Cuban independence.[7]



## AFRO CUBANS

To the concept of Ybor being multicultural, multiethnic, multilingual, the community also came to be described as multiracial. In Cuba, Hispanic Cubans and Afro Cubans were drawn together by a common language and a common industry. The term Hispanic refers to the people, speech, or culture of Spanish according to Merriam-Webster thereby including Spaniards and Afro Cubans. Exclusivity was the rule in the U.S. where in the Jim Crow South of segregation and keeping the races separate, the social implications were harsher. Not only separated from their fellow Cubans by race, Afro Cubans were separated from the Anglo society by language, requiring them to be a stronger and more self-reliant community than all the other immigrant groups. If Afro Cubans needed surgical treatment, their best recourse was to return to Cuba.[8]

The Afro Cuban community strongly supported the Cuban independence movement. They were led by such activists as Paulina and Ruperto Pedroso with whom José Martí stayed in his frequent visits to Ybor City as they generated support for the independence movement.[9]

General Antonio Maceo, the Afro Cuban after whom the group's mutual aid society is also named, was a galvanizing leader for independence and a veteran of the Ten Years' War. In the revolution's War of Cuban Independence in which Martí is killed on the battlefield in 1895, General Maceo led the largest fighting force consisting primarily of Afro Cubans who bore the brunt of the fighting.[10] The struggle for independence would not have succeeded without their critical participation.

The first Afro Cuban society to provide a community in the midst of segregation was formed in 1900. It was later followed by the current organization, a combination of two groups to form La Union Martí-Maceo in 1909. They were most often employed in many stages of the hand-making of cigars alongside their white Cuban counterparts in the cigar factories.[11] 

## ITALIANS/SICILIANS

The Italians began to arrive soon after the Spanish and Cuban immigrants. The surge of Italian immigrants to the US began in the late 1870s and continued up to the beginning of World War I in 1914. Their arrival in Ybor City became noticeable in the late 1880s.

This group came primarily from villages in southwestern Sicily but also some from southern Italy. Among the Sicilian towns heavily represented were Santo Stefano Quisquina, Bivona, Alessandria della Rocca, and Cianciana. The soil was poor, and agriculture was the primary livelihood. Yet the minimal trade markets made such a living unsustainable. Santo Stefano at the higher elevation was primarily engaged in sheep and goat herding, which produced cheese and wool. Bivona and Alessandria della Rocca were more successful in growing crops, especially wheat, while Cianciana residents worked extensive sulfur mines. Italians also came from Naples and the small surrounding villages in southern Italy.[12]



Italians in Ybor began to flow in with the completion of the Henry Plant railroad to Tampa in 1885, and came from the Port of New York, from New Orleans, and from the sugar cane plantations in St. Cloud and Kissimmee where working conditions were harsh and the pay low.[13] They sought the warmer climate of Florida similar to southern Italy, in a geographical location that resembled the Apennine Peninsula of home. Spain had controlled Sicily for hundreds of years, and the Italian and Sicilian cultures developed somewhat differently—both being divided by a related language, similar to the situation with British and US English.

The Italians often arrived in Ybor City with their whole families. This was in contrast to the early days of Ybor City when men from Cuba and Key West arrived singly or without their families and sent for them later once they got settled. A devastating earthquake in Sicily in 1909 further hastened the departure of Sicilians and their family units for Tampa.[14]

The introduction of Italians into the Hispanic-dominated cigar industry was slow and initially involved menial labor or the arduous tobacco-stripping process as they came with no cigar rolling skills, but they managed to work their way up in the process and Italian women also became factory employees. With political conflict brewing over Cuban independence among those identifying as Cuban or supporting Spain, some factory owners preferred Italian workers. With a background in agriculture, many Italians became grocers and were supplied by Italian farms and dairies north and east of the city. They were not averse to taking their wagons of goods into the neighborhoods and by factories to seek out customers. They also managed to occupy as much as 20% of cigar worker employment. Today's descendants are still engaged in those activities and the supplying of other commercial goods.[15]

*Four villages in southwest Sicily, south of Palermo.*

## ROMANIANS

Along with the Italians' arrival in the late 19th and early 20th centuries came Romanian Jews, building on the small Jewish community already developing in Tampa in the 19th century. Jews were also of Austrian and German extraction, from other eastern European countries, and from the Middle East. Jews from Romania were also subject to severe discriminatory treatment in being excluded not only from business opportunities but also generally from the rest of society.[16]

The Romanian people were divided into three regions—one controlled by the Austrian Hapsburgs to the west, a second by Russia in the east, both of which had anti-Jewish policies, and a small area in between the two countries where Romanians were self-governed. Despite the self-government, they were under constant threat from their powerful neighbors.

Traditionally, Romanian Jews were shopkeepers, and they came to set up many shops providing the necessary dry goods for Ybor City's growing populace, just as the Italians gravitated toward growing produce, raising livestock, and establishing groceries as they did in Italy. By 1920 (according to city directory records), there were thirty Jewish businesses on 7th Avenue, providing a range of household items and family necessities. This community gave generously to the cause of Cuban independence as they could relate to the oppressive discriminatory treatment of their homeland.[17]

Word-of-mouth spread through the US then abroad about the community of Ybor City where people could provide a niche in the economy and be accepted as one among many cultural groups attempting to make a new life. The Romanian Jews and other Jewish nationalities came to fit right in with the Latin community and tended to sympathize with cigar workers in their clashes with patrons (the cigar company owners), often extending credit to those working in the cigar industry during strikes.[18]

Many Romanian Jews struggled during the Great Depression and afterward with the decline of the cigar industry and the loss of population in Ybor City as their businesses ceased to prosper. The names of their large and valued enterprises are remembered today and appear faded on buildings now utilized for different purposes. The names include Maas Brothers clothing store, Isidor Kaunitz clothing store, El Sombrero Blanco (housed in the first brick building on 7th Avenue), the Max Argintar Men's Store, Wolfson's, Star Grocery, Blue Ribbon Market, Louis Wohl & Sons (dry goods, equipment, furniture), David Stein Furniture Co., Steinberg's, and Buchman's Department Store.[19]

The Jewish community from many nationalities have provided civic and governmental leadership to Tampa since the days of Vicente Martinez Ybor in such capacities as state legislators, a US Senator, mayors, sheriffs, and judges. This group provided critical leadership that sustained a developing Ybor City.

## GERMANS

The German community in Tampa hovered between 1 and 2% of the population in Tampa in the late 19th and early 20th centuries. Yet in the golden years of the cigar industry (leading up to 1920), they played a significant role far beyond their numbers. The Germans performed such functions as accounting and bookkeeping in the cigar factories and other businesses.[20]

Many Germans became involved in establishing and maintaining the needed Florida Brewery upon which Ybor City would critically depend. They were also teachers. In the cigar industry, Germans played an instrumental role in the design and printing of cigar labels for cigar boxes and the bands on the cigars themselves, which promoted the cigar brand. They used a lithograph process developed in Bavaria, where the image was drawn on a limestone slab; it was a less expensive printing process than metal plates. The Germans created cigar labels and bands in brilliant colors, and many of the vintage labels and bands from a bygone era are available today in Ybor City.[21]

Within the cigar industry, the Germans also made the cigar boxes early on, mostly with selected woods that enhanced the aroma of the cigar product without detracting from it. Some boxes were made out of cardboard of a sturdy thickness to protect the valuable contents. Both types of boxes are used today. During the golden age of cigar rolling, there were three box factories in Ybor. One on Adamo Drive called the Box Factory Lofts is utilized as apartments today.

The German immigrant involvement dropped off in 1917 with the US declaration of war against Germany in World War I. Germans became subjected to discrimination and hate crimes, and were ostracized.[22] They began moving away from Ybor to other larger German communities or to other areas of the country where they could hold themselves out as Americans abandoning those aspects of their culture which identified them as German.

The German-American Club built in 1908 was sold in 1919 as the members who identified as German dramatically decreased. Their community assistance center on Nebraska Avenue had a restaurant serving German foods, which was open to the public and a popular place to eat in Tampa in the pre–World War I years.[23]



## CULTURAL GROUP CENTERS

The centers for the cultural groups were known by many names. Today they are often referred to as "clubs," but they were also known as community centers or mutual assistance centers. They were all there committed to serve the purpose of aiding newly arriving immigrants to become assimilated into the life and world of Ybor City.

The large imposing clubs were an opportunity for the various groups to compete with one another in building the most aesthetically pleasing and impressive, yet functional building. Most clubs came to allow for members to join who were outside their cultural and ethnic group, and the centers supported one another in times of peril. This was especially crucial during the major fires that impacted the community. If one center burned, the others would allow the use of their facilities until a new facility could be built.

Some were set up for different reasons. The Union of Martí-Maceo developed because the Jim Crow laws would not allow the Afro Cubans to be part of the Hispanic Cuban organization, which had been possible in Cuba. The Cuban Club began as a congregating point to support the Cuban independence movement. The Centers included the following:[24]

| Cultural Group | Center Name | When First Organized | Date of Current Building |
|---|---|---|---|
| Asturians | El Centro Asturiano | 1902 | 1914 |
| Spanish | El Centro Español | 1891 | 1912 |
| Italian | L'Unione Italiana | 1894 | 1918 |
| Cuban | El Circulo Cubano | 1902 | 1918 |
| Afro Cuban | La Union Martí-Maceo | 1900 | 1965 |
| German-American | Deutsch Amerikanischer Verein | 1901 | 1909 |

Members from one club would switch to another based on which services they needed or preferred. The centers were funded by member dues. In return, members and their families received a whole range of services and enhanced community involvement:

- Medical services ranged from clinics where one could be seen by the center's doctor(s) to treatment rooms and pharmacies. El Centro Asturiano was known for its surgical center and for the hospital it later built north and west of the club. The medical coverage extended from the cradle to the grave even though Afro Cubans often had to return to Cuba for surgical needs. The medical care provided was the forerunner of today's Health Maintenance Organizations (HMOs) and the concept of universal healthcare for all. The coverage could boast from the "cradle to the grave."
- Education was emphasized with space dedicated to classes including language literacy, and the centers included libraries.
- Lavish ballrooms for social gatherings occupied second floors, and some, like the Italian, Cuban, and Asturian Clubs, had stages for various performances including operas and special entertainers. The Italian Club served as a movie theatre for many years.
- Many included canteens where members could gather for a light meal and relax after work.
- Sports events allowed for intra-club rivalries as well as competition between clubs. Some like the Cuban Club had a gym, bowling alley, and exercise equipment.
- Special cultural celebrations were held in the community's clubs including dances, picnics, and informal gatherings.
- The center community was there to help assimilate newly arriving immigrants, helping them get established. The clubs also provided community at the time of death, for other tragedies, and during periods of adversity:[25]

## CLUBS TODAY

Many of the same functions take place today, and membership in the organization includes those beyond the ethnic group as well as members who represent the fourth and fifth generations of Yborites. Special community-focused events still occur, but the facilities are open for weddings, special occasions, and milestone celebrations. The facilities can be rented out for social, business related, or nonprofit purposes as well.

Classes and education are still an important facet of the clubs. The clubs also sponsor Krewes, whose purpose is to preserve its culture and traditions as well as to participate in the many parades, festivals, and unique cultural events in the Tampa Bay area.

*Photo by David Nankervis. Used with permission.*



## Historical Note

In 1886, the same year that the first cigar workers arrived in Ybor City, the Statue of Liberty was installed on October 28th. It was a gift from France in honor of the country that openly welcomed Europeans to the shores of America. The statue was a joint venture between the US and France. The French provided the statue, and the US raised the money for the pedestal on which it would stand.

The installation of the statue and the poem which promoted it symbolized an immigrant movement to America that had been ongoing since the two continent's first settlements. The statue's opening coinciding with the beginning of Ybor City reinforces the central defining characteristic of US history—immigration.

## *Endnotes Section 6*

1. Steve Rajtar, *A Guide to Historic Tampa Florida* (Charleston, SC: The History Press, 2007), 44-45, 70.
2. Gary R. Mormino and George E. Pozzetta, *The Immigrant World of Ybor City* (Gainesville, FL: University of Florida Press, 2017), 47-49.
3. U.S. Immigration through Primary and Other Sources, The Gjenvick-Gjonvik Immigration Archives, Immigrant Passage Archives 1880s -1920, Immigrant Passenger Information by Port of Call, By Region, By Port of Entry, By Year. Last accessed February 2022, https://www.gjenvick.com/; U.S. National Archives, Records of Immigration and Naturalization Services, 1891-1957: Immigration Records, Passenger Arrival Records by Port of Entry, Last accessed February 2022, https://www.archives.gov/research/immigration/ports/
4. National Park Service, U.S. Department of Interior, El Centro Español de Tampa Ybor City, Tampa, Florida, last accessed February 2022, https://www.nps.gov/nr/travel/american_latino_heritage/El_Centro_Espanol_de_Tampa.html ; Mormino and Pozzetta, *The Immigrant World of Ybor City*, 70-75.
5. Wallace Reyes, *Once Upon a Time in Tampa, Rise and Fall of the Cigar Industry* (Scotts Valley, CA: CreateSpace Publishing Platform, 2013), 81-84; Mormino and Pozzetta, *The Immigrant World of Ybor City*, 102-103.

6. L. Glenn Westfall, *Don Vicente Martinez Ybor, The Man and His Empire* (New York: Garland Publishing Inc., 1987), 20-26; Mormino and Pozzetta, *The Immigrant World of Ybor City*, 73-74.
7. Westfall, *Don Vicente Martinez Ybor,* 20-26.
8. Reyes, *Once Upon a Time in Tampa,* 185-186.
9. Alfred J. Lopez, *Jose Martí, A Revolutionary Life* (Austin, TX: University of Texas Press, 2014), 264-266.
10. Lastra, *Ybor City The Making of a Landmark Town* (Tampa, FL: The University of Tampa Press, 2006), 88-91; John M. Dunn, *José Martí: Cuba's Greatest Hero* (Sarasota, FL: Pineapple Press, Inc., 2015) 70-72.
11. "Afro Cubans in Tampa," Florida History.org, last accessed February 2022, http:/ www.floridahistory.org/ybor6.htm; Isaiah Destee, "Pan-Africanism: Afro Cuban History in Tampa, Florida, last accessed February 2022, https://destee.com/threads/afro-cuban-history-in-tampa-florida.39717/
12. Mormino and Pozzetta, *The Immigrant World of Ybor City,* 17-22.
13. Mormino and Pozzetta, *The Immigrant World of Ybor City*, 32-34.
14. Reyes, *Once Upon a Time in Tampa*, 188-189.
15. Mormino and Pozzetta, *The Immigrant World of Ybor City*, 85-92; Lastra, *Ybor City The Making of a Landmark Town*, 29.
16. Reyes, *Once Upon a Time in Tampa*, 113-122.
17. Reyes, *Once Upon a Time in Tampa*, 119-122.
18. Reyes, *Once Upon a Time in Tampa*, 116.
19. Rob Norman and Marcia Jo Zerivitz, *Jews of Tampa* (Charleston, SC: Arcadia Publishing, 2013), 57-84.
20. Lastra, *Ybor City The Making of a Landmark Town*, 85-87.
21. Reyes, *Once Upon a Time in Tampa,* 189; The Art of the Cigar – Artisans of Leaf and Stone / One Stone, Many Colors – The Incredible Process of Stone Lithography, Museum Exhibit, Ybor City Visitor Information Center, 2000.
22. Lastra, *Ybor City The Making of a Landmark Town*, 86.
23. Reyes, *Once Upon a Time in Tampa*, 190-191.
24/25. "History," The Asturian Club (Centro Asturiano de Tampa) last accessed February 2022; https://www.centroasturianotampa.org ; John A. Ranon, "Our Story," Centro Español de Tampa, last accessed February 2022, https://centroespanoltampa.org; E. J. Salcines, "History," The Italian Club of Tampa (L' Unione Italiana}, last modified April 2018, accessed February 2022, https://italian-club.org/history/; "About the Cuban Club," The Cuban Club (El Circulo Cubano), accessed February 2022, http://cubanclubybor.com/; "Afro Cubans in Tampa," Floridahistory.org, accessed February 2022; "German-American Club, German-American Club Marker, HMdb.org, The Historical Marker Database, last revised January 3, 2020, last accessed February 2022, https://www.hmdb.org/m.asp?m=32372/

# 7 TOBACCO, CIGARS, & CIGAR SHOPS



## A BRIEF HISTORY OF TOBACCO[1]

Tobacco came from the Americas, perhaps originally from the ancient Mayan people of South America, before it extended northward to Central and North America and the Caribbean Islands. Its history goes back as far as 6,000 BCE, but the Indigenous people of America did not begin smoking until closer to the current era.

Columbus found tobacco when he first landed in the Caribbean in 1492, and took it back to Spain. It came into common use in Spain in the 1530s, then spread to Portugal. The French ambassador to Lisbon, Jean Nicot, whose name was used for the scientific name of the plant, sent a sample to Catherine de Medici in Paris. Arriving in England in the late 1560s, the product then moved eastward to the rest of Europe. Spain began importing tobacco seeds in the 1560s for growing the plant in Europe. In the late 1580s, Sir Walter Raleigh brought it back to the court of Elizabeth I from North Carolina. Legend has it that he had her partake of it. Given her intrepid nature, this may well have occurred. Early on in Europe, pipe smoking was popular as the rolling process was in its crude stage and less satisfactory for smoking.

The Indigenous people of America used tobacco for a large variety of **medicinal** purposes including applying it directly to wounds. In addition, it was being smoked in pipes or in tightly rolled leaves lit at one end and drawn into the mouth. It had a strong traditional purpose among America's Indigenous peoples in two respects. First it had a **ceremonial** purpose, confirming agreements between tribes and signifying unity and brotherhood. But it was also used for religious purposes and was believed to have been from the Creator.

In America, the Spanish were the first to cultivate tobacco in Hispaniola and then in Cuba in the 1530s. In Europe, both Philip II of Spain and James I of England attempted to curtail its use but it developed widespread usage and was an ingredient in snuff. Indigenous people of the eastern North America tribes carried tobacco around to **use for barter,** and this practice was also used by the first Europeans to arrive in America because gold and silver were not available. Hence tobacco became a currency standard. Jamestown struggled until John Rolfe arrived later and began to grow tobacco. It became a cash crop for export to England and was the turning point from subsistence farming in America. Tobacco farms were first worked by indentured servants in return for passage to America, then by slave labor.

Today, there are more than seventy species of tobacco. The most common species used for commercial tobacco products are *Nicotiana tabacum* and to a lesser extent, the more potent, *Nicotiana rustica*. Dried tobacco leaves are used in many products, but they're primarily used for cigars, cigarettes, and pipe smoking. They are also consumed as snuff and chewing tobacco.

## A BRIEF HISTORY OF CIGARS[2]

Technically, the first cigars have to be attributed to the Mayans of southern Mexico and Central America even though the rolled tobacco leaves in no way resemble the artistic and intricate process of cigars made today.

While cigars were introduced in America just prior to the Revolutionary War, their production was not significant until the early 19th century with the first cigar factories being established in Connecticut and using Cuban seed tobacco. Cuban cigars also began to be imported at the same time.

Cigar use was accelerated at the time of the Civil War as a status symbol with General (and later President) Ulysses S. Grant often pictured with a cigar in his mouth. Another model of promotion was Edward, Prince of Wales (later Edward VII) who made cigar smoking even more popular in Britain and the US. Vicente Martinez Ybor would create his cigar brand Prince of Wales to build on the popularity created in the English speaking market by the heir to the British throne. Winston Churchill, more frequently photographed with a cigar than without, maintained a large stock of several thousand cigars at his home and is said to have stayed at El Pasaje when it became a hotel.

The introduction of cigars made by mechanization occurred in Cuba in the 1920s, creating the first dampener on the made-by-hand industry. Despite regulatory labels cautioning the use of cigar products sold in the US, the cigar has undergone a gradual increase in popularity, which began in the 1990s.

Tobacco for cigars is not really grown in the middle Atlantic states of Virginia and North Carolina, well-known for its tobacco crop production. Cigar tobacco is principally grown in the Central American countries of Nicaragua, Guatemala, and Honduras, in Mexico, and in the Caribbean, in Cuba, the Dominican Republic, Haiti, and Puerto Rico. Tobacco leaves used as wrappers can come from the northeastern US.

Tobacco for components of cigars, like the wrapper leaf in the US, comes from Connecticut, Massachusetts, southern Vermont, Kentucky, and Pennsylvania. Since the Cuban embargo in 1962, which affected imports from Cuba, domestically sold US cigars are not made from Cuban-grown tobacco, which was the source of Vicente Martinez Ybor's cigar production. However, the seeds of Cuban tobacco have been spread throughout the tobacco-growing world.

The location of where the tobacco is grown has a lot to do with its flavor and taste. No two cigars will taste exactly alike, and when smoking, it is advisable and common practice, not to inhale.

There is proper etiquette in cutting, lighting, burning, and smoking cigars, which makes the process of enjoying the cigar as much of an art as is the making of it.

Cigars are made up of three parts: the filler, the binder, and wrapper.

1. The **filler** (inside) is tobacco of Cuban seed. It's responsible for a significant portion of a cigar's taste, and differences in taste are determined by where it is grown. The blend of filler leaves is called a bunch and can consist of up to five types of filler tobacco and is held together by the binder.
2. The **binder** (outer layer that holds the filler together) is from thicker, rougher leaves, which are selected for flavor and burn quality.
3. The **wrapper** (which gives it a finished visual appeal and contributes flavor) leaf can come from anywhere in the world and usually have some characteristics of Cuban seed tobacco. The different types of wrappers are identified by their colors. The wrapper leaf is usually the most expensive tobacco in a cigar. The tobacco grown in the northeastern US is most frequently used in domestic cigar production as its thin-veined quality makes it a vital component for the outer wrapping of the cigar.

## *Additional Cigar Terminology*[3]

**band** – a ring of paper around the head of most cigars. They are often a color printed label with the name of the brand indicating the originating country and if the cigar is hand-rolled. It serves an advertising purpose and helps keep the wrapper together.

**blend** – the complete selection of tobacco used to make a cigar. It consists of multiple leaves for the filler and binder, and one type of leaf for the wrapper, all of which make up the undisclosed ingredients in a particular cigar.

**box** – the container which holds the cigars which comes in 3 standard sizes: 1) a mini-cabinet of wood with a sliding top which holds up to fifty cigars; 2) an 8-9-8 box has rounded sides and holds three rows of cigars: 8 on the top, 9 in the second row below that, and 8 lying on the bottom; and 3) flat top, 2-layer box with 12 cigars on the bottom and 13 on top.

**bunch** – the combination of binder and filler leaves (long and short) used in a cigar. The buncher assembles the binder and filler leaves for the cigar.

**bundle** – the process by which cigars are wrapped in cellophane packaging.

**cap** – the cover for the head of the cigar from which it is smoked, usually consisting of 2 or 3 circular pieces of tobacco leaf. The cap needs to be cut before the cigar can be smoked.

**Clear Havana** – a cigar manufactured in the US, consisting of a special Cuban tobacco (before the embargo).

**Corona** – a classic size of a manufactured cigar measuring 5 and 5/8 inches with a 42 ring size.

**Cuban seed** – tobacco that refers to plants grown with Cuban seed but not in Cuba.

**curing** – the process by which tobacco is dried in a gradual process to remove moisture from the leaves usually in a curing barn.

**destemming** – the process manually or machine guided by which the stems running through the center of the leaf are cut away.

**Dominican Republic** – the nation regarded as the primary producer of premium cigars.

**Habano** or **Habana** – the term used to refer to a Cuban cigar.

**Honduras** – a large cigar-producing nation along with Nicaragua, the Dominican Republic, and Cuba.

**hand-rolled** – a cigar made entirely by hand.

**head** – the end of the cigar at which one draws the smoke.

**humidor** – a room or boxes of various sizes that preserve the cigar by providing proper storage conditions, including an appropriate humidity level and a temperature in the range of 65° to 70°F.

**machine-made** – cigars made with the assistance of machines, antique or modern. The filler in machine-made cigars is usually of scrap tobacco as opposed to long leaf, and therefore they're cheaper than the hand-rolled cigars that are of higher quality and better draw.

**mold** – the form into which cigar bunches (which include filler and binder leaves) are placed to create the semblance of a rounded cylindrically shaped cigar product.



**Nicaragua** – one of the four leading countries in Central America prominent in tobacco growing and cigar production.

**Pina del Rio** – the most famous tobacco-growing region in Cuba is the westernmost province.

**press** – used in conjunction with a mold to form the cigars into their circular, rounded shape.

**ring gauge** – the diameter by which a cigar is measured in millimeters often characteristic of the cigar's brand.

**Spanish cedar** – the material of which most cigar boxes and humidors are made considered to enhance without conflicting with the cigar blend.

**tabaquero** – the term applied to both tobacco growers and cigar workers.

**wheel** – consists of a bundle of 100 cigars bound by a ribbon.

## CIGAR FACTORIES AND THE CIGARS THEY MADE[4]

### *The Factory*

Cigar factories in 19th century Ybor City were rectangular in shape, and they were built on an east–west axis to provide sunlight all day long. The path of the sun would move east to west across the top of the building, which provided an equal amount of light through the windows of the north and south sides of the building.

Wood structures in the first years gave way to bricks soon after the bricks were imported by train from manufacturers in the southeast, including the closest in Augusta, Georgia. The windows occupied as much space of the building façade as the brick construction between each window. Larger windows on the north side would draw the air into the building, which flowed out through the smaller windows on the south side, providing for steady ventilation and as much cooling as possible.

## *Four Levels*

The cigar factories, of which there are only perhaps 15 remaining structures in Tampa, are used for different purposes today except for one, the J. C. Newman Cigar Factory. There were well over 200 factory buildings consisting of four floors in Ybor City. The basement was partly above ground to allow natural light onto the floor with three levels above the basement.



## *The Cupola*

On most factory buildings, at the very top above the roof line was a cupola. It was a little square room resembling a turret with windows and a roof astride the middle of the building. It was the lookout for a young employee who could manage the narrow staircase to the room above the roof. From this vantage point he could spot ships as they entered the port, which was located off the western side of what is today MacDill Air Force Base. The ships could not be easily seen from Ybor City, but their masts with the country's flags could be seen. If the flags indicated Cuban origin, the probability of Cuban tobacco aboard was high. The youthful employee would race down to the street to a wagon stationed outside the building and begin the race to the port to be as close to the first as possible to get, for example, the Havana Clear tobacco that Mr. Ybor valued for his cigars.

Reproduction of a cigar factory cupola

*Diagram of a Cigar Factory, late 19th, early 20th centuries. Used with permission of Dr.Wallace Reyes.*

## *First Floor (2)*

Bales of tobacco were unloaded from the wagon onto the loading docks of the first full floor above ground level. The leaves were graded according to texture from smooth to course, and by color among other considerations. The factory image reveals the worktables and the sorting process. Management offices were also located on the first floor, and the finished cigars would return here for packaging before departing the factory.

## *Basement (1)*

After the grading or sorting of leaves, the tobacco leaves were moved to the basement (often by elevator), where they would be moistened so that they could be more easily flexible for rolling. Bales of tobacco were also stored there.

*Third Floor (4)*

After moistening, the leaves would be moved to the third floor to begin their conversion from plant to skillfully crafted cigar product. The leaves were carefully stripped of their stems and often children and women were engaged in this process. The third floor contained shelf racks to hold the destemmed leaves.

*Second Floor (3)*

The leaves were then transferred to the second floor referred to as the Galleria where hundreds of cigar rollers at row after row of tables lined the floor. See the diagram showing the gallery of tables and cigar rollers. It was on the second floor while the rollers worked their magic that lectors read to them from newspapers and world literature in Spanish, and loud enough to be heard throughout the factory.

*Return to the First Floor (2)*

The finished cigars which underwent the process outlined below were then returned to the first floor to receive the bands, which included the company name and were the means by which the cigars were branded and promoted. They were boxed in handsomely constructed wooden boxes which had been shipped to the cigar factory from the box factories.



## CIGAR-ROLLING PROCESS[5]

1. Filler and Binder. In a large factory operation, the task of initially forming a cigar is divided between a buncher and a roller. The buncher takes the filler pieces of tobacco leaves and wraps them in leaves designated as the binder. The filler must be uniform in density throughout the length of its wrapping. The buncher then places the initial tube-shaped cigar into a wooden mold.
2. Wrapper. After a period of time, the buncher removes the bound roll of tobacco from the mold, and the product is passed to the roller to apply a wrapper which is the moistened deveined leaf that surrounds the filler, which in turn is held together by the binder leaves.
3. The Rolling. The bunched cigars are then at the roller's table to begin their artful process. The roller has a sharp, curved blade to cut any abnormal pieces from the tube of tobacco, and he cuts the wrapper leaves to the size of the cigar being rolled. The wrappers are usually curved leaf pieces that will spiral around the binder. A little vegetable glue may be applied to make sure the wrapper leaves hold.
4. Capping. The last step involves applying the cap to the cigar, the end that is put in the mouth. This is a small piece of wrapper, circular in shape that is applied to the head of the cigar.

5. Aging. The cigars are aged for a period of at least several weeks so that the various tobaccos are bonded in a uniform blend.
6. Packaging. The cigars are inspected for uniformity in color and without blemish to be grouped together and placed in a box. Cigars are then sold by the box or by quantity from a box.

## CIGAR ESTABLISHMENTS IN YBOR CITY

Cigar manufacturing takes two forms—those that are entirely handmade and those made with the assistance of machinery. National branded cigars can be made with mechanization while the cigars made in the shops in the more than a dozen cigar shops in Ybor City are made by hand. Most of those listed in this section have websites, but some do not and can simply be accessed on and off 7th Avenue with a little exploration. They are all unique in some way and usually have some offering for the visiting public.



### *National Brands*

Two companies in Ybor City are considered to have a national and international presence. Those include, but are not limited to the **J. C. Newman Company**, the site of the last remaining cigar factory in the United states at 2701 16th Street and **Arturo Fuente**. Both cigar manufacturers are headquartered in Ybor City.

*Arturo Fuente international headquarters in its original factory building on 2nd Avenue.*

J. C. Newman is in partnership with other cigar companies throughout the US and sells their own cigar brands and other company brands, at their factory store. J.C. Newman cigar brands are hand rolled in its factory in Nicaragua. Some Newman brands are also made by hand in the Dominican Republic in partnership with the Arturo Fuente family and certain brands are made in the Ybor factory by both hand and antique rolling machines. Arturo Fuente cigars are made in the Dominican Republic close to its primary source of tobacco. Its renovated corporate headquarters and distribution center buildings are located on 2nd Avenue. Their cigars are sold through distributors who include Tampa Sweethearts Cigar Company, King Corona Cigars and J.C. Newman Cigars.





*Local Brands*

The local shops are hand rolling establishments. They have their own unique brand of cigars and may carry others brands additionally. Their offerings are observable by an in-person visit or going to their website. The cigar shops usually have something of a token for a tourist who is not there to buy cigars. Several have a barista or a person who serves a wide range of drinks and light food offerings.

1. **La Faraona Cigars,** 1515 E. 7th Ave.
   *Phone:* (978) 648-1422
   *Hours:* Sun-Sat: 10am-12am
   *Website:* https://www.lafaraonacigars.com/
   La Faraona brand of hand-rolled cigars. Online sales, gift cards available. Cigar Lounge at 1315 E. 7th Ave.

2. **La Herencia De Ybor,** formerly La Herencia De Cuba, 1817 E. 7th Ave.
   *Phone:* (813) 248-6186
   *Hours:* Sun-Sat: 12pm-3am
   Bar opens in the evening.

3. **J. C. Newman Cigar Factory Store,** 2701 16th St.
   *Phone:* (813) 248-2124
   Visiting *Hours:* Mon-Fri: 9am-5:30pm; Sat-Sun: closed
   *Website:* https://jcnewman.com
   Factory store, factory tours, museum, and online sales. Wide variety of cigar labels and accessories. See Section 5 – Museums and Historical Exhibits.

4. **King Corona Cigars, Bar & Café,** 1523 E. 7th Ave.
   *Phone:* (813) 923-7982
   *Hours:* Mon-Thu: 10am-12am; Fri-Sat: 9am-1am; Sun: 11am-11pm.
   *Website:* https://kingcoronacigars.com/
   The café serves a highly rated Cuban sandwich, café con leche and has a light food offering.

5. **Long Ash Cigars,** 1728 E. 7th Ave.
   *Phone:* (813) 374-0346
   *Hours:* Sun: 11am-10pm; Mon-Thu: 11am-12am; Fri-Sat: 11am-2am
   *Website:* https://thelongashcigars.com/
   Serves Cuban coffee, gift shop, and cigar accessories. Supports local artists by displaying their art.

6. **Nicahabana Cigars,** 1605 E. $7^{th}$ Avenue
   *Phone:* (813) 609-3474
   *Hours:* Mon-Tue: 12pm-7pm; Wed-Thu: 12pm-10pm; Fri-Sat: 12pm-12am; Sun: 12pm-8pm
   *Website:* https://nicahabanacigar.com
   Online sales of cigars and accessories

7. **Sterling Cigar Lounge and Bar,** 1531 E. 7th Avenue
   *Phone: (813) 466-5723*
   *Hours:* Mon-Thu: 12pm-12am; Fri-Sat: 12pm-1:30am; Sun: 12pm-11pm
   *Website:* info@sterlingcigarbar.com
   Beautiful surroundings, impressive cigar selection, rooftop view

8. **Tabanero Cigars,** 1601 E. $7^{th}$ Ave.
   *Phone:* (813) 402-6316; email: store@tabanerocigars.com
   *Hours:* Sun-Wed: 10am-7pm; Thu-Sat: 10am-8pm
   *Website:* https://tabanerocigars.com/
   Tours available if indicated on the website. Serves Cuban coffee. Wide selection of cigars in its humidor. Online store includes accessories.

9. **Tampa Sweethearts Cigar Company,** 1603 E. $6^{th}$ Ave.
   *Phone:* (813) 247-3880
   *Hours:* Mon-Fri: 9am-5pm; Sat-Sun: closed
   *Website:* https://www.tampasweethearts.com/
   Distributor of Arturo Fuente brands. Cigar accessories and souvenirs. Online sales.

10. **Tampero Cigars,** 1805 N. $22^{nd}$ St.
    *Phone:* (813) 964-6863; email: info@tampero.com
    *Hours:* Mon-Sun: 10am-8pm.
    *Website:* https://tamperocigars.com/
    Cigar accessories and gift cards. Online sales.

11. **Ybor Cigars Plus**, 1725 E. $7^{th}$ Ave.
    *Phone:* (813) 516-0531; email: sales@yborcigarsplus.com
    *Hours:* Every Day: 10am-3am.
    *Website:* https://yborcigarsplus.com/
    Wide range of cigars categorized from mild to not so mild, online sales.

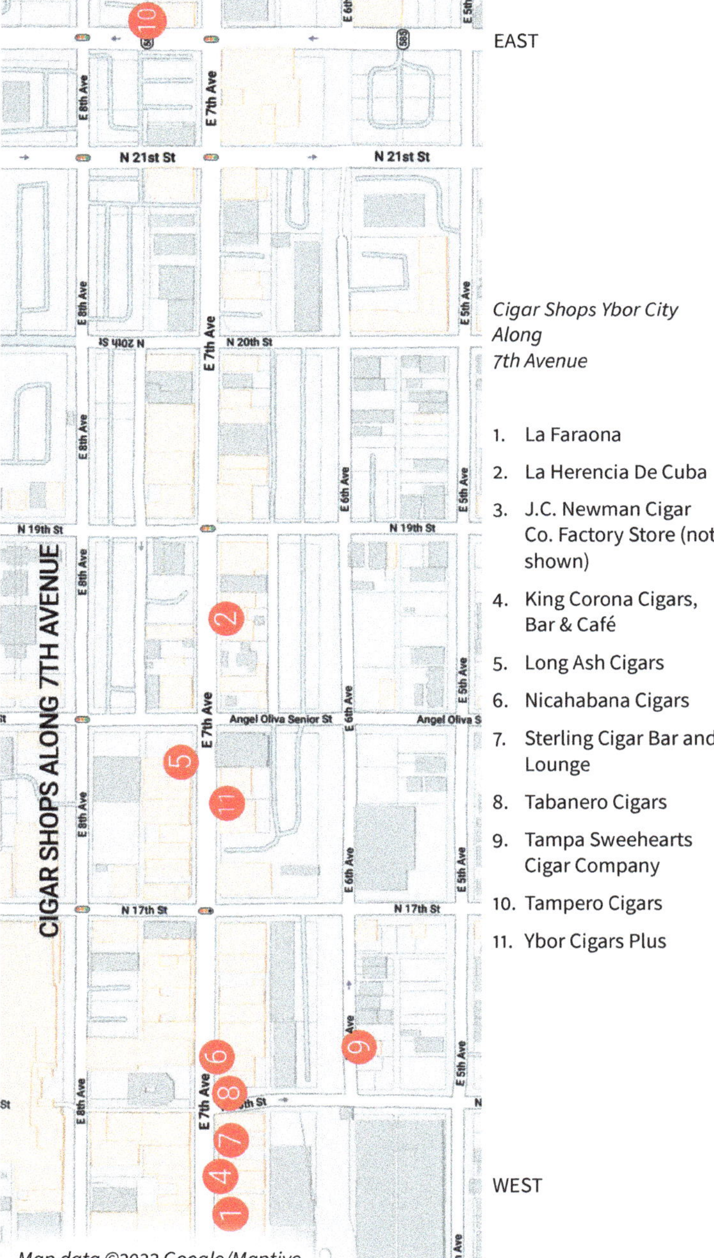


Map data ©2023 Google/Maptive

EAST

*Cigar Shops Ybor City Along 7th Avenue*

1. La Faraona
2. La Herencia De Cuba
3. J.C. Newman Cigar Co. Factory Store (not shown)
4. King Corona Cigars, Bar & Café
5. Long Ash Cigars
6. Nicahabana Cigars
7. Sterling Cigar Bar and Lounge
8. Tabanero Cigars
9. Tampa Sweehearts Cigar Company
10. Tampero Cigars
11. Ybor Cigars Plus

WEST

## *Endnotes Section 7*

1. Joshua J. Mark, "A Brief History of Tobacco in the Americas," *World History Encyclopedia*, last modified February 10, 2021, accessed February 2022, https://www.worldhistory.org/article/1677/a-brief-history-of-tobacco-in-the-americas/.
2. J. Bennett Alexander, "The History of Cigars: When Were Cigars Invented?" Holts Cigar Company, last updated September 17, 2021, accessed February 2022, https://www.holts.com/clubhouse/cigar-culture/the-hisstory-of-cigars-when-were-cigars-invented/
3. See "Cigar Glossary of Terms," Holt Cigar Company for a complete dictionary of cigar terminology, https://www.holts.com/clubhouse/cigar-101/glossary-of-terms; For an Ybor City Cigar Glossary, see "Cigar Terms," Tampero Cigars, accessed February 2022, https://tamperocigars.com/pages/cigar-terms/
4. Tampa Bay History Center, "Model of a 19th Century Ybor City Cigar Factory and the Floor by Floor Process of Making a Cigar," Second level, Cigar City Exhibit.
5. Ybor City Chamber of Commerce Visitor Information Center, Museum Display, "The Art is in the Making: The Process of Making a Hand Made Cigar," 2000; Thomas Tips, "How are Cigars Made: An In-Depth Look at a Rigorous Manufacturing Process," Cigar Cutter Expert, last modified September 15, 2019, accessed February 2022, https://cigarcutterexpert.com/how-are-cigars-made/

# 8
# ORGANIZED CRIME



## INTRODUCTION

While the cigar industry grew and evolved in the early 20th century, there was a parallel development of organized crime. There are plenty of resources to learn more about this chapter in Tampa history such as Dr. Wallace Reyes's book, *Once Upon a Time in Tampa*, and particularly the *Cigar City Mafia* by Scott M. Deitche. What's notable is that the Mafia's growth occurred over an extended period, and it impacted the political and economic life of Tampa as a developing urban area.

From the early 20th century and into the 21st century, the head of organized crime in Tampa was an identifiable person. From the 1920s to the 1970s, politicians and law enforcement alike often looked the other way as a means of coping with organized crime, but also succumbed to taking bribes. Public officials frequently had to receive approval by organized crime leadership to get elected. The power and influence of the Mafia was demonstrated by its interference in election results which were subject to being corrupted by stuffing the ballot box or invalidating votes.[1]

## IMPACT ON THE TAMPA COMMUNITY

The Mafia presence in Ybor City led to many negative impacts on the community and on the average resident.

Tampa civic leaders denied its existence, but Congressional investigations showed infiltration into city administration, law enforcement, and the courts.[2] Mafia leaders, as elsewhere in America, claimed they were legitimate businessmen, and community fear allowed them to be treated as such in places like the Columbia Restaurant and La Tropicana.

Mafia murders were also frequent but remained unsolved. The period from 1930 to the late 1950s was regarded as the Era of Blood due to "Mafia related" homicides, contributing to a large increase in the murder rate. Businesses like the Five and Dime stores were told where to locate, which led to as many as five of them in a three block area of 7th Avenue in the 1940s and 1950s, an arrangement these competing businesses would normally have avoided.

Business had to pay protection money including cigar factories, which were struggling to survive in the years of decline following the Depression, or they were subject to robbery by force.[3] While bolita gambling (discussed in this section) was legal, the discovery of one rigging system after another would simply result in new inventive ways for the Mafia to continue rigging the betting and keep the profiteering going. Even when such gambling became illegal by state law, there was no effective enforcement.[4]

Until 1933, prohibition of alcohol was simply a license for the Mafia to illegally make money and lavishly fund its existence for years to come. Likewise it's now accepted that the tunnels in Ybor City were not built for smuggling liquor during Prohibition but for sewage and storm water drainage, despite what was previously believed. The tunnels were, however, still used by the Mafia and other criminals to store and hide illegal commerce as businesses and residences linked up with abandoned brick tunnels, which had been replaced by more modern piping systems.[5]

## IMPACT ON RESIDENTS

The Mafia control presented a quandary for local inhabitants as they wondered whom they could trust. The societal impact of a Mafia presence precludes people from sharing anything about their lives with the community as information about individual personal and business dealings became a point of leverage for extracting favors and money from individuals.



While evidence shows a large number of public officials taking bribes in the 20th century, the ramifications of refusing to do the Mafia's bidding were severe. As Ybor City's economy declined from the 1930s to the 1960s with businesses leaving and people moving, those who stayed faced high unemployment rates. This, in turn, made working for the Mafia the only paying job in town, allowing for more people to be funneled into illegal activities including protecting the boss's turf. The result being 25-plus years of murderous rage inflicted on the city by competing factions for control of the bolita action and other vices.[6] Deaths of Mafia figures could result in honorable church funerals, burial in consecrated cemeteries, and access to the sacraments, while faithful church members of the Latin community were not so privileged if they were divorced or remarried.

## IMPACT ON TAMPA'S GROWTH

During the course of the 20th century, Tampa was subject to influences which limited its growth. Beyond the decline of the cigar industry and the move to the suburbs, Tampa's reputation as a center for organized crime in the South also impacted the city's growth.

The Era of Blood from 1930 to the late 1950s created a Tampa reputation for not only violent crime and a high murder rate, but also corruption and underworld activity and control. This dangerous reputation was further emphasized by the attention the Mafia received from the Kefauver and McClellan Congressional Committees, which investigated organized crime in the 1950s and 1960s. Such an environment discouraged businesses from moving to Tampa, which could have offset the losses in the cigar industry.

And beyond dampening economic development, this criminal image also stunted Tampa's population growth.

While a direct link to population growth in the 20th century cannot clearly be demonstrated, there is some correlation. It has only been with the decline in organized crime activity, that the city has experienced substantial growth. From 1930 to 1970, during organized crime's heyday, growth was minimal despite growth across the state. The population of Tampa rose from 1950 to 1960 due primarily to annexation, then was stagnant from 1960 to 1990, increasing by only 2% for the 30-year period. It was losing population between the 1970 and 1980 censuses, while the state of Florida grew by 8.7 million.[7]

The two periods of growth dormancy for Tampa were in stark contrast to the state's growth and in cities like Miami, Jacksonville, and Orlando. From 1990 to the present (coinciding with the noticeable decline of Mafia activity in Tampa), the population of the city has increased from 280,826 in 1990 to 404,836 in 2020. Part of the reason for stagnant growth should be attributed to the Mafia's influence.[8]



## *Bolita Beginnings*

At first, there was a gambling game called bolita, which emerged in the ethnic Ybor community as early as the 1880s. It gave wage earners a chance to increase their income. In short, people bought tickets with a number from 1 to 100. One hundred balls were placed in a sack with some variations to selecting the winning ball. The sack could be thrown around and when a bell rang, whoever was holding the bag reached in to select a ball. Without regulation, this gambling lottery process became corrupted at many points. The payouts were small, but it was extremely popular in the Cuban community.[9]

*A set of bolita balls on display at the Ybor City State Museum.*

*Zeng8r at English Wikipedia. CC BY-SA 3.0.*

There was a power struggle for control of the bolita racket among up-and-coming mafiosos who attempted to challenge control. From about 1930 to the mid-1950s, gangland conflict was the rule in Tampa as groups tried to take control of the bolita racket. The Hillsborough River became a dumping ground for Mafia-connected killings as more than a score of slayings of leading Mafia figures took place, characterized by drive-by shootings and other methods.

While some elements of organized crime were involved in bolita gambling, others were engaged in organized criminal behavior in narcotics, and in the illegal import and sale of alcohol during Prohibition. Even though bolita gambling was outlawed by statute, it continued due to minimal enforcement of the law. Organized crime influence is said to have been initiated in Tampa by the criminal activity of Charlie Wall and his period of control of the bolita racket. Subsequent to his death in 1955, the attempt was made to consolidate all organized crime business under one boss in the Tampa area. This came about in the early 1940s and continued under a father then son reign until the latter's death in 1987.[10]



## *Prohibition*

The advent of Prohibition by the passage of the Nineteenth Amendment in 1919 allowed for enhanced funding of organized crime. The Italian community joined the Cuban community in organized crime activities by producing and importing contraband liquor. Contrary to popular belief, organized crime was not restricted to certain ethnic groups but involved participation across numerous communities and backgrounds.

As a port of entry, Tampa became a center for the import of illegal liquor for the nation. Liquor was in great demand throughout the country. The general public was hostile to the enforcement of Prohibition laws, and community involvement in the clandestine smuggling and sale of alcohol was extensive. Additionally, local law enforcement and public officials either turned a blind eye or were intimately involved in the supply business to meet public demand. Old brick tunnel sewage and storm drain lines, no longer in use, were utilized to move and store illegal liquor in Ybor City.[11]

## *Impact on Cuba*

In the 20th century, connections were made with crime families in New York and Chicago. Tampa Mafia leadership also attempted to develop a presence in Cuba. The Cuban government, initially a democratic republic established in 1902 when the US granted independence, had succumbed to corruption and dictatorship. The presence of the Mafia in Cuba only served to accelerate the corruption, and the move was on in the late 1950s for another revolution to reverse corrupt government leadership.[12] Cubans domestically and in the US supported the revolution of 1959 to take their country back, not realizing the radical and violent turn it would take under communist rule.

### *Federal Investigations*

In the 1950s the **Kefauver Congressional Committee** began its investigations on organized crime. But as they centered on Tampa, Mafia leadership became unavailable as they evaded subpoenas by going to Cuba and other overseas locations, or went into hiding. They sought to wait out the congressional mandate for the committee until it expired. And county law enforcement did little to investigate gangland deaths, providing inadequate information for the committee to go on.[13] Subsequent commissions, however, were created including the **McClellan Committee.** The FBI, which was founded in 1908, became involved as their jurisdiction came to include illegal interstate commerce.

### *Conclusion*

The history of the Mafia in Tampa is a colorful one from the turf war between mob bosses from the 1940s to the 1980s. The Tampa community of the past was not a "happy" community because paranoia reigned.

Furthermore, the Mafia's impact is another decisive factor in the decline of the Ybor City community. The Mafia joins the Depression, the advent of cigarettes, the mechanization of cigar production, and the destructive urban renewal process as the fifth horseman of the apocalyptic downturn indicative of Ybor City's 20th century history after 1930.

The influence of the Mafia in Tampa is said to be on the decline in the last few decades. Of course, public officials and mob leaders always denied its existence. Seemingly, there will always be opportunities for exploiting drugs and gambling, among other illegal activities. The Mafia is certainly active in other parts of the state and the country where arrests continue to be made.

Much federal law enforcement funding has been diverted since 2001 from a focus on organized crime to international and domestic terrorism, creating a potential for the Mafia's return in the future.[14] From a reading of Scott M. Deitche's publications on mob activity in Tampa in the 20th and 21st centuries, it's clear that its return would not be a welcome event.

> *"The Mafia has never gone away. It's just the American public's attention was refocused after 9/11... organized crime families have always had their tentacles in South Florida."*[15]
>
> —Joe Cicini Retired FBI Agent, South Florida Organized Crime Task Force, Retired FBI Agent

To learn more, go on the Tampa Mafia Tour in Ybor City with Scott Deitche and read his numerous books, articles, and blogs.

## *Endnotes Section 8*

1. Paul Guzzo, "In the Early 1900s Tampa was Infamous for its Corrupt Elections," *Tampa Bay Times*, November 11, 2018, https://www.tampabay.com/news/politics/local/In-the-early-1900s-Tampa-was-infamous-for-its-corrupt-elections_173492516/
2. Scott Deitche, *Cigar City Mafia, A Complete History of the Tampa Underworld*, "There's No Mafia in Tampa," (Fort Lee, NJ: Barricade Books, Inc., 2005), 224-230.
3. Holden Rasmussen, "Ybor City's Underbelly," Curator's Corner, Cigar City History, J.C. Newman Cigar Co., https://www.jcnewman.com/ybor-citys-underbelly/
4. Deitche, *Cigar City Mafia*, "Bolita," 19-21.
5. "Ybor Tunnels," Abandoned Florida, accessed February 2022, https://www.abandonedfl.com/ybor-tunnels/; Paul Guzzo, "Historians Now Agree: Ybor City's Tunnels were built as Sewers, not Smuggling Routes," *Tampa Bay Times*, December 5, 2018, https://www.tampabay.com/bizarre/historians-now-agree-ybor-citys-tunnels-were-built-as-sewers-not-smuggling-routes-20181204/
6. Dr. Frank Alduino, Paper entitled "The Damnedest Town This Side of Hell: Tampa, From Prohibition to Organized Crime of the 40s," Tampapix, read at meeting of the Florida Historical Society, Tampa, May 11, 1990, http://www.tampapix.com/tampa1940s7.htm
7. Population U.S. Florida Cities, https://www.biggestuscities.com/ from the U.S. Census Bureau; Tampa, Florida Population History 1930-2019, plus Miami, Jacksonville, Orlando, and State of Florida, last updated February 9, 2022; List of most populous cities in Florida by decade as reported by the U.S. Census 1930 to 2020, List of most populous cities in Florida by decade - Wikipedia
8. U.S. Census Bureau, Historical Population Change Data (1990-2020) for Florida, April 2021, https://www.census.gov/data/tables/time-series/dec/popchange-data-text.html
9. Deitche, *Cigar City Mafia*, "Bolita," 19-21.
10. Alduino, "The Damnedest Town," Paper read at meeting of Florida Historical Society, Tampa, May 11, 1990.
11. Alduino, "The Damnedest Town," Paper read at meeting of Florida Historical Society, Tampa, May 11, 1990.
12. Deitch, *Cigar City Mafia*, "The Mob's Playground," 97-102.
13. Kefauver Committee Reports of 1950-1951: Published Reports (3 Interim Reports and a Final Report) and Committee Hearings Testimony (Section 1: Florida, Section 1A: Tampa), The American Mafia, The History of Organized Crime in the United States, Thomas P. Hunt, historical database compiler, Whiting, VT, https://mafiahistory.us/maf-kef.html.
14. Patrick Tucker, "DHS, DOJ Look to Spend Big on Countering Violent Domestic Extremism," *Defense One*, May 12, 2021, https://www.defenseone.com/threats/2021/05/dhs-doj-look-spend-big-countering-violent-domestic-extremism/174002/.
15. Paula McMahon, "Mob Crackdown Shows South Florida is Still Home for Organized Crime, Feds Say," *Sun Sentinel*, August 13, 2016, https://www.sun-sentinel.com/local/palm-beach/fl-mob-arrests-south-florida-20160813-story.html.

# 9 WHAT'S UP WITH THE ROOSTERS?

Running loose and free in Ybor City is a brood of chickens. And twice a year, a clutch of baby chicks can be seen. The chicks hide in shrubs for the most part at the insistence of mother hens, so they are not carried off by predator birds.

So who owns these birds and where did they come from? Well, it's a long story and one as colorful as their tail feathers.

## WHY DID THE CHICKENS CROSS THE STREET...I MEAN THE OCEAN?

Without refrigeration and effective preservatives, it was the practice of Europeans coming to America to bring food on the hoof if the animals could survive the journey. This was particularly true of the Spanish who brought chickens to the Caribbean islands in their first forays into the New World. Since the first explorers of the New World came from Spain, the Spaniards were the group to help the chicken population grow.



## CHICKENS AMONG THE CIGAR WORKERS

As Cuba developed initially as a Spanish base in the New World, chickens became a part of the food chain for their eggs and meat. (Whichever came first is contested.)

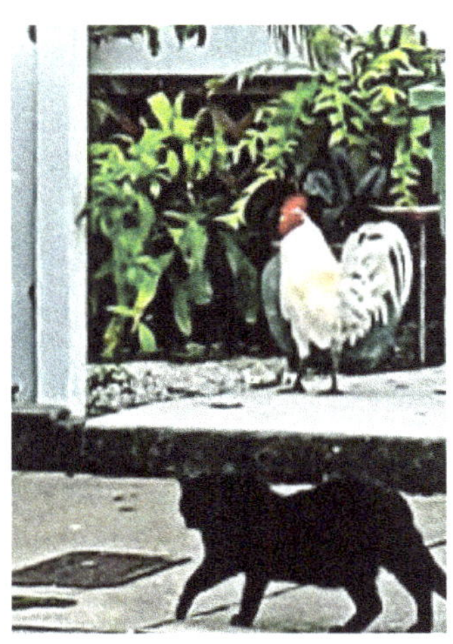

*A black cat carefully proceeds by Ybor City icon white rooster on 5th Avenue.*

Spanish Cuba developed agriculturally, growing Indigenous American crops like corn and tobacco, and manufacturing sugar from sugar cane. The main influx of chickens into cigar-producing areas in Florida began with the Ten Years' War in Cuba from 1868 to 1878. It was an independence movement to separate Cuba from Spanish control and was oppressively put down. This resulted in many Cubans leaving for many points in the US. Cigar producers moved to Key West and areas northward. As a result of a continuous stream of immigrants to America, chickens were brought by cigar industry workers from Cuba to Key West. The domesticated farm foul were becoming established when Vicente Martinez Ybor arrived in Key West in 1869.

## CHICKEN LINEAGE

With the 1886 fire in Key West, large numbers of workers began arriving in Tampa via steamers loaded with all their personal goods including livestock; the workers' families were coming a little later.

Chicken migration occurred from Spain to Cuba to Key West, then to Tampa. But there are those who contend that when Ybor City went into major decline in the 1940s and 1950s, the birds disappeared entirely and were reintroduced in the 1990s.

Dr. Wallace Reyes, Ybor City historian in residence, believes that the roosters and chickens in Ybor today are descended from those brought by the cigar workers in the late 1880s.[1] There are several indicators that support this conclusion. First, if chickens were reintroduced, their lineage from Spanish origin would not be interrupted because the path from Spain to Cuba to Florida is the primary migration route (if you can call it migration since their move was not bird-initiated). Second, roosters started displaying exotic coloring. In some cases, there were as many as eight tail feather colors in the Ybor roosters: red, green, orange, magenta, gold, beige, blue, and white. This indicates several generations of wild breeding. There are few roosters in North America that can compare to this display. Third, all-white roosters in Ybor City have been traced genetically back to Spain.[2]



## CHICKEN CIVIL RIGHTS

The chickens are not appreciated by all in Tampa, or for that matter, in Ybor City. Numbering approximately 200 by some estimates, they tend to be noisy, crowing at all times of the day and night and leaving their calling cards wherever. There have been initiatives to reduce the population, but they are protected by city ordinance passed in 1986.

A subsequent ordinance has categorized the chickens as pets so that people could keep them in their back yards, a throwback to early Ybor City. Some contend that the birds are more protected than the historical sights. They survive by free ranging and the handouts from the locals and visitors even though signage exists discouraging such behavior.

In 1997 a special funeral was held for an outstandingly beautiful rooster whose burial is marked in Ybor City. The funeral was a New Orleans–style parade replete with brass instruments. Yet ever since, rooster status has continued to be elevated, allowing them the run of the town.[3] They benefit from the right of way even in the face of streetcars in addition to being protected against confiscation by humans for food. With their status challenged from time to time, the future for the roosters is not always completely secure, but how can you rid yourself of an icon?

*Mosaic Rooster. Ybor City Visitor Information Center Gift Shop.*



## BIRD HEALTH

The Ybor Misfits Micro sanctuary is a non profit volunteer run animal rescue organization that works with the chickens in Ybor City. It provides care for the feral flock that roams the historic district. The organization rescues, rehabilitates and provides medical care for chickens that are severely injured, sick, or abandoned and can no longer survive on their own.
Web: www.yborchicken.org; FB: #yborchickens

Report injured birds via social media, include a picture or video and a specific location.

# *Endnotes Section 9*

1. Ricky Rodriguez, "Ybor Chickens Are Tampa's Historic District's Oldest Attractions," *Artistic Native*, February 15, 2018, interview with Dr. Wallace Reyes, PhD, https://artisticnative.wordpress.com/2018/02/15/ybor-chickens-are-tampas-historic-district-oldest-attractions/
2. Kristina Killgrove, "Ancient DNA Explains How the Chicken Got to the Americas," *Forbes*, November 23, 2017, https://www.forbes.com/sites/kristinakillgrove/2017/11/23/ancient-dna-explains-how-chickens-got-to-the-americas/?sh=7d9718d856db.
3. Joe Harless, "The Rooster Funeral," *Cigar City Magazine*, November-December 2008, story paraphrased in the Ybor City Visitor Information Center Museum Display, "What's the Deal With the Roosters, The Legend of the Rooster," 2000.

# 10 GUIDED WALKING TOURS

## CIGAR FACTORY TOUR

Visitors can participate in a cigar manufacturing tour at the J. C. Newman Factory. In addition to the tour, there is also a factory store, museum, and online sales.

Being the last remaining cigar factory not only in Ybor City but in the United States, the J. C. Newman Factory is not only a workplace but also one large museum devoted to how cigars are made both by the hand rolling process (the age-old process of Ybor City), and the machine process which came into use near the Depression.

The museum features the history of the J.C. Newman company and their relationship with other manufactured brands. The store on the first floor off the lobby has merchandise to commemorate your visit. Or even better, sign up for a tour at https://www.jcnewman.com/. The tour includes a walkthrough of the factory and steps in cigar making by hand rolling and by antique cigar rolling machines. Three tours are usually scheduled daily Monday through Friday. Significant walking is involved. An elevator facilitates accessibility.

*Location:* 2701 N. 16th St. Free parking available around the factory
*Phone:* (813) 248-2124
*Hours:* Visiting hours Monday through Friday, 9am-5:30pm. Tours occur Monday through Friday. Reservations are made online for tours.
*Cost:* $15 Adults; $12 Seniors, students, and veterans
*Length of Tour:* 1 hour and 15 minute

*Holden Rasmussen, museum associate, company historian and tour leader, begins a tour at the J. C. Newman Factory.*

*Hand rollers in the J. C. Newman factory, creating the artistically beautifully finished cigars.*

*The finished cigar product is aged for a period of time before packaging at J.C. Newman Cigar Factory.*

## TAMPA BAY TOURS

These walking tours—founded and previously managed by father, Lonnie Herman, and now by son, Max—are highly acclaimed and awarded. Their love of history and encyclopedic knowledge of the community is evident in the quality of the tours they provide and the captivating storytelling of their guides. The tours are conducted by Max and the company's team of highly qualified tour guides, and they can be scheduled almost any day of the week. Private tours available upon request. *https://tampabay-tours.com/*

### 1. Ybor City Historic Walking Tour

Register in advance either by going online to make reservations or by phone. If arriving in Ybor City for the day, the Visitor Information Center may be able to assist you in connecting with a tour.

The tour takes you through the heart of the historic district with anecdotes and inside information regarding the places, people, and events of the saga that is Ybor City. Tours convene at the site of Vicente Martinez Ybor's bronze statue on 7th Avenue in Centro Ybor and includes multiple stops to explore.

Step-on bus tours are available if arriving in a bus with a group. The guides can be scheduled to board the bus and conduct the tour. Arrangements must be made in advance. Bus transportation is not provided.

*Phone:* (813) 505-6779 or visit the website for reservations
*Hours:* Tours are conducted Sunday through Saturday, twice a day, at 11am and 2pm, with registration according to availability. Tours during the summer usually take place at 11am only.
*Length of Tour:* 90 minutes
*Cost:* Adults (ages 13 and above) $25; Children (ages 12 and under) $10
*Website:* https://tampabay-tours.com/ybor-city-citywalking-tour/about-this-tour

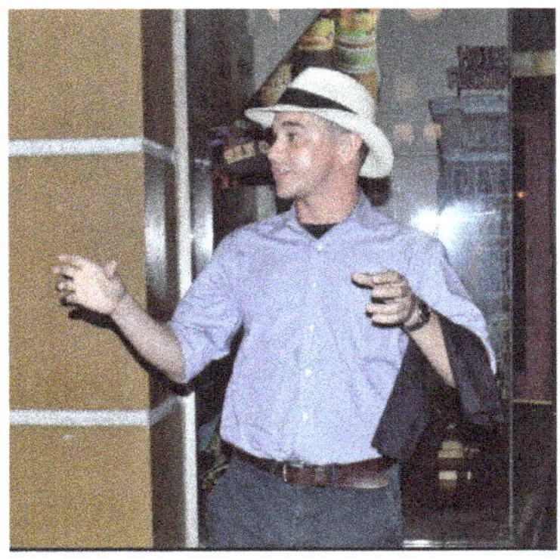

*Lonnie Herman with a tour group. Max Herman setting the scene.*

**2. The Official Ybor City Ghost Tour**

The tours are led by the reputable team of guides of Tampa Bay Tours. The tour is approximately two hours in length. The Official Ybor City Ghost Tour is highly acclaimed and led by expert storytellers who cover the spooky, sinister, criminal, and tragic side of Ybor history and the apparitions of people who were never quite able to move on to the next world. Call in advance or go online to make your reservation. Online reservations receive an email confirmation.
*Phone:* (813) 505-6779
*Hours:* Tours are conducted daily Sunday through Saturday at 8pm, with registration according to availability. They queue at King Corona Cigars at 1523 E 7th Avenue.
*Cost:* Adults (ages 13 and above) $30; Children (ages 12 and under) $10
*Website:* https://tampabay-tours.com/ybor-city-ghost-tour/about-this-tour

**3. The Official Downtown Tampa Ghost Tour**

The history of Tampa proper is replete with stories of death, murder, and mass graves from the Indigenous People to mobsters, to movie stars. Spirits that have never entirely passed on make for an eye-opening evening on the streets of Tampa. Call in advance or go online to make reservations.
*Phone:* 813-505-6779
*Hours:* Tours are conducted week nights at 8:00pm , with registration according to availability. They convene at the Tampa Theatre.
*Cost:* Adults (ages 13 and above) $30; Children (ages 12 and under) $10
*Website:* https://tampabay-tours.com/downtown-ghost-tour/about-this-tour/

**4. Downtown Tampa Historic Walking Tour**

The history of Tampa comes alive from the Native Americans who lived along the rivers and coast 6,000 years ago to the present. From the establishment of Fort Brooke at the mouth of the Hillsborough River after U.S. possession of Florida, to the arrival of the cigar industry, to the Spanish-American War staged from Tampa, events jump-started the sleepy little town of Tampa from a population of 700 to the rapidly growing metropolis of three million today. See the sights of historic Tampa and the historical figures who made a mark on the Tampa Bay region. The tour meeting location is the Fort Brooke Garage, 107 N. Franklin Street. Call in advance or go online to make reservations.
*Phone:* (813) 505-6779
*Hours:* 2pm, 90 minute tour, conducted Tuesday through Sunday, with registration according to availability.
*Cost:* Adults (ages 13 and above) $25; Children (ages 12 and under) $10
*Website:* https://tampabay-tour.com/downtown-history-tour/about-this-tour

## CIGAR INDUSTRY HISTORY TOUR

This cigar industry history tour is conducted by Wallace Reyes, PhD, Ybor City's resident historian and an expert on the cigar industry. Dr. Reyes was brought up in the cigar industry, learning every phase from the growth of tobacco to becoming an expert roller and head of the Gonzalez Habano Cigar Company, which is part of his family's heritage. His history tour is acclaimed as a captivating learning experience. He is well published with articles and books on the history of the cigar industry, Ybor City, and Florida.

You must call in advance to make reservations for this tour with Dr. Reyes. The point of origin for the tours is the Ybor City Museum State Park at 1818 9th Avenue, across the street from Centennial Park.

*Phone:* (813) 550-5220

*Cost:* $19.95 for Adults; $12.95 for Children ages 6 to 12; Free for children under 6 years. The price includes free admission to the museum.

*Length of Tour:* 90 minutes includes visiting 12 historical sights.

## YBOR CITY FOOD TOURS

These highly rated tours allow you to experience Ybor City through the taste and smells of the unique Ybor culture. The tours are led by a group of knowledgeable, professional guides and include stops at restaurants and cafes that feature the food of Ybor City's diverse history. Those participating in the tour have the opportunity to try Spanish, Cuban, Italian, and German cuisines. The different food tours include taste tests of a variety of foods and introduce you to the cultural and ethnic flavor of this community. There are several types of food tours from which to choose. You must call in advance to make reservations or go online to make your reservation. Tours convene at Jimmy John's Restaurant in Centro Ybor adjacent to the bronze statue of Vicente Martinez Ybor.

*Phone:* (813) 408-1078

*Email:* info@yborcityfoodtours.com

*Hours:* Usually the original food tour is conducted daily at 12:30pm. See online calendar for availability.

*Cost:* $89.00 per person

*Length of Tours:* 3 hours with multiple food stops

*Website:* https://yborcityfoodtours.com/

*Cindi Hughlett leading a Food Tour at the Ybor Visitor Information Center.*



## TAMPA MAFIA TOUR

Scott M. Deitche, an expert on Mafia history in Tampa and the US, conducts the tour. At times the tour is conducted by Scott's fellow seasoned historian colleagues. The tours cover the Ybor City haunts of Mafia kingpins on specified Saturdays. It queues at the King Corona Cigars at 1523 E. $7^{th}$ Avenue. Happy hour and private tours are also conducted.

Reservations required in advance, no walk-ins. Information of future tours can be obtained by calling, emailing, or checking the website. Tickets may be purchased online. Trolley Tours go beyond Ybor City to locations not accessible by foot.

*Phone:* (813) 358-3455

*Cost:* $30 per person, tours are for adults only, ages 21 and older.

Trolley tours are $65 per person.

*Length of Tour:* 1.5 to 2 hours and is approximately a one mile walk.

*Email:* info@tampamafia.com

*Website:* https://www.tampamafia.com

# 11 EATING



## DINING CONSIDERATIONS

Ybor City is known as a Tampa location for fine dining and good eating. Latin food is a staple but by no means is a limitation on the menus or variety of eating establishments throughout the district. Eating in Ybor City falls into several categories—restaurants, cafés, and pubs—many of which are highly rated.

The eateries range from historic to recent arrivals and are moderately priced as all are competing for the same tourist and local patron dollar. Most are located along 7th Avenue or just off 7th, and almost all have their menus posted on the outside of the premises. So if you're strolling the avenue, check the menus to get inspiration for your next meal. Not all establishments serve breakfast and those that do are noted in the listings which follow. Most are open for lunch and dinner. Some are open for one meal daily.

The Columbia Restaurant provides on-site parking at no cost, but most establishments are accessible from the Centro Ybor Garage located at 5th Avenue with entrances at 15th and 16th streets. Public parking lots are available on the adjacent 8th Avenue across from Centennial Park and Centennial Park Station. On-street parking in the evening is usually unavailable. See the map of eating places at the end of the chapter. Since the Historic District runs primarily from west to east along three or four avenues, **eating places are listed according to their location from west to east, from 13th Street to 24th Street.**

The list is not exhaustive. Reservations are indicated as either required, suggested, or not needed. If your group is 6 or more, calling ahead is recommended. The link to site menus is provided.

Food service hours for individual restaurants are subject to change. All establishments are casual and while some state that there is no dress code, shirt and shoes are required in most places. A few have vegetarian and vegan offerings and those are indicated in the menus of which links are provided. Many offer takeout.

Average cost of a dinner entrée is as follows:

- $ - under $10
- $$ - between $10 and $15
- $$$ - over $15

Many eating venues have live music entertainment in the evenings especially from Thursday nights through the weekend, and information can be obtained from the listed website. But first, a word on the Cuban sandwich.

## ABOUT THE CUBAN SANDWICH

A delectable representative of Cuban cuisine is the Cuban sandwich (or should I say, the Ybor Cuban sandwich) as presented here. We will avoid, for the moment, the controversy over whether Miami or Tampa has the best Cuban, or the sandwich's origin being traced to Cuba or the US. Let's just say it's called the Cuban sandwich because it was made by Cubans and that its makeup has evolved over time.[1]

The Columbia Restaurant was founded in 1905 and served initially as a lunch place for cigar workers. According to tradition, the cigar factory owners noted a decrease in production following the midday and were looking for a fortifying meal full of protein that would sustain the workers for the rest of the day. It is not known where or when the first sandwich was served in Ybor following its establishment in 1885 to 1886. It is known what some of the major ethnic groups contributed to make it what it is known for today.

There is no better representative of the "melting pot" in Ybor City than the ingredients found in an Ybor Cuban sandwich.

The **German** niche in the cigar industry were their factories, which produced cigar boxes and humidors for the cigar manufacturers. This included the magnificent labels which are part of the beauty and character of the boxes. This segment of the community is said to have contributed the mustard for the sandwich spread on the bottom layer of the **Cuban bread.** The bread was specially made by including three types of flour and baked with a palmetto leaf on the top and center of the bread so that it would toast evenly. The glazed ham contribution came from the **Spanish** community. The pork prepared in the Cuban cuisine fashion was included by the **Cuban** immigrant constituency. The salami of Genoese origin was the **Italian** offering and is the primary ingredient difference between the Miami and Tampa Cuban sandwich. Lastly, the Swiss cheese and the pickles were also German influences to the sandwich.[2]

The sandwich is often pressed, which is not exactly like a panini but similar. The pressed Cuban does not have the grill markings of a panini, but it is pressed by weighing down the sandwich. In the early days this was accomplished by a hot brick or a heavy skillet with the goal of melting the cheese, and bringing out the juices of the various meats.[3]

Many of Ybor City's restaurants serve a Cuban sandwich. Each year a **Cuban Sandwich Festival** is held in the spring in which restaurants and other vendors compete to make the best sandwich and a winner is proclaimed. So enjoy your Cuban! It epitomizes the melting pot of the US when immigrant groups have come together to give the nation unique products which can only be described as American. A great Cuban sandwich can be found at Carmine's, the Columbia Restaurant, La Segunda Bakery, and Café Quiquiriqui in the Hotel Haya.

## THE TRADITIONAL FOODS OF YBOR CITY

What are the traditional foods of the Latin Ybor Community that are not to be missed? Here's a short list for your culinary exploration:

| **Spanish and Cuban** | **Italian / Sicilian** |
|---|---|
| Black beans and rice | Pasta with fish, squid |
| Spanish bean soup | Tripe with red sauce |
| Cuban black bean soup | Pasta and succo |
| Chicken and yellow rice | Pasta with ricotta |
| Deviled crab croquettes | Focaccia |
| Boliche (eye of round stuffed with chorizo) | Minestra soup with multiple pastas & vegetables |
| Gazpacho | Brasciole |

## DIAGRAM OF A CUBAN SANDWICH

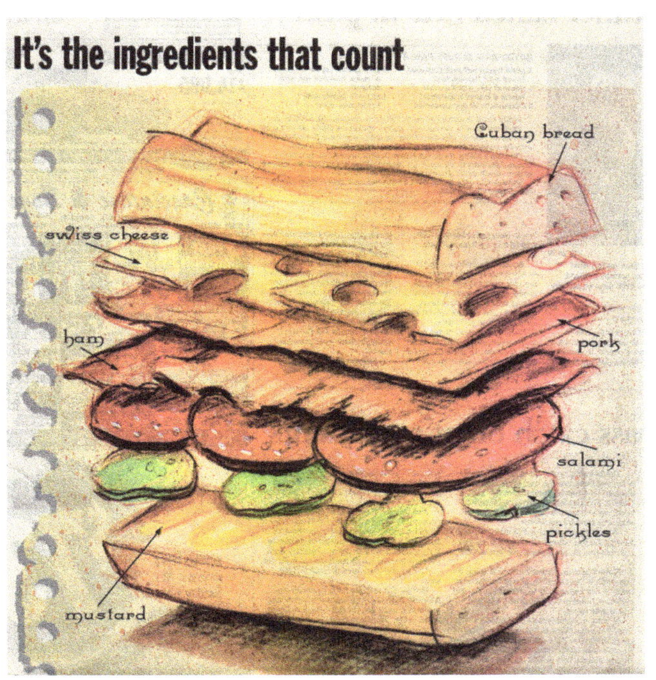


*From Tampa Tribune ©2021 Tampa Bay Times. All rights reserved. Used under license.*

## RESTAURANTS ON THE WEST SIDE

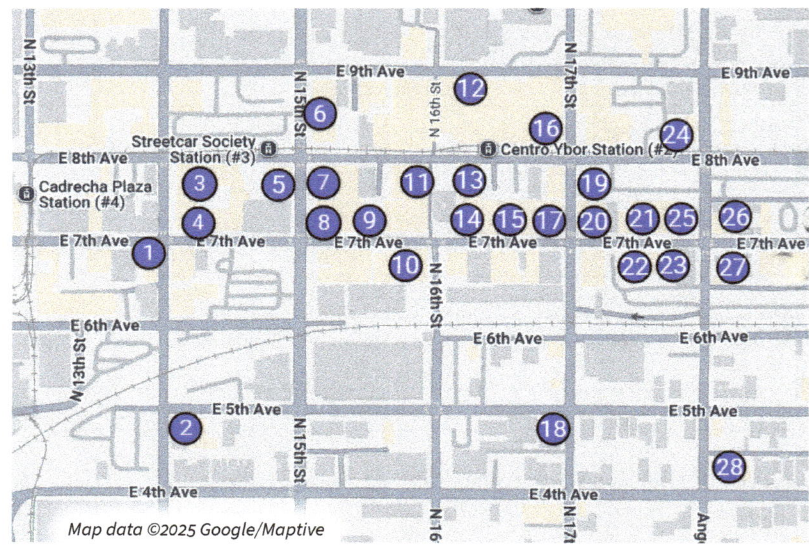


1. The Bricks
2. BarrieHaus Beer Co.
3. Flor Fina, Hotel Haya
4. Cafe Quiquiriqui, Hotel Haya
5. Cigar City Cider and Mead
6. SpookEasy Lounge
7. Barterhouse Ybor
8. Copper Shaker
9. New York New York Pizzeria
10. Ybor Seoul
11. Samurai Blue & Saki Bar
12. Tampa Bay Brewing Co.
13. Asiatic Street Food & Noodle Bar
14. Ybor City Society Wine Bar
15. Jimmy John's
16. Game Time
17. Ocean Ink
18. El Puerto Restaurant & Grill
19. Rasoi Indian Cuisine
20. Bernini
21. Due Amici
22. La Terrazza Ristorante Italiano
23. La Creperia Café
24. James Joyce Irish Pub and Eatery
25. Geo's Fine Wine and Champagne Bar
26. Carmine's
27. Gaspar's Grotto & Pirate Bar
28. Pete's Ybor.

See Cheesology under Specialty Foods, p. 114.

See restaurant descriptions for 26-29 under East Side Restaurants, next section.

**RESTAURANT HOURS ARE SUBJECT TO CHANGE. PLEASE CALL AHEAD TO CONFIRM.**

1. **$$ The Bricks**, 1327 E. 7th Ave.
*Phone:* (813) 247-1785
*Hours:* Mon-Wed, closed; Thu-Fri, 5pm-11pm; Sat, 12pm-11pm; Sun, 12pm-7pm;. Kitchen closes before closing time.
*Cuisine:* A cozy quiet corner in Ybor with music entertainment at night. Well prepared bar food, American with an ethnic touch. Serves as a coffee stop and brunch locale.
*Website:* https://www.thebricksybor.com/

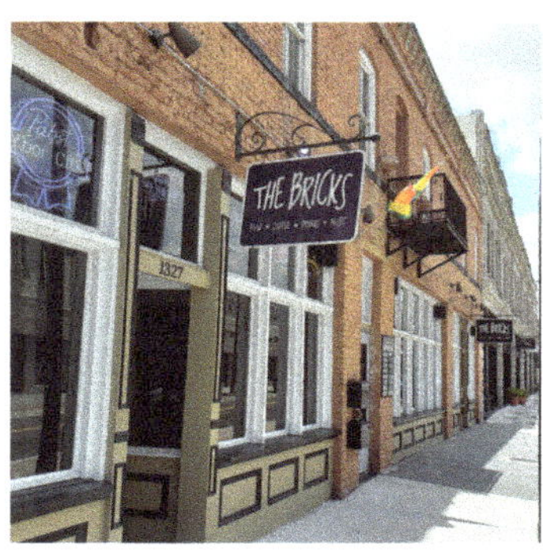


2. **BarrieHaus Beer Co.**, 1403 E. 5th Avenue
*Phone:* (813) 242-2739
*Hours:* Mon-Thu, 3pm-10pm; Fri, 12pm-10pm; Sat, 12pm-11pm; Sun, 12pm-8pm
*Cuisine:* German Food offerings, Octoberfest celebrations. German style lagers
*Reservations:* Needed for private events
*Website:* https://barriehaus.com/about

3. **$$$ Flor Fina**, Hotel Haya, 1412 E. 7th Ave.
*Phone:* (813) 462-9660
*Hours:* Brunch - Tue-Fri, 11am-3pm; Dinner - Tue-Sat, 5pm-10pm
*Cuisine:* The chef prepares signature dishes blending the various cuisines of Ybor City's ethnic communities.
*Reservations:* recommended
*Website:* https://hotelhaya.com/food-drink/ flor-fina/

4. **$$ Café Quiquiriqui**, Hotel Haya, 1412 E. 7th Ave.
*Phone:* (813) 568-1200
*Hours:* Mon-Sun, 7am-4pm
*Cuisine:* This gem serves classy upscale café food for breakfast and lunch.
*Reservations:* not needed
*Website:* https://hotelhaya.com/food-drink/ café-quiquiriqui/

5. **Cigar City Cider and Mead**, 1812 N. 15th St.
*Phone:* (813) 242-6600
*Hours:* Mon-Tue, closed; Wed-Fri, 5pm-12am; Sat, 12pm-12am; Sun, 12pm-10pm
*Cuisine:* This locale offers a selection of craft brewed ciders and meads.

*Reservations:* not needed
*Website:* http://www.cigarcitycider.com/

6. **$$ SpookEasy Lounge**, 1909 N. 15th St.
   *Phone:* (813) 373-6452
   *Hours:* Mon-Thu, 3pm-1am; Fri, 3pm-3am; Sat, 11am-3am; Sun, 11am-1am
   *Cuisine:* Unique enticing and well-prepared food offerings. All day breakfast, lunch, and dinner. Botanical teas, kava, and coffee. Alcohol free lounge
   *Reservations:* not needed but call ahead for groups of 10 or more
   *Website:* https://www.spookeasylounge.com

7. **$$ Barterhouse Ybor**, 1811 N 15th Str, Suite A
   *Phone:* (813) 542-1710
   *Hours:* Mon-Tue, closed; Wed-Thu, 4:30pm-10pm; Fri-Sat, 4:30pm-11pm; Sun, 4:30pm-9pm
   *Cuisine:* varied and unique offerings of American cuisine and creative craft cocktails. Happy Hour specials.
   *Reservations:* recommended
   *Website:* https://www.barterhouseybor.com

8. **$$$ Copper Shaker**, 1502 East 7th Ave.
   *Phone:* (813) 344-4012
   *Hours:* Mon, closed; Tue-Thu, 4pm-1am; Fri, 4pm-2am; Sat, 3pm-2am; Sun, 3pm-1am
   *Cuisine:* a bar with a wide range of craft cocktails and a kitchen supporting a food menu ranging from creative appetizers and shareables to entrees comprising a full dinner meal.
   *Website:* https://www.coppershakerybor.com

9. **$$ New York New York Pizzeria**, 1512 E. 7th Ave.
   *Phone:* (813) 248-1845
   *Hours:* Sun-Wed, 11am-10pm (dining), closes at 12am; Thu-Sat, 11am-12am (dining), closes at 3am.
   Hours subject to change.
   *Cuisine:* This location offers a large selection of pizzas including signature pizzas; noteworthy selection of subs, sandwiches, and pasta dishes.
   *Reservations:* not needed
   *Website:* https://nynypizzeria.com/locations/ybor-city/

10. **$$ Ybor Seoul**, 1531 E 7th Ave.
    *Phone:* (813) 248-0788
    *Hours:* Sun-Thu, 11am-10pm; Fri-Sat, 11am-12am

*Cuisine:* popular Korean street fare, dine in and take out, self-serve ordering by kiosk and food served when ready. Convenient for people on the go.
*Website:* https://yborseoul.com

11. **$$$ Samurai Blue & Sake Bar**, 1600 E. 8th Ave., C208 in El Centro Español, Entrance on 7th Ave. and midway between 7th and 8th Ave., second floor.
*Phone:* (813) 242-6688
*Hours:* Dinner, Sun-Tue, 5pm-11pm; Wed-Thu, 5pm-12am; Fri-Sat, 5pm-1am; Lunch, Mon-Fri, 11:30am-2pm.
*Cuisine:* Known for their sushi, they serve a wide variety of Japanese dishes as well.
*Reservations:* Accepted, recommended for dinner
*Website:* https://samuraiblue.com/

12. **$$ Tampa Bay Brewing Co.**, 1600 E. 8th Ave.,
*Phone:* (813) 247-1422
*Hours:* Mon-Thu, 11am-10pm; Fri-Sat, 11:00am-11pm; Sun,11am-10p; Summer Schedule, closed possibly Mon, Tue.
*Cuisine:* This brewery serves well prepared American bar food and is known for its gourmet hamburgers, beer-infused dishes, and a craft beer sample tray. It's dog friendly and has outdoor/indoor seating. Call for brewery tour.
*Reservations:* needed for parties of ten or more
*Website:* https://www.tbbc.beer/ybor

13. **$$ Asiatic Street Food and Noodle Bar**, 1600 E. 8th Ave., #D101 in Centro Ybor
*Phone:* (813) 284-5317
*Hours:* Mon-Tue, 11:30am-9:30pm; Wed-Thu, 11:30am-10pm; Fri-Sat 11:30am-11pm; Sun, 11:30am-10pm
*Cuisine:* This locale serves commendable stir fry dishes with rice and noodles, and a family group menu.
*Reservations:* only needed for large groups
*Website:* https://asiaticstreetfood-noodle.com/

14. **$$ Ybor City Society Wine Bar**, 1600 E. 8th Ave. (food); see menu for wines and beers
*Phone:* (813) 999-4966
info@yborcitywinebar.com
*Hours:* Mon-Thu, 4pm-10pm; Fri-Sat, 12pm-12am; Sun, 12pm-8pm
*Cuisine:* Over 200 wines for purchase by the bottle or glass and more

than 60 craft beers served alongside gourmet food plates that make for a complete experience. The establishment provides weekly wine tasting, a wine club to learn about new wines, and special events.
*Website:* http://www.yborcitywinebar.com

15. **$ Jimmy John's**, 1600 E. 8th Ave., Unit D
*Phone:* (813) 241-9600
*Hours:* Sun-Thu, 11am-9pm; Fri-Sat, 11am-3am
Cuisine: This chain location offers subs and clubs, and design-your-own-sandwich options. Delivery available.
*Website:* https://www.jimmyjohns.com

16. **$$ Game Time**, 1600 E. 8th Ave., at 17th St. corner
*Phone:* (813) 241-9675
*Hours:* Mon-Wed, 4pm-11pm; Thu, 4pm-12am; Fri, 4pm-2am; Sat, 10am-2am; Sun, 10am-11pm
*Cuisine:* This American eatery features some ethnic food and snacks for family dining with kid friendly meals and entertaining. It includes a sports bar, 120 game attractions and simulators, and numerous TVs for sporting events.
*Reservations:* Party events need to be booked
*Website:* https://www.gametimeplayers.com/locations/tampa

17. **NEW! $$ Ocean Ink**, 1632 E. 7th Ave.
*Phone:* (813) 215-2280
*Hours:* Mon, closed; Tue-Sun, 5pm-11pm
*Cuisine:* This restaurant is a raw bar that features fresh and local seafood. The menu includes a range of oyster dishes and peel yourself Key West pink shrimp. It opened in September 2025 and is a welcome addition to Ybor City and 7th Avenue.
*Reservations:* suggested
*Website:* https://www.oceaninkraw.com

18. **$$$ El Puerto Restaurant and Grill**, 1623 E. 5th Ave.
*Phone:* (813) 248-8222
*Hours:* Mon, 11am-3pm; Tue, 11am-9:30pm; Wed-Thu, 11am-10pm; Fri-Sat, 11am-11pm; Sun, 12pm-9:30pm
*Cuisine:* This eatery offers Latin flavors featuring seafood, meat, salad, and pasta dishes from South America, Central America, and Cuba.
*Reservations:* suggested
*Website:* http://www.elpuertoybor.com

19. **$$$ Rasoi Indian Cuisine**,1701 E. 8th Ave.
*Phone:* (813) 241-0003
*Hours:* Lunch, Mon-Fri, 11:30am-2:30pm; Sat-Sun, 11:30am-2:30pm; Dinner, Mon-Thu, 5pm-10pm; Fri-Sat, 5pm-10:30pm; Sun, 5pm-9:30pm
*Cuisine:* This restaurant serves Indian food with a weekend buffet, and vegetarian options. Indoor/outdoor patio seating is also available.
*Reservations:* recommended
*Website:* https://www.rasoitampa.com

20. **$$$ Bernini**, 1702 E. 7th Ave.
*Phone:* (813) 242-9555
*Hours:* Mon-Thu, 11:30am-10pm: Fri-Sat, 11:30am-11pm; Sun, 11am-9pm
*Cuisine:* This historic eatery serves Italian cuisine with locally acclaimed sauces and dishes, and offers a daily martini special.
*Reservations:* suggested
*Website:* http://berniniofybor.com



21. **$$ Due Amici**, 1724 E. 7th Ave.
*Phone:* (813) 443-0906
*Hours:* Mon-Sun, 11am-3am (every day)
*Cuisine:* This locale serves Italian with highly rated pizza and other well prepared entrées. Their world famous sauces are available for purchase in the restaurant or online.
*Reservations:* suggested
*Website:* https://www.dueamiciybor.com/

22. **$$$ La Terrazza Ristorante**, 1727 E. 7th Ave.
*Phone:* (813) 248-1326
*Hours:* Thu-Sat, 5:00pm-10pm
*Cuisine:* This upscale restaurant serves signature Italian dishes by a renowned chef.
*Reservations:* accepted but not required
*Website:* www.laterrazzayborcity.com

23. **$$ La Creperia Cafe**, 1729 E. 7th Ave. next to the Italian Club
*Phone:* (813) 248-9700
*Hours:* Mon, 10am-3pm; Tue-Wed, closed; Thu-Fri, 10am-3pm; Sat-Sun, 9am-4pm
*Cuisine:* This well-established café is an Ybor favorite featuring savory entrees and sweet deserts in crepes, Parisian sandwiches, paninis, and pasta dishes. It also serves breakfast.
*Reservations:* recommended for groups of six or more.
*Website:* http://www.lacreperiacafe.com

24. **$$ James Joyce Irish Pub and Eatery**, 1724 E. 8th Ave. next to Centennial Park
*Phone:* (813) 247-1896
*Hours:* Sun-Sat, 11am-3am
*Cuisine:* This locale serves standard quality Irish and American pub fare, gourmet burgers, and an assortment of beers including craft beers.
*Reservations:* not needed
*Website:* https:ybornow.com/places/the-james-joyce-pub/

25. **$$$ Geo's Fine Wine and Champagne**, 1730 E. 7th Ave.
*Phone:* (813) 284-7331
*Hours:* Mon-Wed, closed; Thu-Sun, 5pm-2:30am
*Cuisine:* Charuterie boards (cheese and meat), extensive list of wines and champagnes, live music nightly
*Reservations:* accepted online
*Website:* https://geosfwc.com



## RESTAURANTS NEARBY (West Side, outside the historic district)

**$Flan Factory, 1718 N. Nebraska Ave.**
*Phone:* (813) 402-2400
*Hours*: Mon-Tue, closed; Wed-Fri, 10am-8pm; Sat, 9am-8pm; Sun, 9am-6pm
*Cuisine:* Cuban inspired entrees, bowls, and sandwiches with a passion for extraordinary flan desserts, all day breakfast
*Website:* https://flanfactory.com/

**$Los Chapos Tacos Ybor, 951 E. 7th Ave.**
*Phone:* (813) 277-8999
*Hours:* Mon-Sat, 11am-11pm; Sun, closed
*Cuisine:* Authentic Mexican Street Food
*Reservations:* for group special events
*Website:* https://loschapostacos.com

## RESTAURANTS ON THE EAST SIDE

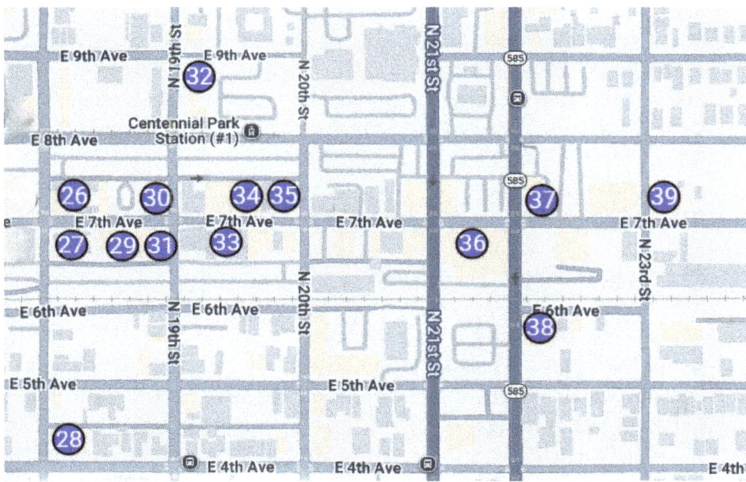


*Map data ©2025 Google/Maptive*

26. Carmine's
27. Gaspar's Grotto
28. Pete's Ybor
29. Blind Tiger Café
30. Barrio Ybor City
31. Acropolis Greek Taverna
32. Ybor City Coffee and Tea
33. LARA, Apothecary Bar and Bazaar
34. Roast and Madame Fortune
35. 7th + Grove
36. Columbia Restaurant
37. Shrimp and Co. Restaurant
38. Casa Santo Stefano
39. Al's Finger Licking Good Bar-B-Que & Soul Food
40. Coppertail Brewing Company (not shown on map)
41. 22nd Street Coffee (not shown on map)

See Tico's Bakery under Specialty Foods, p114.

**RESTAURANT HOURS ARE SUBJECT TO CHANGE. PLEASE CALL AHEAD TO CONFIRM.**

26. **$$ Carmine's**
    1802 E. 7th Ave., diagonally across from the Italian Club
    *Phone:* (813) 248-3834
    *Hours:* Mon, 10am-5pm; Tue-Thu, 10am-10pm; Fri-Sat, 10am-11pm; Sun, 10am-8pm
    *Cuisine:* This well-established Ybor City restaurant features Spanish, Cuban, and Italian with a creative blend of the cultures in some dishes. Known for its devil crab and Cuban sandwich.
    *Reservations:* accepted
    *Website:* https://carminesybor.com

27. **$$ Gaspar's Grotto,** 1805 E. 7th Ave., on the corner across from the Italian Club
    *Phone:* (813) 248-5900
    *Hours:* Sun, 11am-2am; Mon-Sat, 7am-2am
    *Cuisine:* Gaspar's Grotto offers reliable cuisine with a wide variety of Cuban and American bar food. It's Ybor's take on the Gasparilla Festival, replete with a pirate theme enthralling for all ages. Enjoy indoor/outdoor bar, eating, and dancing. Serves breakfast six days and brunch on Sundays. Serves a commendable Cuban sandwich.
    *Reservations:* for large groups
    *Website:* https://gasparsgrotto.com/about-us/

28. **$$ Pete's Ybor**, 1804 E 4th Ave.
    *Phone:* (813) 392-1005
    *Hours:* Daily, 8:00am-2pm
    *Cuisine:* All day café, well made bagels and coffee, tea, wine, breakfast and lunch menu
    *Website:* https:// petesgeneral.com

29. **$$ Blind Tiger Cafe,** 1823 E. 7th Ave.
    *Phone:* (813) 540-2233
    *Hours:* Mon-Thu, 7:30am-5pm; Fri, 7:30am-8pm; Sat, 8am-8pm; Sun 8am-5pm
    *Cuisine:* This speak easy has extensive coffee and tea offerings and creative café fare.
    Reservation: not needed
    *Website:* https://www.blindtigercoffeeroasters-3/ybor-city/

30. **$$ Barrio Ybor City,** 1822 E. 7th Ave.
*Phone:* (813) 342-2452
*Hours:* Sun-Thu, 11am-12am; Fri-Sat, 11am-1am
*Cuisine:* Creative Mexican fare. Build your own tacos, bowls, and nachos with a wide range of savory meats, cheeses, sauces and side items. Commendable dietary labels. Drink specials Monday and Tuesday.
*Reservations:* for group special events
*Website:* https://barrio-tacos.com/locations/yborcity/

31. **$$ Acropolis Greek Taverna,** 1833 E. 7th Ave.
*Phone:* (813) 242-4545
*Hours:* Sun-Thu, 11am-11pm; Fri-Sat, 11am-1am
*Cuisine:* This chain has a solid presence in Ybor with a full range of authentic Greek food, drink specials, and belly dancing.
*Reservations:* recommended
*Website:* http://www.acropolistaverna.com/Tampa/



32. **$$ Ybor City Coffee & Tea,** 1907 N. 19th St. near Centennial Station
*Phone:* (813) 242-0855
*Hours:* Sun-Wed, 7am-3pm; Thu-Sat, 7am-5pm
*Cuisine:* Selected hand picked and locally roasted coffees and hand blended teas served with commendable light fare for breakfast and lunch in an inviting environment
*Website:* https://www.yborcitycoffeeandtea.co/

33. **NEW! $$ LARA, Apothecary Bar and Bazaar,** 1919 E. 7th Ave.
*Hours:* Mon-Wed, closed; Thu-Sat, 12pm-12am; Sun, 12pm-6pm
*Cuisine:* An apothecary bar provides craft cocktails, both alcoholic and non-alcoholic. The restaurant has tempting flavors of comfort food from around the world, an appropriate theme introduced by chef Suzanne Lara for a historic district with international connotations.
*Reservations:* needed for large groups
*Website:* https://www.tampalara.com

34. **$$ Roast and Madame Fortune,** 1930 E. 7th Ave., Suite C
*Phone:* (813) 242-0572
*Hours:* Mon-Tue, Closed; Wed-Thu, 5pm-10pm; Fri-Sat, 4pm-1am; Sun, 4pm-10pm
*Cuisine:* Roast Deli, Bakery, and Social Bar serves as a dessert and coffee shop. Madam Fortune is a hidden speakeasy behind the Roast Deli which highlights Caribbean soul fare and crafted cocktails. It is in honor of Tampa historical figure, Madam Fortune Taylor.

*Reservations:* Required for Madam Fortune
*Website:* https://madamefortunetpa.com/

35. **$$$ 7th and Grove,** 1930 E. 7th Ave.
*Phone*: (813) 649-8422
*Hours*: Mon, closed; Tue-Thu, 11am-10pm; Fri, 11am-2:30am; Sat, 11am-3am; Sun, 11am-4pm; Late night hours, Thu-Sat.
*Cuisine*: Creative Southern signature dishes excellently prepared and presented.
*Reservations*: recommended
*Website*: https://7thandgrove.com

36. **$$$ Columbia Restaurant,** 2117 E. 7th Ave.
*Phone:* (813) 248-4961
*Hours:* Sun-Thurs, 11am-9pm; Fri-Sat, 11am-10pm
*Cuisine:* A highly acclaimed historic dining experience, the Columbia has an extensive menu of Spanish and Cuban dishes, and it's vegetarian and vegan friendly. Flamenco shows occur twice evenings except Sunday and Monday. Lunch and dinner are served daily, and live music is featured on Fridays and Saturdays.
*Reservations:* recommended for lunch and dinner. Flamenco shows occur Mon-Thu at 7pm with a prior dinner reservation and on Fri-Sat at 7pm and 9:30pm with a prior dinner reservation. See website for details. Reservations required for dinner and show.
*Website:* https://www.columbiarestaurant.com/flamenco-show-ybor-city



37. **$$$ Shrimp and Co. Restaurant,** 2202 E. 7th Ave.
*Phone:* (813) 374-0192
*Hours:* Mon, closed; Tue-Thu, 11am-8pm; Fri-Sat, 11am-9pm; Sun, 12pm-7pm
*Cuisine:* This locale holds the niche in Ybor of exclusively serving seafood with Caribbean and New Orleans Cajun seasoning.
*Reservations:* recommended for lunch and dinner
*Website:* https://shrimpandco.com/

38. **$$$ Casa Santo Stefano,** 1607 N. 22nd St.
*Phone:* (813) 248-1925
*Hours:* Lunch, 11am-4pm; dinner, 4pm-10pm. Santo's Drinkeria: Fri-Sat, 5pm-10pm.
*Cuisine:* Casa Santo Stefano serves inspired traditional Italian/Sicilian pasta dishes from Old World Sicily with the excellent quality of food and service of the Columbia Restaurant organization.

*Reservations:* no reservations necessary
*Website:* https://casasantostefano.com/

39. **$$ Al's Finger Licking Good Bar-B-Que and Soul Food,** 2302 E. 7th Ave.
*Phone:* (813) 515-5036 - (813) 956-0675
*Hours:* Mon-Tue, closed; Wed-Thu, 11:30-5:30pm; Fri-Sat, 11:30am-7pm; Sun,12pm-5pm
*Cuisine:* Well prepared and commendable southern cooking.
*Reservations:* not needed
*Website:* https://www.alsybor.com/

40. **$$ Coppertail Brewing Company,** 2601 E. 2nd Ave.
*Phone:* (813) 247-1500
*Hours:* Mon-Thurs, 11am-11pm, Fri-Sat, 11pm-12 am; Sun, 11am-9pm; Hours subject to change.
*Cuisine:* This locale offers quality pub food and craft beer tasting.
*Reservations: not needed*
*Website:* https://coppertailbrewing.com/main-page/

41. **22nd Street Coffee**, 402 N. 22nd Street, 2 blocks south of IKEA ($$ - packaged coffee)
*Phone:* (813) 304-0373; Inquiries: customer@22ndStreetCoffee.com
*Hours:* Mon-Fri, 7am-2pm; Sat, 8am-2pm
*Cuisine:* This café serves specialty crafted, freshly ground coffees as well as light café fare. Their coffee is sold online.
*Website:* https://22ndstreetcoffee.com/

*Casa Santo Stefano*

1. **La Segunda Central Bakery (1915)**, 2512 N. 15th St.
   *The historic bakery of Ybor City in its fourth generation of family ownership*
   *Phone:* (813) 248-1531
   *Hours:* 6:30am-3pm daily
   *Specialties:* Bakery and café fare serving authentic Cuban bread shipped throughout the United States, memorable pastries and cakes, including flan; delicious deli sandwiches including for breakfast; cookies, and beverages. Menu includes tasty offerings for breakfast and lunch. Catering menu and online ordering.
   *Website:* https://www.lasegundabakery.com

2. **NEW! $ Tico's Bakery**, 2209A E. 7th Ave.
   *Phone:* (786) 569-1924
   *Hours:* Mon-Sat, 7am-8pm; Sun, 8am-3pm
   *Specialties:* Just beyond the Columbia Restaurant, this bakery specializes in goods that are fresh every day and often unique in America. Baked goods from signature croissant filled sandwiches to pastries, all very inviting with a South American twist.
   *Website:* http://ticosbakery.com

3. **Cheeseology**, 1527 E. 7th Ave.
   *Phone:* (813) 557-6464
   *Hours:* Mon, closed; Tue-Thu, 12pm-8pm; Fri-Sat, 10am-10pm
   *Specialty:* The making and enjoyment of cheese through scheduled cheese making classes with an exceptional selection of in-store cheeses and accompanying wines and beers. The shop promotes humanity's love affair with this age-old international staple of the world's diet.
   *Website:* https://cheeseology.net

4. **Chill Bros. Scoop Shop**, 1910 E. 7th Ave., Suite 101
*Phone:* (813) 247-2767
Hours: Sun, 12pm-9pm; Mon-Thurs, 12-9:30pm; Fri-Sat, 12-11pm
*Specialties*: This shop features homemade ice cream with all fresh ingredients, seasonal specialties, toppings, cookies, cookie sandwiches, shakes, and pints to go.
*Website*: https://www.chillbros.com

5. **Mayday Ice Cream**, 1600 E. 8th Ave., Suite E100
*Phone*: (813) 644-4289; General corporate Inquiries: info@maydayicecream.com, or call (904) 401-7515
*Hours*: Sun-Thu, 11am-10pm; Fri-Sat, 11am-11pm
*Specialties*: Unique Ice Cream Flavors, online store.
*Website*: https://www.maydayicecream.com

## NIGHTLIFE AND ENTERTAINMENT

Ybor City rocks with live entertainment all week long, but especially on the weekends in the Tampa version of Bourbon Street. The district is teeming with bars, nightclubs, restaurants, and pubs, all of which have been instrumental in the resurgence of Ybor City. They all seek to go above and beyond in providing an entertaining evening from the flamenco show and vocal artists at the Columbia Restaurant, to Funny Bone, previously the Improv Theatre, to live bands, DJs at pubs and bars, and dance music.

For a listing of Ybor City bars and nightclubs go to: https://www.yborbars.com

The GaYbor District, centered at E. 8th Avenue and 14th Street, is a coalition of gay supporting businesses, restaurants, and retail shopping along with gay-owned businesses, bars, and clubs. Ybor has always welcomed a diverse community and the LGBTQ+ community adds greatly to that heritage. GaYbor is part of the Ybor tradition of accepting, supporting, and welcoming ALL who seek community as it has done for more than 135 years.

### Personal Safety Considerations

As with any urban environment at night, visitors should be proactive regarding their personal safety. Walking in groups is encouraged. Parking near the point of destination is recommended. Securing money in a belt purse is a good idea.

**DRINK RESPONSIBLY – HAVE FUN – BE SAFE.**



### *Endnotes Section 11*

1. Loren McCollom, “Miami vs Tampa: The “Original” Cuban Sandwich”, Chain Store Guide, April 16, 2015, https://chainstoreguide.com/offthechain/2015/04/miami-vs-tampa-the-original-cuban-sandwich/
2. “The Original Cuban Sandwich Columbia Restaurant Recipe”, Columbia Restaurant, last accessed February 2022, https://www.columbiarestaurant.com/The-Columbia-Experience/Recipes/Cuban-Sandwich; Adela Hernandez Gonzmart and Ferdie Pacheco, *The Columbia Restaurant Spanish Cookbook* (Gainesville, FL: University Press of Florida, 1993), 27-28, 105.
3. “The Original Cuban Sandwich Columbia Restaurant Recipe,” columbiar-estaurant.com.

# 12 EXPLORING YBOR CITY

Tourism industry experts, like Rick Steves and the late Silvia Griffin, advocate that the best way to learn about a historical area is to spend some time on your own exploring a locale. This section is devoted to encouraging visitors and natives alike to do just that. This section includes points of interest within Ybor City's West Side, East Side, and North side.

## WEST SIDE SIGHTS

Here are some sights of Ybor City's West Side, closest to Tampa proper, with an explanation of their historical significance. See some or all of the sights or use this checklist as a jumping off point to explore side streets on your own. A map is included at the end of this section.

Rough Riders Park – The Gateway to the Latin Quarter
Sociedad La Union Martí-Maceo (Martí-Maceo Society)
Friends of José Martí Park – Ybor Square – El Pasaje
Circulo Cubano (Cuban Club) – The Castle – Tampa Bay Brewing Co.
Ybor City Chamber Visitor Information Center – El Centro Espanol
(Spanish Community Center) – Ybor Statue – Tabanero Cigars

1. For exploring the West Side of Ybor, including any of the sights above, park in the **Centro Ybor Parking Garage**, located between 5th and 6th Avenues with entrances on 15th and 16th Streets.

2. Up 16th Street two blocks north on 7th Avenue, Café con Leche, Ybor City's favorite coffee is available from baristas at **King Corona Cigars** (1523 E. 7th Ave) or **Tabanero Cigars** (1601 E. 7th Ave.).

3. Proceeding west to 14th Street and 7th Avenue are three eateries where you could start your day with a meal or snack: **The Bricks** (1327 E. 7th Ave.) serves brunch on Saturday and Sunday at 12pm (page 103). **Café Quiquiriqui** at the Hotel Haya (1412 E. 7th Ave.) in the stunning boutique hotel, is open at 7am and serves café food (page 103). **Flor Fina** Restaurant (1412 E. 7th Ave.) also at the **Hotel Haya** serves lunch beginning at 11am and brunch on Saturday and Sunday (page 103). Also a couple of blocks from the Centro Ybor Garage is **Pete's Ybor** on 4th Avenue an all-day café open at 8am (page 110) and known for its bagels.

4. **Rough Riders and Spanish-American War Memorial Park** isn't far from the previous eateries. This park commemorates the service of the veterans of the Spanish-American War, especially that of the Rough Riders. The war was precipitated by the sinking of **the USS Maine** in Havana harbor, and by the Cuban War of Independence which started in 1895. In **1898**, the Rough Riders, under the leadership of **Theodore Roosevelt**, made their famous ride from assembling near the location of what was to become the Columbia Restaurant at 7th Avenue and 22nd Street and proceeded down 7th Avenue to the cheers of the crowd. They turned south just past this park to ride down to the port and board ships for the trip to Cuba. War material and logistics were staged out of Ybor City and Tampa. The war was over in just three months following Roosevelt's famous charge up San Juan Hill, and Cuba began its journey toward a democratic republic.

*Col.Theodore Roosevelt stands on San Juan Hill, Cuba after its capture by his "Rough Riders" during the Spanish-American War. Theodore Roosevelt Association, Library of Congress, and Public Domain, PD-US*

*Memorial Plaque, Rough Riders Park, Ybor City.*

5. **Gateway to the Latin Quarter** is an archway just outside the park, announcing the entrance to the Latin Quarter of Ybor City. A historic marker exists on the left pillar as you enter the neighborhood. The archway is on the world's list of freestanding structures.

6. **Afro Cuban Club, Sociedad La Union Martí-Maceo,** across the street from Rough Riders Park, was named after two heroes of the Afro Cuban community—José Martí and General Antonio Maceo. Martí was the voice of Cuban liberty, while Antonio Maceo, a Black general, represented the movement militarily. Both men died on the battlefield. Through the segregation policies of the US, the group had to negotiate their social standing where language and color were both barriers to Afro Americans and other Cubans, alienating them from the social fabric. They began meeting in the home of **Ruperto and Paulina Pedroso** (where the Martí Park is now located) before moving into a spacious building on 6th Avenue in the early 1900s. Eventually urban renewal and destruction of their community aid building resulted in another move to the current location on 7th Avenue. The group was a merger of two societies. Most of the community was employed in the cigar factories, including the women. Many moved northward during the Great Depression due to less segregated social policies.

In recent decades, many of the older generation have moved back to Tampa.[1] Note the historic marker located in front of the building. For further information, visit:
http://floridahistory.org/ybor6.htm and
http://ybor.org/sociedad-la-union-Martí-maceo/

7. **Friends of José Martí Park (1956)** is up 13th Street at the corner with 8th Avenue. Be mindful of the tracks and passing streetcars. The soul of Ybor City belongs to José Martí. He was a frequent resident of Ybor City and stayed with the Pedroso couple in a house once situated at this spot. Martí was at once a poet, political scientist, journalist, professor, political essayist, and advocate of democratic government. (See the short biography of Martí in Section 3.) He campaigned all of his adult life for Cuban independence from the oppressive Spanish regime that governed Cuba. As a **political theorist**, he realized that the success of a democratic government in Cuba would be based on the creation of strong institutions. However, without him, Cuba did not have the improved chances of developing healthy democratic institutions once Cuban independence was fully obtained in 1902. **He died at the Battle of Dos Rios in Cuba in 1895** in the Cuban War of Independence, and his death had lasting consequences for Cuba. He is often referred to as the "George Washington of Cuban independence," but he was also its political philosopher or "American Rousseau."[2] Tragically, the Cuban fledgling democracy succumbed to corruption and infiltration by the Mafia leading to dictatorships and the revolution of 1959.

*Statue of José Martí in the Friends of José Martí Park.*

*About the park*



Once you're inside the park, you are on Cuban soil. However, **passports are not required**. It's located at the site of Paulina and Ruperto Pedroso's boarding house, where Martí stayed during his numerous visits to Tampa and where they helped Martí recover from an assassination attempt in 1892. Look for the historical marker just inside the park entitled LA CASA DE PEDROSO 1893.

Note: The park is only open Monday to Friday from **8am-1:30pm**, but due to its small size, all of the park can be seen from the front gate and fencing. If you arrive late, a hand through iron fence still puts you in Cuba.

8. **Ybor Square and the Ybor Factory.**
   Ybor Square is located across 8th Avenue from the Marti Park. The Cigar Factory entrance, located on N. 14th Avenue near 9th Avenue, is one of three buildings comprising Ybor Square that occupies a city block between 8th and 9th Avenues and 13th and 14th (Avenue Republica de Cuba) Streets.

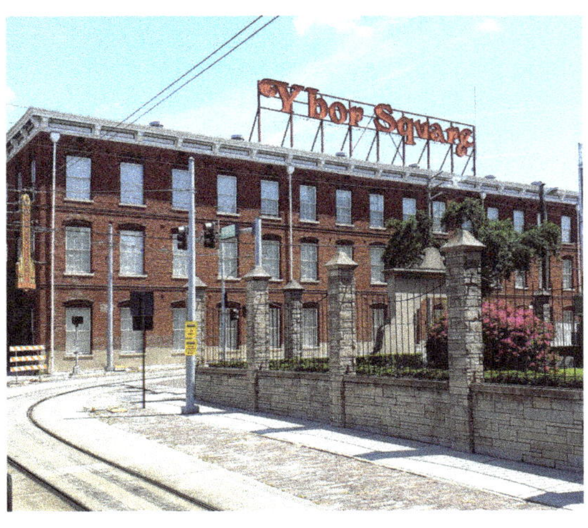


*South side of Ybor Square across from the Martí Park.*



**Factory Building.** If the soul of Ybor City is José Martí, the heart of Ybor City is represented by Vicente Martinez Ybor. Ybor struggled in the cigar business under Spanish oppression in Cuba, moved to Key West in 1869, then in 1886, he moved his cigar business to Tampa giving the little fort town, population 700, its reason for being. The building has four floors, each dedicated to certain tasks in cigar production.

*The Ybor Factory.*



José Martí spoke to the cigar workers from the steel steps at the front entrance of the factory. Ybor was at one with Martí in wanting Cuban independence. A famous impassioned speech given here by Martí 130 years ago (as of 2023) is commemorated by a marker in front of the iron stairwell. The speech called for aid from the cigar workers to fund an uprising in Cuba. This was just one of many speeches and public appearances he made in Ybor City.

The marker, in Spanish, translated to English reads:

> FROM THIS STAIRCASE IN 1893, JOSÉ Martí, THE APOSTLE OF CUBAN FREEDOM, WITH ELOQUENT WORDS ASKED THE CUBAN CIGAR WORKERS THAT HAD EMIGRATED HERE FOR THEIR HELP IN GAINING THE INDEPENDENCE OF THEIR COUNTRY BY PROVIDING MEN, WEAPONS AND MONEY. MANY WORKERS EXCHANGED THEIR TOBACCO CUTTING KNIFE FOR A MACHETE AND OTHERS DONATED HUNDREDS OF THOUSANDS OF PESOS TO HELP SAVE THE PEOPLE OF CUBA FROM OPPRESSION AND TO CREATE THE REPUBLIC OF CUBA.

*In this 1893 photo, Martí is in the center with open coat and white shirt, with cigar workers from the factory. State Archives of Florida, Florida Dept. of State, Division of Library & Information Services. Florida Memory Collections, Public Domain.*

A second marker **FOUNDING OF THE CIGAR INDUSTRY** is at the corner of the factory building at 9th Avenue and 14th Street.

9. **El Pasaje** (later known as the **Cherokee Club) (1886)** means "passageway." Across 9th Avenue from the factory is a building architecturally styled like those of the Italian Renaissance. It was built to house the offices for Vicente Martinez Ybor's companies as he planned Ybor City, then ran his cigar factory and other businesses. El Pasaje was the second brick building in Ybor City and has been home to many establishments since including the Cherokee Club, a hotel, a bar, a restaurant, newspaper offices, and an armed forces recruitment center.[3]

*El Pasaje, the Vicente Martinez Ybor office complex, and later the Cherokee Club.*

Within El Pasaje, Ybor maintained guest accommodations for visiting VIPs to stay overnight. Among them was José Martí. Subsequently, other famous people have been recorded as staying here including Theodore Roosevelt, President Grover Cleveland, and Winston Churchill who more than likely checked out the cigar shops.



10. **El Circulo Cubano** (The Cuban Club) (1917) located at 2010 Avenida Republica

*The Cuban Club.*

de Cuba at Palm Avenue, was a multipurpose community center. The major ethnic groups developed mutual aid societies, which served a social function for community gatherings and provided medical assistance in the form of clinics and pharmacies. The Cuban Center located on 14th Street behind El Pasaje is the second structure on this site, the original having burned in 1916 and replaced by the present building in the neoclassical style erected in 1917. At the time of its construction, it housed a 2-story theatre, pharmacy, library, ballroom, and cantina, along with a swimming pool, bowling alleys and locker rooms.[4] Today the club continues to serve its community with its elaborate interiors of marble, stained glass, and other elegant architectural features for social gatherings and as a venue for all kinds of celebrations.



11. **The Castle,** or Ybor City Labor Temple (1930) located two blocks east of the Cuban Club on 9th Avenue, is the most important preserved building associated with labor and unionism in general in the Tampa Bay area and is located at the corner of 9th Avenue and 16th Street. It was a place where members of multiple unions came together including Ybor City's cigar worker and restaurant unions.[5] Today it's a dance club and bar with a dark theme. People of all ages are attracted to its nightlife and the medieval architecture that reflects one of the many styles found in Ybor City. The facility is closed during the day, but a photo in front of its main tower has European implications.

*The Castle Nightclub, formerly served as the Union Hall for various union organizations.*



12. **Tampa Bay Brewing Company** is one of Vicente Martinez Ybor's dreams brought to life. As he planned his company town in 1885, Ybor made sure a brewery would be developed, which began Tampa's heritage not only of cigars but the development of local craft beers.[6] **There are several breweries in Ybor City among the more than 45 in Tampa as a whole.** No tour of Tampa or Ybor City would be

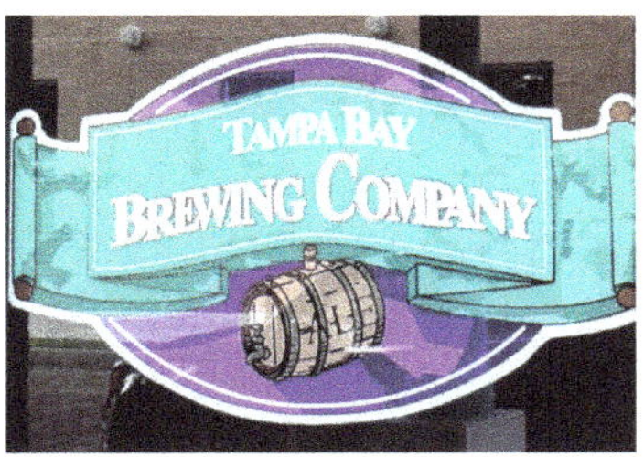

complete without a brewery stop. The 11 craft beers brewed on-site at the Tampa Bay Brewing Company are highly rated by long-standing patrons. It has indoor and outdoor bars and seating perfect for people watching. It's a friendly location for families, and for dogs in its outdoor area, and it has a varied and dependable pub fare like great American-style hamburgers. It opens at 11am. Tours of the brewing facility can be arranged by calling ahead at (813) 247-1422.

13. **Ybor City Chamber of Commerce Visitor Information Center** is located at 1600 E. 8th Avenue, B-104, across the street from TBBC and half a block to the west. The "VIC" is command central for info about accommodations, events, shopping, dining, and entertainment in Ybor City and Tampa. It disseminates tourist information and serves as a history center, gift shop, and museum all rolled into one. The center is surrounded by art depicting the scenes and history of Ybor City, a historical film theater, and brochures and books offering numerous ideas for planning a Latin Quarter experience. Informative staff is on site to answer questions. Browse the books and pamphlets on Ybor City. Ask about the next showing of the short historical film. Pick up a one-of-kind souvenir from its gift shop which received "Best of the Bay" designation by Creative Loafing for 2025. Obtain maps of Ybor City, the streetcar system, and Tampa.
    Phone: (813) 241-8838
    Website: https://www.ybor.org/vic/
    Hours: Mon-Sat: 10am-4pm; Sun: 12-4pm
    Email: info@ybor.org

*VIC cigar box information counter.*

*The VIC has the world's largest cigars overhead, but could this possibly be the world's largest cigar box?*

14. **Centro Español de Tampa** (The Spanish Club) (1912) located around the corner from the Visitor Center fronting on 7th Avenue, is the second building on the site, dating back to 1912 with Spanish immigrants organizing the first mutual aid society in 1891. The building is heavily influenced by Moorish architecture, adding yet another style to Ybor City's character. The center provided a ballroom, a theatre, a cantina, and a health insurance system for its members. Due to the cost of the upkeep of the facility and other financial woes, the building was sold in 1983 and is the home of restaurants. However, its flavor and landmark attraction are unique. it was the first community center to be established and was the model for those mutual aid societies that followed. Its heritage lives on in its repurposed use. See the historic marker in front of the building. Read more in Section 15 - Arts and Culture.

*El Centro Español de Tampa Public Domain Image, National Park Service. Wikimedia Commons. Tampa AGS Media, Creative Commons Share Alike 3.0 Unported license (CC BY-SA 3.0)*

**Don Vicente Martinez Ybor was born in Valencia, Spain in 1818, thereby making 2018 the 200th anniversary of his birth; and it was definitely celebrated in Ybor City!**

**December 14, 2021 marked the 125th anniversary of his death.**

15. **Statue of Don Vincente Martinez Ybor**

At fourteen, Don Vicente Martinez Ybor was sent to live in Cuba to escape military service in Spain. There he learned the cigar business and was able to start his own cigar-making business, producing a cigar he called **The Prince of Wales,** a brand always associated with Ybor. The Ten Years' War began in 1868 between the Spanish and those seeking Cuban independence. Ybor was accused of supporting the independence movement, and he fled Havana to escape arrest, moving his operation to **Key West** in 1869. While in Key West, Ybor had transport issues due to the port's limitations, conflict between Cuban and Spanish workers, and other labor issues which led him and his colleague, **Ignacio Haya**, to seek other sites from 1884 to 1885. After considering various locations along the gulf coast, they settled on Tampa Bay where Fort Brooke existed in what initially was a swampy area infested with mosquitos, alligators, and snakes. His factory and many others in Key West were destroyed by a fire in 1886, hastening the departure of cigar workers to Tampa. Ybor and Haya enticed workers with the promise of their own homes and good wages. They attracted other factory owners with cheap land, a good harbor, and great transport provided by Henry Plant's newly constructed railroad to Tampa. In 1886, in a little more than a year, Ybor had built his 4-floor brick cigar factory, the largest in the world at that time. See Mr. Ybor's brief bio in Section 3.[7]



16. **Roland M. Manteiga's** (1920–1998) marker and statue is located leaning against the Centro Español building. He was the owner and publisher of **La Gaceta** newspaper, where he influenced power politics in Ybor City in support of human rights. His bronze statue stands in an informal pose reading a newspaper. See more in Section 15 - Arts and Culture under "Statuary."

17. To understand and appreciate the craft of cigar making, experience the **Ybor cigar shops**. Along La Setima on the west side are a variety of cigar shops some of which show rollers at work hand rolling cigars at desks created for that purpose. Rollers are glad to demonstrate their craft. A barista may be on hand to serve you a café con leche, Ybor's famous coffee with steamed milk, or other beverages including beer or wine.

From west to east beginning on the West Side of Ybor, these shops include **La Faraona Cigars** (at 1515 7th Ave), owned by Odelma Matos with a bar that serves beer and wine and other beverages and cigar rollers at work.

**Tabanero Cigars** (at 1601) serves a great café con leche and displays a large humidor locker for patrons.

Next door is **Nicahabana** (at 1605) promoting itself as the cigar link between Havana and Ybor City.

A block away is **Ybor Cigars Plus** (at 1725) with its claim on a great mojito and Cuban music. Across the street is **Long Ash Cigars** (at 1728) with its front window roller, its tobacco leaf bar, and impressive humidor. Additional shops are identified in section seven.

**Nearby Eating.** See Section 11, Eating, "Restaurants on the West Side"

**Nearby Shopping.** Consider a shopping stop at either a vintage clothing shop like *La France* near Mr. Ybor's statue, or *Agora's,* an import and export shop, with an Old World feel and the Visitor Information Center's Gift Shop on 8th Avenue.

**Cuban Sandwich and Cuban Coffee:**

- The Bricks Café
- King Corona Cigars, Bar, & Cafe
- Café Quiquiriqui
- Flor Fina and Café Quiquiriqui at Hotel Haya
- Gaspar's Grotto
- Carmine's
- Tampa Bay Brewing Company

# YBOR CITY – WEST SIDE

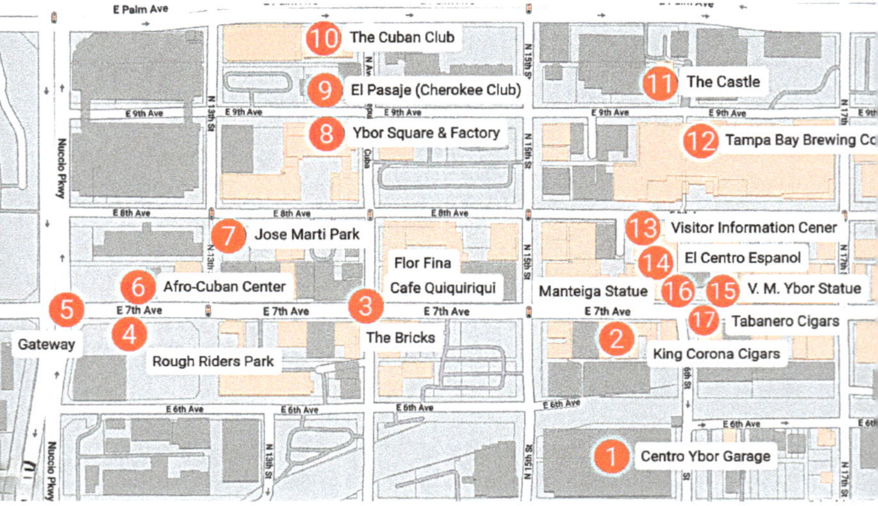


*Map data ©2024 Google/Maptive*

| | |
|---|---|
| 1. Centro Ybor Garage | 9. El Pasaje/Cherokee Club |
| 2. King Corona Cigars , Tabanero Cigars | 10. The Cuban Club (El Circulo Cubano) |
| 3. The Bricks Cafe, Café Quiquiriqui, Flor Fina | 11. The Castle |
| 4. Rough Riders Park | 12. Tampa Bay Brewing Co. |
| 5. Gateway to Ybor City | 13. Visitor Information Center |
| 6. Afro Cuban Center (Sociedad La Union Marti-Maceo) | 14. El Centro Español |
| 7. Friends of José Martí Park | 15. Ybor Statue |
| 8. Ybor Square & Factory | 16. Roland Manteiga statue |
| | 17. Tabanero Cigars* |

*Other nearby cigars shops include La Faraona Cigars, Nicahabana Cigars, Ybor Cigars Plus, Long Ash Cigars

## EAST SIDE SIGHTS

Here are some sights to see in the East Side of Ybor City with an explanation of their historical significance. See some or all of the sights or use this checklist as a jumping off point to explore side streets on your own. A map is included at the end of this Section. **Note: The Ybor City Museum is open Wednesday through Sunday. The Tampa Baseball Museum at the Al Lopez House is open Thursday through Sunday.**

Centennial Park – Tampa Baseball Museum at the Al Lopez House
Ybor City Museum State Park – Casita Tour – Ybor mural
Blind Tiger Cafe – Restaurant Central
L'Unione Italiana (Italian Club)
Ybor statue – Shopping – Centro Ybor Station
Centennial Station – Columbia Restaurant

20. Park in one of the three public parking lots just south of Centennial Park and the **Centennial Park Streetcar Station (#1)**. The two on the south side of E. 8th Avenue are accessible by 8th Avenue and 19th Street. They lie between N. 18th (Angel Oliva Senior) Street and N. 20th Street.

21. **Centennial Park** has many features. The brick-surfaced park was created to commemorate the 100th Anniversary of Ybor City in 1986. There is a statue of an immigrant family in honor of all those that have made Ybor City a great community to live and work. The park is the center of monthly festivals, events, and exhibits in addition to being a recreational and picnic space. The Ybor City **Saturday Market** occurs every Saturday from 9am to 1pm (May-September) and from 9am to 3pm (October-April). Websites for events: https://www.ybormarketonline.com/ and https://ybormarket.com/

*Tents at Centennial Park for the weekly Saturday Market.*

The park is in front of the museum and is the home base for the **roosters** who do not like being displaced on Saturdays. See Section 9 for the story of the roosters and Section 15 for details under "Saturday Market."

22. **The Tampa Baseball Museum at the Al Lopez House,** located above Centennial Park at 2003 N. 19th Street, hours of operation are Thu-Sat, 10am-4pm; Sun, 11am-5pm; Mon-Wed, closed.

With the arrival of Vincente Martinez Ybor and the cigar industry, Tampa's 135 years of baseball history began in earnest when Cuban cigar rollers formed their first team in Ybor City in 1887. They shared their passion for the sport, leading to the formation of early leagues including the Inter-social, and Negro leagues. The local spring training tradition began In the early 20th century the local spring training tradition began, as well as the formation of three minor league teams. Over 90 players from Tampa have made it to the pros beginning with the legendary Al Lopez, and in 1995, Tampa Bay got its own Major League team, the Tampa Bay Devil Rays, now the Tampa Bay Rays.

Exhibits are showcased in the 1905-era rehabilitated childhood home of Al Lopez. See also under Section 5, Museums and Exhibits, for additional description.



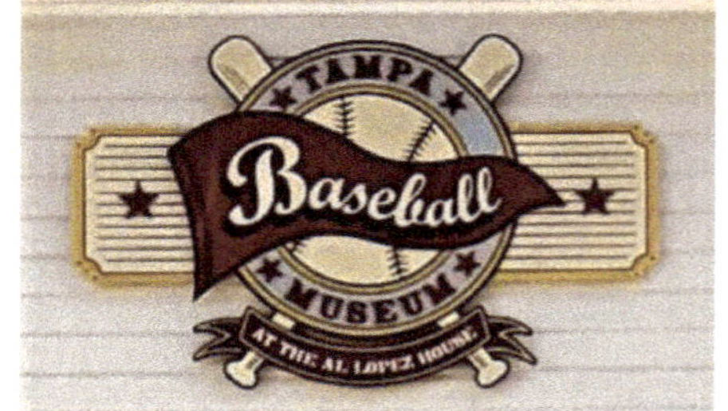

*Tampa Baseball Museum logo. Used with permission.*

The Ybor City Historical Society operates the Tampa Baseball Museum at the Al Lopez House. It provides a traveling museum experience of Ybor City's history to the Tampa Bay region. This educational program is entitled, Rollin' Through History , and offers multiple lessons from Ybor City's founding to Tampa's baseball legacy. The Historical society has expanded from its previous namesake, the Ybor City Museum Society to its successor organization, the Ybor City Historical Society, with an expanded mission, to restore the character of historic Ybor City by promoting and preserving its heritage. Contributions to the Ybor City Historical Society benefit the baseball museum, the mobile museum and the advancement of efforts to maintain and restore the cultural integrity of the historic district.

*Ybor City Museum on 8th Avenue across from Centennial Park.*

23. **Ybor City Museum State Park,** across 19th Street at 1818 E. 9th Avenue is housed in the 1920s **Ferlita Bakery building**. It features pictorial displays, artifacts, and a video about the founding and development of Ybor City, the beginning of the cigar industry, and the growth of the town. The entrance fee for the museum is $4.

    **Hours of Operation:**
    Wednesday-Sunday, 9am-4pm;
    Monday-Tuesday, closed.

    Next to the museum is a beautiful garden. In the adjacent garden containing a wide range of plantings native to Florida is a bust of Vicente Martinez Ybor. Inquire inside the Museum about a guided tour of a neighboring casita.

24. **The Casita Tour** (conducted from the Ybor City Museum) features one of thousands of these homes that were built of which approximately 400 remain. The *casita* or "little house" was a sturdy wooden structure built on bricks to elevate the building from snakes, alligators, and other wild animals. The air circulated through a shotgun hallway that connected all the rooms. Bedroom netting was essential to escape mosquitos. The kitchen was at the rear and water was accumulated from runoff from the roof. The cigar factory owners enticed workers to move and settle in Ybor City by offering interest-free home ownership. Payment was deducted from weekly earnings. Thousands of Cuban and Spanish cigar rollers immigrated and settled down. They were followed by Italians and Germans who either became factory workers or were involved in businesses which supported the cigar industry. They formed a multiethnic population that came together as one community. See also 'Casitas" under Architecture, section 15.

*Casitas on 8th Avenue next to the Ybor City Museum.*

Unlike many communities set up by American moguls of the same period, Ybor City was not a typical company town by any means. Vicente Martinez Ybor paid the highest wages to attract workers. And he established worker home ownership opportunities rather than company housing. He invited competitors to come and establish their cigar businesses in Ybor City too. Ybor lived among his workers a few blocks away in a home once located at 12th Avenue and 17th Street where he frequently entertained his workers.



25. **The Viva Ybor mural** between 19th and 20th Streets on 7th Avenue depicts many of the symbols and icons of Ybor City as part of a historic Tampa. How many can you identify? See a description of this outdoor work under Murals.

26. **Blind Tiger Cafe,** 1823 E. 7th Avenue, is a great stop for signature café food reflective of Ybor City's culinary heritage and for an array of coffees and teas. See "Restaurant List on the East Side" in Section 11.

27. **Restaurant Central** is a term used to describe the number of amazing eateries within two blocks in all directions of 18th Street and 7th Avenue, including but not limited to Bernini, Du Amici, La Creperia, La Terrazza, Carmine's, Gaspar's Grotto, and The Acropolis. The intersection is the geographic center of Ybor restaurants with 9 being within a block of the intersection, and 21 being within 2 blocks. Get something to drink or a light repast while exploring the East side of Ybor. Consider making dinner reservations at one of the previously mentioned locations or at the historic Columbia Restaurant.

28. **L'Unione Italiana** (The Italian Community Center) (1918) is on 7th Avenue at the SW intersection of 7th Avenue and 18th Street. It's the neoclassical imposing Italian Union, now more of a social club and a venue for special events. But back in the first quarter of the 20th century, it was one of several mutual aid societies.

*The Italian Club on 7th Avenue at 18th Street.*

**At the turn of the 20th century, there were six mutual aid societies in Ybor representing the different cultural groups**. These societies were a hallmark of Ybor's tobacco industry. They were often referred to as clubs for they constructed opulent premises for the social and cultural aspects of their individual cultures. However, the **mutual assistance** aspect included education classes for cigar workers and medical clinics on the property supported by the dues paying members. The clubs often maintained pharmacies and established a system of medical insurance benefits for injury, sickness, and death, far exceeding anything existing in most of the US at the time.[8]

After observing the imposing exterior facade, take a step inside the front door to get a feel of the place. There are currently no tours of the facility unless you are interested in renting the venue for a special event. However explore the brochures on a table just inside the left entrance and consider heading upstairs to look at the ballroom and other spaces. See also "Architecture" within Section 15 - Arts and Culture.

29. **Long Ash Cigar Shop,** 1728 E. 7th Avenue, is a cigar shop of beautiful and comfortable surroundings enhanced by local art and leather chairs. It features a cigar lounge with a tobacco leaf bar counter. The cigar roller at the front window is a place to stop and see how cigars are hand-rolled. Enjoy an authentic cup of café con leche or other libations. It has tables for playing cards and dominoes, and flat screens to enjoy sporting events. The elegant humidor is where they store their impressive inventory of handmade cigars. They sell an extensive line of cigar accessories and other items to remember your trip to Long Ash and Ybor City.

    Other cigar shops nearby have a unique presence of their own and include **Ybor Cigars Plus** across the street (at 1725), **La Herencia De Cuba** (at 1817), and near the Columbia Restaurant on 22nd Street is **Tampero Cigars**. Also check out the neighboring **Dysfunctional Grace Art Gallery** referred to in Section 15.

30. **The Kress Arts Building** at 1624 E. 7th Ave. houses artist studios, galleries and organizations of Kress Contemporary on the second and third floors. Their galleries are open according to posted schedules at the building and on the Kress Contemporary website. On the first floor is the Florida Museum of Photographic Arts which is open Tuesday through Saturday. See the Kress Arts Building under Section 15, Arts and Culture.

31. **Vicente Martinez Ybor's bronze statue** is where the east side of Ybor meets the west side. Vicente Ybor is the man who at age 68 decided to start cigar manufacturing all over again in a new place called Tampa. See item #15 under West Side Sights within this section. The plaque below the statue provides a brief biography. A short biography of his illustrious life is in section 3.

32. **Shopping** at La France (1612 7th Avenue), a vintage clothing store for men and women known throughout the southeast and celebrating its 50th anniversary in business in 2024. Agora (1517 7th Avenue) is an "Old World" store with products from all over the world. The Visitor Information Center Gift Shop (on 8th Avenue, next to Funny Bone) is the place to find the perfect souvenir of your trip to Ybor whether for yourself or friends back home.

33. From 7th Avenue, take the walkway immediately adjacent to the Ybor statue to 8th Avenue. Immediately across the street is the **Centro Ybor Streetcar Station (#2)** which will return you to **Centennial Park Streetcar Station (#1)**.

34. Walk or take your vehicle to the **Columbia Restaurant,** 2117 E. 7th Avenue, to check out its Spanish heritage decor and its gift shop. You can also get a light meal or dinner. Reservations needed for dinner.
    *Phone:* (813) 248-4961
    *Website:* http://www.columbiarestaurant.com/
    See three Historical Markers in front of Restaurant:

    - COLUMBIA RESTAURANT FOUNDED 1905
    - THE ROUGH RIDERS RODE BY HERE 1898
    - THE KREWE OF THE KNIGHTS OF SANT' YAGO

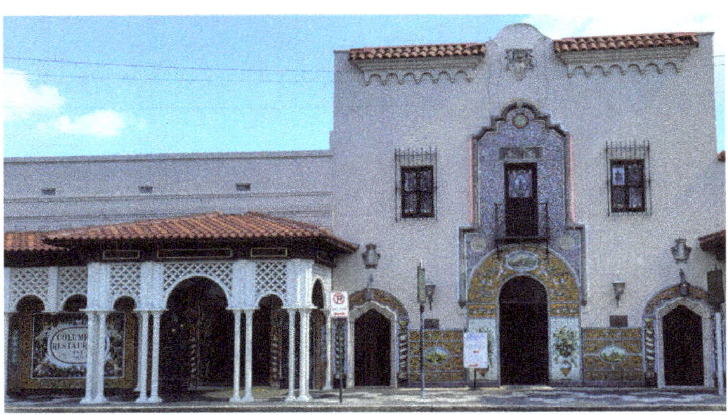

*Front façade of Columbia Restaurant.*

Founded in 1905, the Columbia Restaurant is the **oldest restaurant in Florida**, and is the largest Spanish restaurant in the world with a seating capacity of 1,700 in 15 dining rooms. The restaurant has been the steward of introducing Spanish food to the US since its start. Go to the website and check its incredible menu, read about its illustrious history and the **Hernandez/Gonzmart** five-generation family ownership. While Ybor City went into decline following the Depression, this institution continued to courageously expand for the day when it would lead a resurgence. The successful Columbia was the forerunner for the revitalization of Ybor City, and it reestablished the appreciation for the community's heritage. Make reservations for a flamenco dance show. Reservations needed for dinner and recommended for lunch. Enjoy the amazing decor of period pieces and architectural features, making a visit there a complete experience into the Ybor City of the past. See Section 15 for details on artistic features.

## YBOR CITY - EAST SIDE

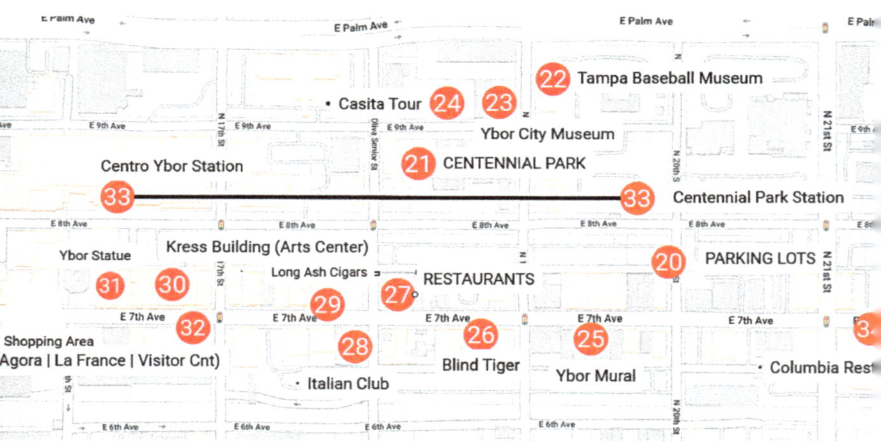


Map data (C) 2023 Google/Maptive

| | |
|---|---|
| 20. Parking (3 lots) | 28. The Italian Club (L'Unione Italiana) |
| 21. Centennial Park | 29. Long Ash Cigars* |
| 22. Tampa Baseball Museum at Al Lopez House | 30. Kress Contemporary Arts Center |
| 23. Ybor City Museum State Park | 31. Vicente Martínez-Ybor Statue |
| 24. Casita Tour | 32. Shopping |
| 25. Viva Ybor Mural | 33. Centro Ybor Station to Centennial Park Station |
| 26. Blind Tiger Cafe | 34. Columbia Restaurant |
| 27. RESTAURANT CENTRAL | |

*Other nearby cigar shops include Ybor Cigars Plus and La Herencia De Cuba

## NORTH SIDE SIGHTS

Here are some sights to see on the North side of the Ybor district beyond walking distance of 7th Avenue and best traveled by car, with an explanation of their historical significance.

The **Queen Isabella statue** resides in Centro Asturiano near its front entrance. It is a historic artifact worth taking in at this, the largest of the community center buildings. The building's design and architectural features are noteworthy. See Centro Asturiano under Architecture. The statue was commissioned by Vicente Martinez Ybor and crafted in Cuba according to historian Anthony Pizzo. It was utilized at cigar exhibitions in the United States and abroad to promote the Spanish heritage of cigar making. The sculpture of several kinds of wood has a history all its own worth reading about on a visit to the building. Queen Isabella financed Christopher Columbus's expeditions to the new world which found tobacco being used by indigenous people of Cuba. The Queen stands on a round ball representing the globe which rests on a humidor like pedestal. Photo by Ansley Blackwell Wrigh, courtesy of Centro Asturiano. Cristal Lastra, President of Centro Asturiano stands next to the statue.

35. **Centro Asturiano de Tampa** (1914) is at 1913 N. Nebraska Avenue, and was the club organized for Asturian immigrants. Beginning in the late 1880s, many immigrants who came to the Americas from Spain were from the Spanish province of Asturias. The community center was organized in 1902 by those immigrants whose heritage was from this province on the northern coast of Spain along the Bay of Biscay. It was one of two Spanish centers founded in Ybor City in the first decades of Ybor City. The original building was destroyed by fire and the current structure dates from 1914 in a neo-Graeco-Roman style. When completed, it was characterized by an "unbiased" local

paper as "the most beautiful building in the South."[9] The primary focus of the club was the healthcare of its members, so the club built a hospital which contained a state-of-the-art operating room. Club members were provided lifetime, low-cost medical care. When the structure opened, it contained a cantina with bowling alleys, a theatre, a ballroom, education rooms, and a library. Today it's a venue center for special events including wedding receptions, theatre productions, recitals, and it remains open for membership and hosting events.

*El Centro Asturiano de Tampa*

36. **The German-American Club (Deutsch Amerikanischer Verein) (1908)** at 2105 N. Nebraska Avenue was organized in 1901. This community center served the German, eastern European, and Jewish communities during its heyday. The building was completed in 1908 and originally contained a stage for various productions, a swimming pool, a gymnasium, and educational classrooms. For an interim period, it was utilized by Tampa's Labor Temple Association. It has been undergoing significant restoration by a health center that now occupies the building and promotes inclusive healthcare. Its classical style is reminiscent of Old South architecture. A historical marker is on the corner.

*The German-American Club.*

37. **Hillborough College, Ybor Campus, Visual & Performing Arts** located in the Performing Arts Building includes an impressive visual arts Gallery 114 presenting rotating exhibits, some of which have depicted the heritage of Ybor City. It is free and open to the public. The gallery promotes not only local and regional artists but also national and international exhibits as well. Gallery hours are Monday through Wednesday 9am-4pm; Thursday 9am-7pm; and Friday 9am-2pm. Hours may be subject to change when classes are not in session. The performing arts present an annual schedule of plays, concerts, and dance performances in its two theatres also located in the Performing Arts Building. Performances permit the school's visual and performing art students to work under the direction of professionals in environments that duplicate the real work of artistic productions. For exhibitions, hccyborgallery114

38. **La Segunda Central Bakery (1915),** at 2512 N. 15th Street, is the historic bakery of Ybor City and run by a fourth-generation Cuban family. It makes authentic Cuban bread for Tampa and beyond. It has wonderful baked goods and other prepared foods including a highly rated Cuban sandwich. It makes the legendary Cuban bread with 3 kinds of flour and uses a palm leaf on top of bread so the top browns evenly. Go in, learn about Cuban food, and let your taste buds try something new.

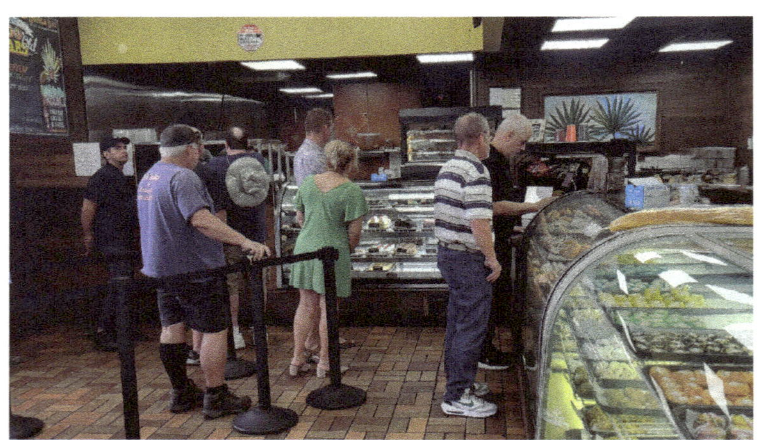

*La Segunda Storefront at 15th Street & 15th Avenue*



39. **The J. C. Newman Factory (1910),** of 2701 16th Street, is the last remaining cigar factory in the United States. Its iconic clock tower can be seen from miles away. In 2020, the company celebrated the **125th year in the cigar business,** which moved from Cleveland in 1954, and the 110th anniversary of the building which once originally housed **Regensburg Cigar Company**. The anniversaries have been marked by a complete renovation of the building.[10] This newly renovated factory features a not-to-be-missed tour, which highlights the company's history as well as the making of cigars by hand and by machine. The historic building features a cigar store with souvenir merchandise and cigar accessories. Its fully functioning factory operation is reflective of the large scale cigar production of Ybor City in its heyday. See section 10, Guided Walking Tours.

## MAP OF NORTH SIDE OF YBOR CITY – 5 SIGHTS

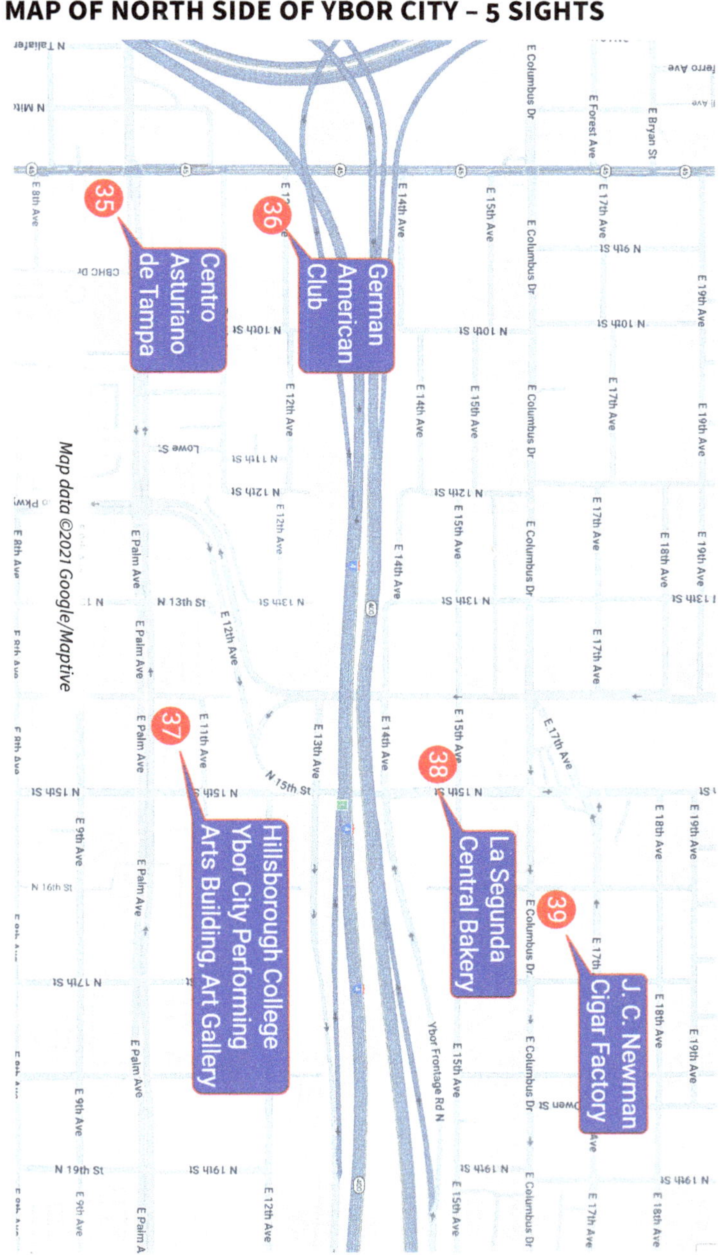


Map data ©2025 Google/Maptive

## *Endnotes Section 12*

1. Andrea Christou and the Tampa Historical Team, “Sociedad La Union Martí-Maceo,” Tampa Historical, accessed February 2022, https://www.tampahistorical.org/items/show/112.
2. John M. Dunn, *José Martí: Cuba's Greatest Hero*, (Sarasota, FL: Pineapple Press, Inc., 2015), 4.
3. Wallace Reyes, *Cigar City Architecture and Legacy* (Scott Valley, CA: CreateSpace Independent Publishing Platform, 2015), 325-326.
4. “History,” The Cuban Club, accessed February 2022, http://cubanclubybor.com/history/
5. Kenneth Burt, “Cigar Makers Pioneered Hispanic Labor Organizing,” Kenneth Burt's Blog, August 28, 2010, http://kennethburt.com/blog/?p=827.
6. Wallace Reyes, *Cigar City Architecture and Legacy*, 367-373.
7. See section 3 for a short biography on Don Vicente Martí Ybor with endnotes for further reading.
8. Wallace Reyes, *Once Upon a Time in Tampa*, 104-112.
9. “History,” Centro Asturiano de Tampa, accessed February 2022, https://www.centroasturianotampa.org/history.
10. “Cigar Factory Renovations,” J.C. Newman Cigar Company,” accessed February 2022, https://www.jcnewman.com/cigar-factory-renovations/.

# 13 SELF-GUIDED TOURS

For a meaningful and enlightening tour of Ybor, it is recommended that you utilize one of the expert historical tours set out in Section 6. If for some reason you are not able to arrange that or are just in Ybor for a few hours, the following is a two-to-three hour self-guided tour you can do on your own. Utilize the numbered site information in parentheses located in the previous section for information on the stop. This tour is circular so that it may be started at any point in the sequence. In this section, you'll find a self-guided walking tour and a car tour.

## SELF-GUIDED WALKING TOUR –15 SIGHTS – 2 to 3 HOURS

Friends of José Martí Park – Ybor Factory – El Pasaje – Tampa Bay Brewing Co. Ybor City Visitor Center – Centro Ybor to Centennial Park Streetcar Stations – Centennial Park – Ybor City Museum State Park Tampa Baseball Museum at Al Lopez House Casita Tour - Restaurant Central – L'Unione Italiana (Italian Club) – Long Ash Cigars – Kress Contemporary Arts Center – Ybor Statue – Tabanero Cigars Centro Ybor to Cadrecha Streetcar Stations

**NOTE: The Ybor Museum is open Wednesday through Sunday. The Tampa Baseball Museum is open Thursday through Sunday.**

This self-guided tour includes sights from both the West and East sides of Ybor, as discussed in Section 12. The number in parentheses refers to the paragraph in the preceding section. The course of this walk may be impeded by street closures. See the following map.

A. Park in the **Noriega Garage** at the 8th Ave. entrance near N. 13th St.

B. The **Friends of José Martí Park** (#7) is diagonally across from the parking deck. The entrance is on 8th Avenue at the corner with 13th Street. See numbered item in parenthesis in the previous section for commentary.

C. The **Ybor Factory Complex** (#8) is across the street from the park. After departing the park, turn right and go to Avenida Republica de Cuba (14th St.) and walk up the street to the factory entrance with its metal staircase.

D. **El Pasaje** (Cherokee Club) (#9) is the brick colonnade building located on 9th Ave. across from the Ybor Factory.

E. **El Circulo Cubano, The Cuban Club** (#10) is the yellow brick community center located behind El Pasaje, fronting N. 14th St.

F. From the Cuban Club, the **Tampa Bay Brewing Company** (#12) is located on 9th Ave. at the 16th St. walkway two blocks from 14th Street as you turn left onto 9th Avenue.

G. The **Ybor City Chamber of Commerce Visitor Information Center** (#13) is on 8th Ave. across the street from Tampa Bay Brewing Co., a half a block to the right.

H. After a stop at the Visitor Information Center, ride the streetcar from **Centro Ybor Station** (stop #2) to **Centennial Station** (stop #1).

I. At Centennial Park, you'll see the **Immigrant Statue**, and **Roosters** (#21). The park is to the left as you deboard the streetcar.

J. Across the street from the Immigrant statue in Centennial Park on 9th Avenue is the **Ybor City Museum State Park** (#23) and the neighboring

K **Tampa Baseball Museum at the Al Lopez House** (#22). These two museums are on either side of 19th St. off 9th Ave. The Hillsborough Sheriff's Office History Center on the corner of 9th Avenue and 19th Street is referred to in section 5.

L. The **Casita Tour** (#24) takes place from the Ybor City Museum State Park and is included in the price of admission. The casita is next to the museum and requires a tour guide. Call or check the museum's website for the times of the Casita Tour. From the row of casitas on 9th Ave., proceed down 18th St. to 7th Ave.

M. A 2-block square area (from E. 7th Ave. and 18th St.) is regarded as the **core restaurant area** with 20+ restaurants. See Restaurant Listing and map in Section 11 to determine which of these eateries would make a good pit stop for you. There are options for indoor or outdoor eating, an informal café experience, a child friendly establishment, (Gaspar's Grotto, Game Time), and the cuisine you have a taste for—Italian, Spanish/Cuban, American, etc.



N **L'Unione Italiana** (#28), the Italian Club is on the south corner of 7th Ave. and 18th St.

O **Long Ash Cigar Shop** (#29) is a sample of what cigar shops have to offer for visitors seeking knowledge about the cigar business. It is located across the street from the Italian Club.

P. **Kress Arts Building** houses artist studios, galleries and organizations of Kress Contemporary on the second and third floors. Their galleries are open according to posted schedules at the building and on the Kress Contemporary website. On the first floor is the Florida Museum of Photographic Arts which is open Tuesday through Saturday. See the Kress Contemporary and the Florida Museum of Photographic Arts under Section 15, Arts and Culture.

Q. A bronze statue of **Vicente Martinez Ybor** (#15) is one and half blocks further down 7th Avenue near 16th Street.

R. Tabanero Cigars and nearby **cigar shops** La Faraona Cigars (at 1515 7th Ave), Nicahabana (at 1605) provide the context of the historic district's heritage of cigar making by hand.

S. Three shops in the area will be of interest: Agora at 1517 E. 7th Avenue, Suite A (S marker); and La France at 1612 E 7th Avenue (S marker); the Ybor City Visitor Information Center Gift Shop, located at 1600 E. 8th Avenue, Suite B-104 (G marker) which can be found under the **Vintage Shopping** in Section 15, Arts and Culture.

T. See "H" on the map for **Centro Ybor Station** #2. Use the walkway adjacent to the Ybor statue to 8th Avenue and board the streetcar westward (to the left) for the return to parking if you parked in the Noreiga Garage. Deboard the streetcar at the Cadrecha Station #4. The Noreiga Garage is adjacent to the station.

SELF-GUIDED WALKING TOUR ROUTE NEXT PAGE

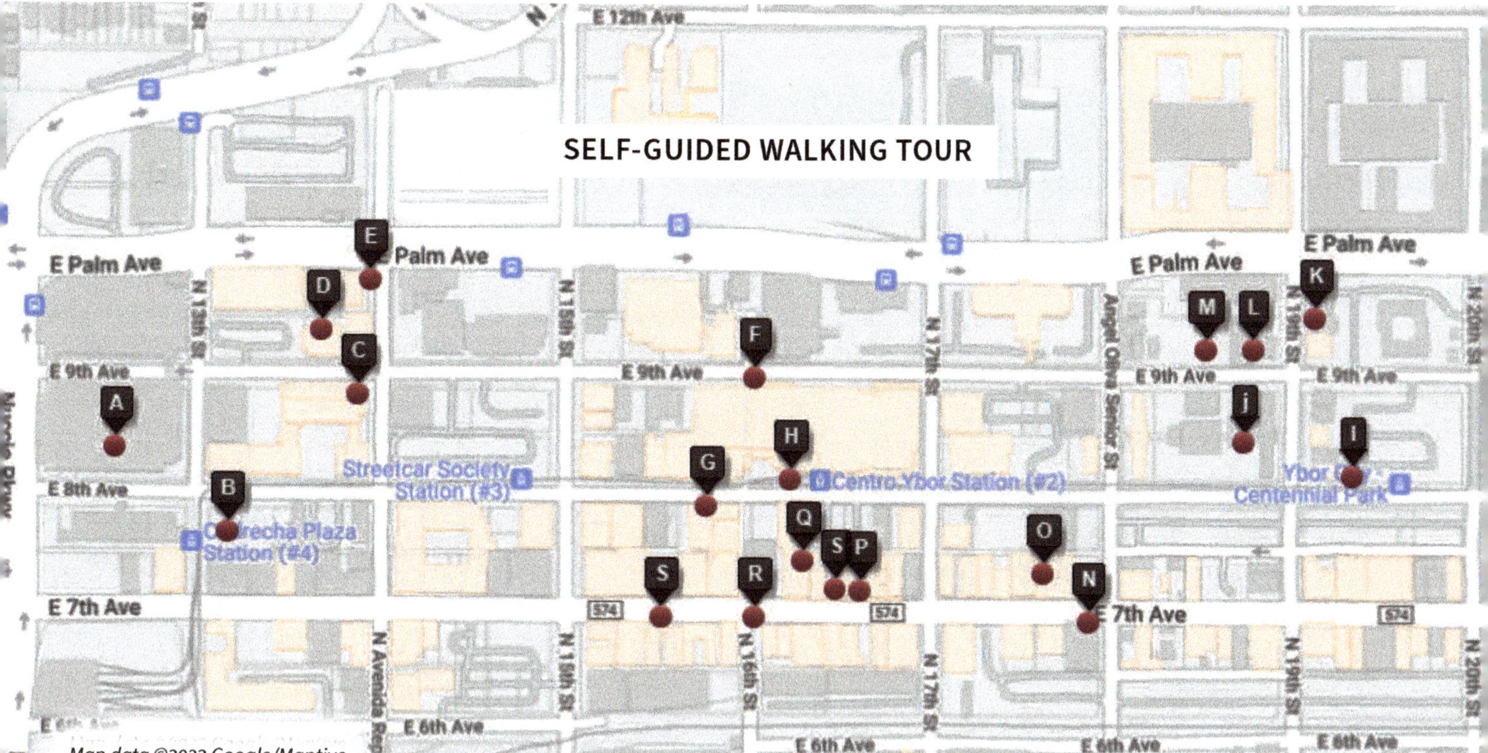

## SELF-GUIDED WALKING TOUR



Map data ©2023 Google/Maptive

## DAY CAR TOUR – 14 VIEWS – 1 TO 2 HOURS

For those preferring a car tour of Ybor City, this option may be a great fit for you. You can choose to make a few stops, which are suggested, or not stop at all. The car tour enables you to see some sights that are on the periphery of the historic district and not within easy walking distance. The route may be affected by closed streets due to construction. See map at end of this section. The numbers in parentheses refer to the complete description of the sight in the previous section.

**Gateway to the Latin Quarter – Sociedad La Union Martí-Maceo (Martí-Maceo Society) – Friends of José Martí Park – Ybor Factory El Pasaje – Circulo Cubano (Cuban Club) – Centro Asturiano (Asturian Spanish Club) – German Club – La Segunda Bakery J.C. Newman Cigar Co. Factory/Museum – Ybor City Museum State Park Tampa Baseball Museum at Al Lopez House – Casitas 9th Ave. L'Unione Italiana (Italian Club) – Kress Arts Building – Tabanero Cigars Ybor Statue – Centro Español (Spanish Community Center)**

*Freestanding steel archway announces the entrance to the Ybor City district. Photo by PamElla Lee Photography.*

**View 1.** This car tour begins at the intersection of the Nuccio Parkway and 7$^{th}$ Avenue. There is a marker on the left side of the archway that tells you about the historical district you are entering and a dedication marker on the right side. The gateway marker on the left side as you enter is difficult to read from the car but includes the following information.

Vicente Martinez Ybor, a wealthy Spanish cigar manufacturer from New York and Key West, began development of Ybor City in 1885. On April 12, 1886, 500 Cuban cigar markers boarded the sidewheeler *Hutchinson* in Key West and sailed for Tampa. Over 3,000 workers arrived by the end of 1886. Cigar factories and home construction flourished and business thrived. Ybor City became known as the "Cigar Capital of the World."

The Ybor City Historic District includes more than 1,300 buildings, nearly a thousand of which are historic. The buildings include the largest collection of cigar factories and related industrial structures in the United States; a major collection of commercial and commercial-residential structures; a group of ethnic clubhouses; and historic worker housing. Many structures, built between 1886 and World War I, display Spanish and Cuban influences, such as wrought-iron balconies, even though many architects in the area were "Anglos."

The Ybor City Historic District was listed in the National Register of Historic Places in 1974. For its importance in the nation's immigration movement, the National Park Service declared Ybor City a National Historic Landmark District in 1990.



To Read the Text on Historic Markers Along the Route more clearly, input the following Link Prefix on your phone: https://www.hmdb.org/search.asp?SearchFor= and then insert the number of the marker listed at the end of each View section. Example: at View 2 input the number that follows the marker title, 31708, immediately after the equal (=) sign. Replace the number for each subsequent marker. https://www.hmdb.org/search.asp?SearchFor=31708

**View 2.** The heritage of the Afro Cuban community was portrayed on a mural on the west side of the building of Sociedad La Union Martí-Maceo (#6), the community center for this immigrant group. The mural is no longer viewable due to construction but can be seen under Ybor City Murals, pages 164-165. On your right is **Rough Riders Park (#4)**, which commemorates the veterans of the Spanish-American war and in particular memorializes the Rough Riders who in 1898 rode down 7th Avenue from their encampment west of 22nd Street, just east of where the Columbia Restaurant was to open in 1905. They proceeded to the area of this park before making a left turn to ride down to Port Tampa and board ships to Cuba. Markers: Sociedad La Unione Marti-Maceo 31708 / Rough Riders 32795.

**View 3.** Proceed down 7th Avenue and make a left on to 14th Street (Avenida Republica de Cuba), at 8th Avenue make another left. (If the way down 8th Avenue is blocked by construction, continue on to 9th Avenue and make a left onto 9th Avenue and proceed to 13th Street and make a left to get to the park.) On the corner of 8th Avenue and 13th Street is the **Friends of José Martí Park (#7)**—Martí was the revolutionary who worked for the independence of Cuba from Spain, leading up to the Spanish-American war. He visited Ybor City some 20 times in the first half of the 1890s, and the cigar workers in Ybor City contributed heavily to the cause. Marker: José Martí Apostle of Cuban Freedom 32132.

**View 4.** Across from the park is the south side of Ybor Square, which includes the buildings of Mr. **Ybor's Factory Complex (#8)**. Return back up 13th Street to 9th Avenue and turn right onto 9th Avenue. Proceed slowly down the street. On the right is the main building of the factory built in 1886 and on your left is **El Pasaje (The Cherokee Club) (#9)**. At the corner of 14th Street, pause at the intersection and note the historical markers in front of El Pasaje and the one on the corner of the factory building. El Pasaje and the factory were two of the first brick buildings in Ybor City. El Pasaje was the office building of Mr. Ybor where he conducted many of his various enterprises, which included enhancing the infrastructure of the city. After his death, the building became a hotel, a men's club, a restaurant, and a military recruiting center. Looking down to your right is the front of the factory building with its iron steps leading up to the front door. Mr. Ybor allowed José Martí to speak to his factory workers from these steps to show his mutual support for the Cuban independence movement. Markers: José Martí (Stone Marker in front of Factory) 14431 / Founding of the Cigar Industry in Tampa 31704 / The Cherokee Club and "El Pasaje" 176195.

**View 5.** Turn left onto 14th Street. Behind El Pasaje on 14th Street is **The Cuban Club (El Circulo Cubano de Tampa) (#10).** Markers: El Circulo Cubano 31710 / Attempt on the Life of José Martí 14545.

**View 6.** Proceed down N. 14th Street to Palm Avenue and turn right. At 15th Street or thereabouts make a U turn to go west on Palm Avenue. Continue to Nebraska Avenue and turn left. On the left is **Centro Asturiano de Tampa.** See **#35** in the previous section and under "Architecture" in Section 15. Turn into the parking lot across the street from the club to turn around. Marker: El Centro Asturiano de Tampa 32185.

**View 7.** Continue north on Nebraska Avenue to **The German American Club** at E. 11th Avenue, the white building on the right now used as a clinic. See **#36** in the preceding section and under "Architecture" in Section 15. Turn right onto 11th Avenue to read the historic marker and admire the architecture of the building. Marker: German-American Club 32372.

 **View 8.** Proceed up Nebraska Avenue to E. Columbus Dr. and turn right onto Columbus Dr. Proceed to N. 14th Street (N. Avenida Republica de Cuba) and turn right. At 15th Avenue, turn left. On the right at the corner of 15th Street is **La Segunda Central Bakery (#38)**, the historic bakery of Ybor City. Parking is available off both 15th Street and 15th Avenue. It has wonderful baked goods including pastries and other prepared foods such as the highly rated Cuban sandwich. It makes the legendary Cuban bread with 3 kinds of flour and uses a palm leaf to evenly brown the top. This stop will help you learn about Cuban food and could offer a new culinary experience. For starters buy a loaf of Cuban bread and some guava turnovers.

**View 9.** Upon leaving the bakery, continue up 15th Street to E. Columbus Drive, turn right and proceed to the **J. C. Newman Cigar Co. Factory (#39).** The iconic factory known as El Reloj, the Clock, will come immediately into view . In 2020, the company celebrated the 125th year of the company, which moved from Cleveland in the 1950s and the 110th anniversary of the building, which once originally housed Regensburg Cigar Company. The anniversaries have been marked by a complete renovation of the building. Its factory tour, which includes cigars made by hand and by machine, requires reservations online in advance. The historic building features a cigar store with souvenir merchandise and a museum which can be seen at no charge. Marker: The El Reloj Cigar Factory and J.C. Newman Cigar Company 236056



**View 10.** To see the **Columbia Restaurant (#34)**, continue on East Columbus Avenue to N. 21st Street and turn right. Proceed down 21st Street and turn left on to E. 7th Avenue and drive in front of the block-long restaurant. There is a lot across the street at 22nd Street where you can park to admire the front tile façade of the building. See also the Columbia Restaurant under “Arts and Culture” in Section 15. Marker: Columbia Restaurant Founded (1905) 231639.

**View 11**. The next stop is the **Ybor City Museum State Park (#23)**, whose exhibits illustrate the start and development of Ybor City and the cigar industry. It is run by the State of Florida Park Services. Proceed back down 7th Avenue and turn right onto 19th Street. Proceed up 19th Street to 8th Avenue. If you wish to stop in this area, parking lots exist to your right and left at 8th Avenue. Proceeding past 8th Avenue, on your immediate left is **Centennial Park (#21)** where the roosters tend to hang out. Two museums are up ahead on 9th Avenue. At the 9th Avenue intersection, The Ybor City Museum State Park is on the left on 9th Avenue and the **Tampa Baseball Museum (#22)** at the Al Lopez House is on the right side of 19th Street. Upon turning left onto 9th Avenue, you will be right in front of the Ybor City Museum State Park. It is housed in a 1920s bakery building and is identified by its yellow brick and historical marker in front. The museum is compact with minimal walking and a stop here is recommended either now or later. A **casita** ("little house") tour **(#24)** of an adjacent cigar worker home is conducted from the museum and included in the $4 admission. Across the street from the museum is the **Immigrant Statue**, which memorializes all who came to America to seek a new start. The park is the location for the weekly **Saturday Market**. Marker: La Joven Francesca Bakery (Ybor Museum) 8703.

**View 12.** From the museum, proceed further down 9th Avenue to 18th Street and turn left. Cross 8th Avenue, looking out for the streetcar crossing. **La Septima (7th) Avenue** and 18th Street is the heart of restaurants and cigar shops. There are numerous restaurants and cigar shops both east and west from this intersection. At the intersection with 7th Avenue is the geographic center for Ybor restaurants with 20 within two blocks in all directions. Turn right onto 7th Avenue. Immediately on your left is the **Italian Club (#28)** with its neoclassical architecture and its historical markers out front. Read more at Item #28 of the preceding section and in Section 15 under "Architecture." Marker: L'Unione Italiana 8769.

**View 13.** On the right as you travel west on 7th Avenue is the **Kress Arts Building** which houses artist studios, galleries and organizations of Kress Contemporary on the second and third floors. Their galleries are open to the public according to posted schedules at the building and on the Kress Contemporary website. On the first floor is the Florida Museum of Photographic Arts which is open Tuesday through Saturday. See the Kress Arts Building under Section 15, Arts and Culture.

**View 14.** As 16th Street is approached, **Don Vicente Martinez Ybor's bronze statue (#15)** resides in front of Centro Ybor on the right, which is the center of Ybor's commercial district. Immediately on the left is **Tabanero Cigars (#16)** which has a barista serving a great café con leche. It is one of more than a dozen cigar shops on and just off 7th Avenue**.** Marker: Vicente Martinez Ybor statue 171087.

**View 15.** Just past Mr. Ybor's statue on the right is a large brick building of Moorish architecture which housed the **El Centro Español de Tampa (#14)** at the turn of the 20th century. To the left of the Spanish community center across the street is **La Faraona Cigars t**he only cigar shop in Ybor City owned and operated by a woman. Proceeding ahead you will see the entrance gateway at which you began your journey. Marker: Centro Español de Tampa 31711

## MAP OF DRIVING TOUR ROUTE

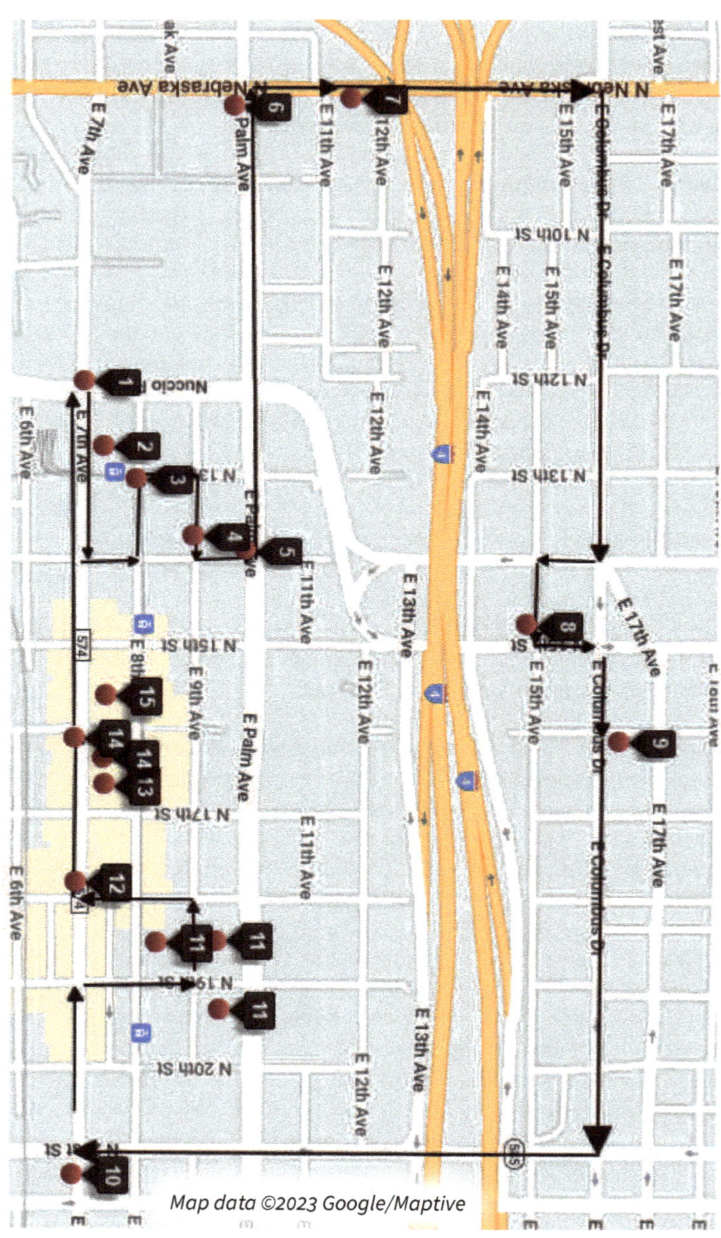


Map data ©2023 Google/Maptive

# 14 YBOR FOR KIDS

Learning about Ybor City as a community where more than seven immigrant groups came together to live and work is a unique story that needs to be passed on to the next generation. So it's important to consider those aspects of Ybor City that would be appealing to people of all ages but especially children.

Here are some suggestions to engage kids in the history of Ybor City and Tampa.

1. The **Ybor City Museum State Park and the Tampa Baseball Museum at the Al Lopez House** are small and easily manageable experiences for children. At the museum they will note that the early pictures of Ybor with its wooden structures and sandy streets resembled a western frontier town except for one thing—the people crossing the street on foot had to accommodate the snakes and alligators using the thoroughfares as well. The Tampa Baseball Museum features many of the famous players from Florida through displays of the history and historic memorabilia of the game that was very much a part of the fabric of Ybor City community from the very beginning.

2. **Gaspar's Grotto** is a pirate-themed restaurant and Ybor's take on the Gasparilla Festival, commemorating Tampa's inclusion in pirate lore.

3. Ybor has its share of great **pizza** places, with many making their ingredients from scratch with the love that only an Italian grandmother would give to the process. Some of these places include Du Amici and Bernini on 7th Avenue.

4. Explore Ybor on a **history walking tour** with a professional guide from Tampa Bay Tours as identified in section 10.

5. Utilize the currently free **streetcar** system in Ybor to get around, and consider going south of Ybor to the Florida Aquarium and the Tampa Bay History Center that feature interactive displays. Fares may be resumed in 2025.

6. The **J. C. Newman Cigar Factory** should prove very interesting for children with a cigar shop that includes souvenirs, tours of the factory facility, and an area to relax and take a break and restrooms. Enjoy a lunch in the park across the street from the factory with bakery food from La Segunda Central Bakery located two blocks away on 15th Street at 15th Avenue.

7. **Ybor City Chamber of Commerce Visitor Information Center** has numerous resources for determining what to explore next in Ybor City and Tampa as well as a short seven-minute video on the history and background of Ybor City that has obtained favorable responses from children and adults alike. Information can be obtained to further explore the historic district, and there is a wide selection of items in its gift area to commemorate your visit to Ybor City.

8. **DRIP Ybor, "Do Really Inspirational Projects"** is a fun and creative space for people of all ages. Participants can learn to express themselves in one of many mediums offered with materials and guidance from staff. A great environment for kids and families, DRIP offers two locations on 7th Avenue, at 1620 and 1910 E. 7th Avenue. Numerous creative classes and workshops for all ages of various lengths offered including single sessions. https://drip-ybor.com
**Phone:** 813-407-1294
**Reservations:** needed for weekend or large group session
**Hours:** Mon: 12pm-10pm; Tue-Wed: 3pm-10pm; Thu: 12pm-10pm; Fri: 12pm-12am; Sat: 12pm-12am; Sun: 1pm-6pm

9. **Game Time Ybor** is an amusement center and sports bar featuring interactive video and electronic games, big-screen TVs, and comfort food. It is a welcome respite for parents and kids alike.

10. The value of a young person's experience in visiting Ybor City cannot be underestimated. It conveys the rich history of our diverse nation and that we all have a point of origin beyond these shores. Also, it teaches toleration of all Americans throughout this hemisphere and beyond. It makes us one in appreciating the liberty, equality, and fraternity that we all share.

# 15 ARTS AND CULTURE

## YBOR CITY RECLAIMED BY ARTISTS[1]

A significant contribution to the revitalization of Ybor City in the 1970s and 80s was the emergence of visual and performance artists, musicians, poets, and craftsmen in the district. Seeking studio spaces, these creatives began to rent vacated factory spaces and retail storefronts. Painters, printmakers, ceramicists, and glass artists exhibited artwork and held art openings for the public.

During the 1970s world renowned Pop artists James Rosenquist, Jim Dine, Malcolm Morley, and John Chamberlin, among others, worked in studios throughout the district. In the 1980s two large artists' collectives strongly impacted the arts scene in Tampa: **El Sama**, located in the Lozano Building (a Ybor factory building), and **Titanic Anatomy**, located in the Corral-Wodiska Cigar Factory Building, provided numerous studio spaces and large public events. Renowned photojournalist Bud Lee, along with artists David Audet, Paul Wilborn, and others, formed the Artists and Writers Group. They created a series of annual art-themed events including **The Artists and Writers Ball** (held at the Cuban Club), **Deep Carnivale Literature Festival, The Ybor Festival of the Moving Image, and The Cuban Sandwich Show**.

Numerous music venues provided performance space for a robust alternative rock scene, enhanced by WMNF Radio's extremely popular **Tropical Heatwave**, a massive music showcase of musical groups from around the world, held at venues throughout Ybor.

Theo Wujcik, a nationally acclaimed artist who taught at the University of South Florida, would lead a "movement" in Ybor City in the 1980s and 90s called **Mododado**, combining punk rock with dance, performance, and salvage art.

Artist Arnold Martinez painted historic images of Ybor City using tobacco and coffee tints on paper or canvas, working in his 7th Avenue storefront window.

And Hillsborough College Ybor City Campus offered an array of art classes introducing art students to the Ybor community.

The many artists who have worked and resided in Ybor City over previous decades have contributed to our renewed awareness of Ybor City's historic significance and to a renaissance for the arts, bringing crowds into the district for events and openings.

An important part of the arts in Ybor City has been the Ybor Art Colony which was a presence for more than 50 years. The community was made up of artists using a variety of materials for visual art from pencil to brush, from portraiture to landscapes, from traditional impressionism to modern art. While its gallery and studios on the second floor above King Corona Cigars and Cafe were their permanent base for many years, the building needing extensive renovation and the members have moved on to join other art groups in Ybor and Tampa. Today traditional artists thrive, while a new generation of creatives grows including digital designers, music studios, and tattoo artists—all furthering Ybor City as a flourishing arts community.

The following information offers insights on this vibrant arts community as it continues to evolve today.

### *Kress Contemporary*

1624 E. 7th Avenue
Phone: (813) 340-9056
Email: contact@kresscontemporary.com
KRESS CONTEMPORARY is an important center for the arts in Florida. It is dedicated to cultivating a robust arts community centrally located in the heart of Ybor City. Its purpose is to provide local, emerging, early-career, and mid-career artists with access to studio space, exhibition opportunities, and engaging events that highlight the visual, performing, and literary arts.

The programs of Kress Contemporary support artists and arts organizations of diverse backgrounds. It serves the community by providing spaces for their creative pursuits, and Kress Contemporary engages the community through public events, including film screenings, performances, exhibition, artist talk, poetry readings, and workshops. This art organization welcomes groups for tours, field trips, meetings, and private or public events. Its website states a purpose to "promote and celebrate all forms of art."

The artists of Kress Collective presently include these personalities who are both local and from beyond our region.

Benjo Blocks - Karol Batansky - Marc Brechwalk - Ashley Cantero - Dave Decker - Elizabeth Fontaine-Barr - Mary Helen Horne - Sarah Hull - Nat Pagan - Chase Parker - Carlos Pons - Kim Radatz - Lisa Ramudo - Lynn Rattray - Marilyn Binder Silverman - Jessica Veguez

The organizations of Kress Contemporary include:

VISUAL ARTS
Honey Gallery - The Coalition of Hispanic Artists (CHA) - Remember Wynn Productions - Art Noire Gallery - Reverb: University of South Florida College of Design, Art & Performance - OXH Gallery - Dave Decker Photography - Florida Museum of Photographic Arts (FMoPA) - Pop Yarn - Tempus Projects

PERFORMING ARTS
The Fringe Theatre - Tampa Repertory Theatre

LITERARY ARTS
Hear 'Em Say Youth Arts Collective - Kitchen Table Literary Arts

The Kress Contemporary arts hub includes galleries that have their own exhibition hours which can be consulted at kresscontemporary.com/visual-arts. Multiple exhibits are often occurring and Thursday is the best day of the week to visit Kress Contemporary. To meet those in the Ybor arts community is a great way to connect with the Tampa arts. It is an opportunity to see contribution of time and money at work enriching the community Ybor City and Tampa. The Kress Contemporary Schedule of Events can be accessed at kresscontemporary.com/events.

## *Florida Museum of Photographic Arts (FMoPA)*

1630 E. 7th Avenue
*Phone:* (813) 221-2222
*Hours:* Monday, closed; Tuesday-Saturday, 11am-5pm; Sunday, 12pm-5pm
*Admission:* Free for Museum members; $12 for adults, $10 Students, Military with ID, and Seniors
*Website:* https://www.fmopa.org Facebook has up to date information

FMoPA collects, preserves and exhibits historic and contemporary works and is one of few such museums in the United States devoted solely to photography. FMoPA exhibits span the evolution of photography from vintage to contemporary. The Museum's main gallery features rotating exhibits encompassing diverse genres and styles, ensuring a great experience with each visit. The FMoPA Community Gallery is dedicated to showcasing the Tampa Bay community and regularly features work from local photographers from its educational programs.

The Museum provides popular workshops and classes for children, adults, and seniors, providing camera instruction and demonstrating how photography can be used to inspire, educate and express.

## *Hillsborough College Ybor Campus Arts*

Performing Arts Building, 2204 N. 15th Street at Palm Avenue.

*HC, Ybor Campus Performing Arts Building*

**Gallery114**
*Phone:* 813-253-7674
*Hours:* Mon-Wed, 9am-4pm; Thu, 9am-7pm; Fri, 9am-2pm
Closed Friday – Sunday during summer.

The gallery is located on the first floor of the Performing Arts Building and is free and open to the public. It features contemporary fine art in various mediums in the college environmment which promotes visual artistic literacy for both students and the public at large. Rotating exhibits are scheduled regularly and some exhibits are displayed virtually. Exhbititions may also reflect Ybor City heritage. Website: https://www.hccfl.edu/campus-life/arts/hcc-art-galleries/gallery114/visit-gallery114 visit-gallery114
All HC Art Galleries - https://www.hccfl.edu/campus-life/arts/galleries-hcc

**Performing Arts**
Performing arts are presented through the Mainstage Theatre and a smaller, intimate theatre. An active schedule of performing events includes concerts, dance and theatre productions. hccfl.edu/theatre, hccfl.edu/dance, hccfl.edu/music

## *Marcolina's Fine Arts Gallery*
1517 E. 7th Avenue, Suite B
*Email:* info@marcolinas.com
*Hours:* Monday-Sunday, by appointment

Arriving from the dynamic art scene of New York, Guillo Perez III and Marcolina Mercado-Perez bring a unique cultural influence to Ybor City. The gallery includes art education through an Academy of the Arts. This program offers a spectrum of weekly classes encompassing a wide range of disciplines: portraiture, sculpture, print making, and drawing, as well as art history.

 The gallery is the only space in the area to host nude life drawing sessions twice a month. The gallery is deeply engaged in the mural scene of Tampa Bay. Art enthusiasts may acquire artworks both online and at the gallery on 7th Avenue and at other affiliates found through their website. The gallery's collection spans a wide range of artistic mediums from the classical to the avant gard and it draws from the talents of the national and international spheres and from the local community including contributions from their Academy of the Arts showcasing class creations. https://www.marolinas.com/pages/about-us Photo courtesy of the gallery.
Artists include: Guillo Perez 3 (Gallery Artist), Blake Emory (Recurrent Artist) and Featured Artists: Greg Latch, Delaney Bend, Deidra Leigh Kling, John Gurbacs, James Luedde, Elizabeth Fontaine-Barr, Artysta Lulu, Gina Novendstern, Eric Ondina, Sal Patalano, Jason Shiver

## *Dysfunctional Grace Art Gallery*

The ambiance of the Dysfunctional Grace Art Gallery is comparable to a Ripley's Believe it or Not as the merchandise on display is not only art but the oddities of both life and death. Many of the items for purchase reflect on the nature of life and death itself, making its items unique and interesting. Inquisitive kids love this place, and it provides a unique taste on what can be considered decor in the home or as keepsakes. To be shocked by what is bizarre and somewhat of an oddity is to reflect on the unusual nature of life.

*Co-owner Liz Furlong stands below an array of birds above a display case at Dysfunctional Grace.*

*Phone*: (813) 842-0830
*Location*: The gallery which has art for display and for sale is located at 1704 ½ E. 7th Avenue, second floor above Big Easy.
*Hours*: Monday-Saturday, 11am-5pm; Sunday closed
*Parking*: Pay lot options are available at 19th St. and 8th Ave. as well as at 7th Ave. and N. 20th St.
*Website:* https://www.dysfunctionalgrace.shop

*Viva Ybor Mural on 7th Avenue. Current version of mural by Chico Garcia.*

**The *Viva Ybor* Mural** is a brilliantly colored mural in the heart of Ybor City on 7th Avenue between 19th and 20th Streets on the right side of the street, when traveling east. It was painted by artist Chico Garcia in 2012 and represents some of the major icons of Ybor City's history. From the left is the Ybor City Rooster who enjoys protected legal status in Ybor City. Their avian ancestors made their way from Spain to Cuba to Key West, then Tampa as they provided a valuable source of food on the hoof in the late 19th century before refrigeration. At the bottom left is the tombstone of the famous rooster, James E. Rooster, a remarkably beautiful rooster, who was buried in Ybor City in 1997 amid a New Orleans–style funeral procession featuring brass instruments.[2]

The iconic lamppost of Ybor is positioned above the rooster. Its five enormous bulbs illuminating the streets of Ybor first as lit lamps, then gas, then electric, inadvertently representing the five major cultural and ethnic groups of Ybor: Spanish, Cubans, Italians, Romanians, and Germans. Through the upper middle of the mural Henry Plant's Tampa Bay Hotel with its exotic onion shaped minarets and rounded cupolas of Moorish architecture, which was popular during the Victorian era. Below the Tampa Bay Hotel (now the Plant Museum on the University of Tampa campus) is the yellow streetcar. In front of the streetcar is the logo of the Have-A-Tampa Cigar Company, which moved to the Dominican Republic in 2009. Overlooking the scene in the upper right is a very serious Vicente Martinez Ybor who arrived in Tampa to start his new enterprise at age 68 and oversaw its first ten years of development until his death in 1896.

164 **The *Tampa Town* Mural**, David Audet and Joe King Carter created Tampa Town in 2013 as an homage to the city of Tampa and, more specifically, to celebrate the relationship of Ybor City to Tampa and to celebrate the work of New York artist Red Grooms.[3] Grooms, an artist who often works in dioramas and 3-D, had been an influence on both artists. At the time of the mural's creation there was no thought to the work's longevity or its future. They thought it might be exhibited for a few months. It was crafted site specific to fit in a 16 foot wide glass enclosed window displaying the front of King Corona Cigars & Cafe on 7th Avenue. The owners Don and Brenda Barco loved the work so much that they requested that it remain, and it did so for the next twelve years. During that time it found a home in the hearts of residents and visitors alike. Being viewed from the sidewalk, it became over time another of the elements of 7th Avenue's vibrant evolution, photographed by tourists from around the world. In 2025 King Corona was purchased by a new owner who had different plans for the display window. Joe and David gifted Tampa Town to Ybor City developer and arts patron, Darryl Shaw, who had long been an admirer of the piece. It will be exhibited in the Hillsborough College, Ybor City Campus Library sometime in early 2026. David

and Joe are revamping, restoring and recreating parts of the piece currently in studio. And they are excited and pleased with this new phase in the life of this historical work which has great cultural significance for the Tampa community. [The pictures below are of the two artists, David Audet (standing) and Joe King Carter at work reconditioning Tampa Town for its new location.]

**The *American Journey* Mural** (top of page 166) was created under the direction of Michael Parker who utilized students from Ybor City's Hillsborough College. The project involved extensive planning, funding, and preparation of the two-block metal warehouse surface. It has multiple themes: The Journey Through Life, The Conflict Between Tradition and Progress, and The American Experience.[4] Featured in the mural are Don Vicente Martinez Ybor, Dr. Frank Adamo, and Tony P. Pizzo. The mural was the result of donations and contributions of materials from Tampa businesses, individuals, and the Ybor City Community. The surface of the work is the corrugated metal of a warehouse, occupying 12,000 square feet. The mural is the largest outdoor work of art in Florida.[5]

*"The Journey Through Life," "The Conflict Between Tradition and Progress," and "The American Experience." Image capture February 2021© Google 2021.*

***Arrival of the Spanish Expedition in the New World.*** The Tile Mural is located near the Café entrance to the Columbia Restaurant close to 22nd Street and was installed during the stewardship of Cesar Gonzmart, who purchased tiles on a trip to Seville, Spain, in the early 1970s and had them installed on the exterior of the building.[6]

*Painted Tile Mural of the Arrival of the Spanish in the New World.*

***This 1937 Antifascist Women's March Mural*** is on the west side of the building located at 2015 E. 7th Avenue. It features the leaders of the march in Tampa and activists who led political opposition to the brutal fascist movement in Spain and elsewhere in the 1930s. The phrase "no pasarán" means "they shall not pass," a reference to the slogan of the democratic forces that held their positions in the Spanish Civil War. The mural depicts three women. Dolores Ibárruri Gómez, on the left, was a Spanish antifascist activist who was a leader of the movement abroad. In the middle is Luisa Moreno and on the right is Margot Falcón Blanco. Both were activists in Tampa advocating for labor and women's rights, as well as opposing fascism, and were leaders of the demonstration. The local artist is Michelle Sawyer. The mural and marker are an important stop on the trail of understanding Ybor City and what brought immigrants to America, a place where they would have the freedom to follow their aspirations. The mural was commissioned by historian Sarah McNamara, who authored *Ybor City: Crucible of the Latina South,* released in 2023. The book includes a chapter about the Antifascist Women's March of 1937 in which McNamara's aunt, Margot Falcón Blanco, was a march organizer. The mural and historical marker were dedicated to the memory of those who participated in the march.[7]

 In the Roosevelt Room at Hotel Haya resides an oil-on-canvas painting of Theodore Roosevelt entitled ***The Charge of the Yellow Rice Brigade***. The line refers to the traditional story of the arrival of Lt. Colonel Teddy Roosevelt and his “Rough Riders” (a nickname for the first US Volunteers Cavalry Regiment) in Ybor City. In early June 1898, the troops descended in masse upon a café known as Las Novedades, once housed in the property adjacent to the hotel, and now owned by it, at 7th Avenue and 15th Street. The troops were enthusiastically welcomed by the local population and were served the well-known Cuban dish of yellow rice and chicken. The event is humorously referred to as the opening salvo in the brigade’s involvement in the Spanish-American War. In the mural, Teddy Roosevelt sits on his horse, Texas, who along with his dog, Cuba, accompanied him to Cuba. Also pictured are two other mascots of the Rough Riders, a golden eagle and a mountain lion cub. Following their arrival, many of the troops encamped on the eastern side of Ybor in the vicinity of what would later be the site of the Columbia Restaurant. Within weeks of the troops’ arrival, the invasion flotilla disembarked from Port Tampa to the war that would last approximately three months and free Cuba from Spanish control.[8]

On the campus of Hillsborough College, Ybor City Campus, are two murals reflecting the heritage of the Ybor community in which the school is embedded. **The *Living Shades* Mural** is located on the east side of the Ybor Campus Visual Arts Building on 11th Avenue and spans the length of the building. It was created by artists Jay Giroux and Edgar Sanchez Cumbas. The vibrantly colorful mural contains many symbols and representations of the Historic District.[9]

*Image courtesy of HC Ybor, Department of Visual and Performance Arts. https://www.hccfl.edu/campus-life/arts/galleries-hcc/grounds4art, below.*

A second heritage mural located on the HC Ybor campus entitled ***Generations*** by artist Trinity Rivard is located in the bi-level passageway between the campus's Ybor Building and the Faculty Building off 9th Avenue. The mural reflects the generations of immigrants who have lived and worked in the Ybor neighborhood. It blends the history of Ybor with the vital presence of the school in the Historic District. The mural is a creation of faculty and students at HC Ybor executing the design of Rivard.[10]

*Generations mural, courtesy of HC Ybor, Department of Visual and Performance Arts.*

## STATUARY

Ybor City's statuary tells the history of its important leaders, influencers, and change agents.

**Don Vicente Martinez Ybor** (1818–1896) has prominent statuary in Ybor City:

A marble bust of Vicente Martinez Ybor is displayed in the garden adjacent to the Ybor City State Museum.

The bronze statue of Vicente Martinez Ybor was sculpted by Steven Dickey. At the base of the statue is a historical plaque providing a short bio of Mr. Ybor, along with a note of those responsible for funding the plaque and statue. It is located in Centro Ybor on 7th Avenue near the intersection of 16th Street.

The **José Julian Martí Perez** (José Martí) (1853–1895) statue is a white painted, larger-than-life statue. It's the central feature of the Friends of José Martí Park (Parque Amigos de José Martí). The entrance to the park is located on E. 8th Avenue at the corner of N. 13th Street, adjacent to the Cadrecha Plaza Streetcar Station on 13th Street. The inscription on the plaque below the statue is in both English and Spanish.

A bust of José Martí is situated on the property of the Cuban Club (El Circulo Cubano de Tampa). The bust alongside the adjacent historical plaque commemorates an attempted poisoning of Martí near the Cuban Club in December 1892.

*Statue of José Martí. Friends of José Martí Park.*

**General Antonio Maceo Grajales (Antonio Maceo)** (1845–1896) is honored with a bust in the Friends of José Martí Park, just to the left of José Martí's statue. The general was a major military leader in the wars for Cuban independence and led the largest contingent of forces comprised principally of Afro Cubans in the final insurrection initiated in 1895, which culminated in the Spanish-American War in 1898 and resulted in Cuban independence.

*Bust of General Antonio Maceo in Friends of José Martí Park*

The inscription in both English and Spanish reads as follows:

> *Born in Santiago de Cuba 14 June 1845. Rose from Private to Major General during the Ten-years' War of Independence 1868-78. During the final War of Independence, he led the 1896 [1895] invasion of Cuba from Oriente across 750 miles of continual combat. Famed*

*for brilliant guerrilla tactics, his many victories roused the Cuban people against the Spanish Colonial regime. He perished in combat on 7 December 1896 at Punta Brava, Province of Havana, Cuba.*

*Statue of Roland Manteiga leaning against Centro Español Community Center in Centro Ybor.*

The **Roland M. Manteiga** (1920–1988) statue honors the life of the owner and publisher of *La Gaceta* newspaper. A bronze sculpture of the editor leans against the Centro Español de Tampa. The statue is located on 7th Avenue directly across from where 16th Street ends in Centro Ybor. The newspaper published weekly included his column, "As We Heard It," broke stories of the immigrant community of Ybor, which were of national importance and stood in support of human rights. Started by his father in 1922, the newspaper continues to be published by his son, Patrick Manteiga, and is the only paper in the country to be printed in three languages, English, Spanish, and Italian.[11]

Next to the bronze statue is a bronze plaque.

**Mayor Nick C. Nuccio's** (1901–1989) bronze statue commemorates the first Latin mayor of Tampa. It's located in Centennial Park and is situated on a marble base near Angel Oliva Senior (18th) Street and faces 8th Avenue. It is within sight of and just to the east of the Pizzo statue. Nuccio, twice elected mayor of Tampa, was born and raised in Ybor City. He was Tampa's first Latin mayor being of Italian descent, specifically Sicilian. He was known for his accessibility to the electorate of Tampa and for many public work projects improving the infrastructure and adding neighborhood amenities such as libraries, parks, and pools.[12]

*Statue of Mayor Nuccio in Centennial Park facing 8th Ave.*

**Historian Anthony (Tony) P. Pizzo** (1912–1994), an Italian American from Ybor City and great civic leader of Tampa, was the historian of his time. His life is memorialized by a bronze statue located in Centennial Park facing 8th Avenue. near the corner of Angel Oliva Senior (18th) Street. It's to the west of and within sight of the Nuccio statue.

A well respected civic leader and businessman, Tony P. Pizzo was dedicated to preserving the history of Ybor City and the immigrant groups who settled and made a life here. Much of his historical research is in a special collection at the University of South Florida. He was a tenured professor in American studies, and he produced an award-winning ten-part television documentary entitled *Tony Pizzo's Tampa*. He was a member of a score of civic associations dedicated to the Tampa community, its heritage, life, and the preservation of its history. He was responsible for the erection of more than 80 historical markers throughout Tampa. He also founded the Tampa Historical Society. The Tony Pizzo award is given annually to those involved in the education and preservation of the history and heritage of Tampa. His statue features him in the pose of a lecturer, which was his common vocation whether he spoke to civic groups, college students, or other gatherings. He is also featured in the nearly half mile long mural on Adamo Drive entitled "American Journey" created by Michael Parker in collaboration with art students from Ybor City's Hillsborough College.[13]

*The Immigrant Statue in Centennial Park.*

**The Immigrant Statue**, dedicated in 1992, was the first commissioned to be created by Steven Dickey in Ybor City. The bronze statue features four members of a family arriving in the US. More specifically the statue is dedicated to the immigrants arriving in Ybor City. The statue located in Centennial Park faces north onto 9th Avenue across from the Ybor City Museum. The four family members are two parents, a son, and daughter. The daughter is looking upward to her father as if to inquire if this new move is going to work out. She reaches upward with her left hand to reach her father's hand, and his hand is open to receive hers. His countenance is one of stern determination. The mother lovingly has her hands on both of her son's shoulders to reassure his uncertainty as he looks down to the ground. They are dressed in early 20th century clothing and are arriving in Ybor in the first decade of the new century. The four stand on a base of dark pink marble.[14]

They represent all immigrants who came for any number of reasons—religious persecution, economic hardship, and the hope for a better future. At the time of the dedication, two of the oldest living immigrants of Ybor City were honored, both having arrived in the first decade of the 20th century. Many of the first immigrants are listed on the base of the monument. The monument represents the more than seven cultural and ethnic groups that came to Ybor City. They included the Spanish, Hispanic Cubans, Afro Cubans, Italians, Sicilians, Romanians, Germans, and others. Some in these groups were Jews. It was a multiethnic, multiracial, and multinational community incorporating four major languages and three religious groups (Catholics, Protestants, and Jews). Each nationality filled a niche in the cigar economy of Ybor City, and learned how to communicate with one another. This makes Ybor City a landmark example of the immigrant story of America.

## ***Steven Dickey,*** *Sculptor*



Steven Dickey has created more than 50 busts and statues, most of which are of the illustrious people of Tampa, both living and dead. Five of his sculptures appear in Ybor City and include the statues of Vicente Martinez Ybor, Nick C. Nuccio, Anthony Pizzo, Roland Manteiga, and the Immigrant Statue. He is considered the unofficial sculptor laureate of Tampa, and his works are characterized by the artistic style of realism. Dickey engages in the study of the life of his subjects and if they are living, he interviews them and creates a 360-degree image of them. He seeks to capture the energy of his subject's persona as a means of portraying an accurate resemblance of the person in life.[15]

Ybor stands in Centro Ybor as the master of all he surveys. Nuccio holds his Fedora, dressed in a trench coat holding a cigar in his right hand. Pizzo stands at a lectern relaying the history of Tampa he has so meticulously researched. Manteiga leans against the Centro Español de Tampa reading a recent issue of *La Gaceta* he has just published.[16]

The process of creating the bronze image, which was the medium of the final stage of his sculpture, is a challenging and painstaking process. It begins with the creation of a clay model of the subject. The image is then cast in bronze. From a mold of the clay sculpture, a wax duplicate is made. A ceramic coating is applied over the wax image, and it's placed in an oven until the coating hardens. The wax interior is melted to leave a hollow form. The liquid bronze is then poured into the ceramic mold. The last step involves removing the ceramic casing from the bronze. The large sculptures that exist in Ybor City are created in sections which are then welded together. Many of Dickey's busts line Riverwalk.[17]



## *Fearless Champions Statue*

The 9/11 Fallen Heroes Memorial is entitled "Fearless Champions," and displays wreckage from the destruction of Tower 2 in NYC. It is located on 8$^{th}$ Avenue at the beginning of the Streetcar line at Centennial Station, and is appropriately displayed in front of the Hillsborough County Sheriff's Office.

The sculpture was created by Becky Ault to honor the First Responders and those who they helped survive that fateful day. The medium used is stainless steel, similar to the beam recovered from the wreckage. The steel beam is incorporated into a scene of four individuals covered in ash. Three are lending aid to the fourth person emerging from the disaster. The sculpture was dedicated on September 11, 2014, the thirteenth anniversary of 9/11 in a solemn ceremony at the location.[18]

Fearless Champions Sculpture.

## ARCHITECTURE

For those interested in architecture, Ybor City will not let you down. The forms of architecture are representative of the diverse nations from which its settlers came.

The Cuban Club and bust of José Martí.

**El Circulo Cubano (the Cuban Club) (1917)** was built in 1917 following a fire that destroyed the original building. It served as the gathering place for the Cuban immigrants. The building's architect was M. Leo Elliott. It is located on 14th Street at Palm Avenue, and it was added as a national historic landmark in 1972.[19]



The four-story yellow brick building presents an architectural style that is neo-Greek-Classical in nature with two rounded columns enhanced by several minimalist columns on either side of the doorway crowned by Corinthian capitals. The entrance is approached by dual stairways. The front façade duplicates the column effect on the second floor with a traditional neo-Greek-Classical triangular pediment that does not encompass the entire roof line. The long northern side fronting Palm Avenue resembles the façade of a palazzo with its symmetrical design. The interior is a must-see with elegant staircases, stained glass, marble, and richly colored tile with paintings and murals by Cuban artists.

*The Cuban Club, stained glass window, third floor.*

**Centro Español de Tampa (The Spanish Club) (1912)** or the Spanish Community Center is one of the historic buildings which documents the immigration of Spaniards to Ybor City. It became a national historic landmark in 1988.

It was the first of several mutual assistance organizations and now the western anchor of the Centro Ybor district. It was built in 1912 to replace the original building, which it had outgrown. The building was designed by architect Francis J. Kennard and bears features characterized by the revival of several European styles of architecture including French Renaissance, Moorish elements, and Spanish Mediterranean.[20]

The Moorish style is evident in its 7th Avenue entryway with alternating colors of red brick and white stone design of the archway extending to the rest of the building. The building extends upward to a third floor as it reaches 8th Avenue. The east face of the rectangular building reflects the symmetrical white stone elements also reminiscent of Byzantine architecture. The Moorish front facing is adorned with a cast iron trim supporting a balcony for the balance and repetition of pattern of a palazzo, which was featured in many large residences and public buildings in Italy. The neo-French Renaissance influence avoided classical Greek and Gothic features and instead combined 19th century elements.

*El Centro Español, Wikimedia Commons, w:en:GNU Free Documentation License, v.1.2.*

**L'Unione Italiana (The Italian Club) (1917)** was the Italian mutual assistance center or club created in 1894; it was the second club to be formed in Tampa. Its first club building was dedicated in 1912, but burned down in 1914. The current building was built across the street facing north on 7th Avenue and was dedicated in 1918. It should be noted that when the initial buildings were being replaced due to fire as many were, the other clubs offered the use of their facilities to those club members temporarily displaced. The record shows that the 116 charter members of the club were Italians and Sicilians.[21]

*The Italian Club, east side*

The new building was designed by architects M. Leo Elliott and B. C. Bonfoey with Elliott having designed the new Cuban Club, which had been completed the year before. The building incorporated the Italian Renaissance style using the red brick of Ybor City with Greek columns.[22] The exterior is accented with marble and rounded Greek columns. The capitals on the columns are Corinthian in style, and the windows which grace the building between the columns are squared off on the second floor and rounded on the third floor. The lower ground floor exists half above ground, allowing natural light into the area that was originally and is still referred to as the cantina. The second floor has specially designed cartouches above the windows, which were introduced by the French Renaissance builders and are unique to the building. Third floor windows contain mini balconies in keeping with the various Mediterranean styles. The building includes elements of the Greek revival style and Italian Renaissance style with the added French Renaissance feature of the cartouches and the dominant masonry framed windows. The cartouche depicts an oculus—a round eye-like disc which anticipates the future and is supported on either side by a cornucopia representing the abundant life of the move to America.

**El Centro Asturiano de Tampa** is a historic site located at 1913 N. Nebraska Avenue. It was another collaboration between the architectural firm of Bonfoey and Elliott. It has a distinctive European style with a grace that has been deemed to be somewhat southern by US standards.

The mutual assistance center was to serve the Asturian-Spanish immigrants whose home of origin was the province of Asturias on the northern coast of Spain on the Bay of Biscay. The organization was a branch of the Asturian community in Havana, and these immigrants usually came to the area from Cuba. The club was originally located in a small wooden structure on 7th Avenue and moved to this location fronting Nebraska Avenue at Palm Avenue.

In 1912 the building burned and was replaced by the current structure constructed in 1913 and opened in 1914. The newly built mutual assistance center was known for its high level of medical care, which included an operating room at one point and the establishment of a hospital and cemetery later.[19] The style of the building is Renaissance Mediterranean with influence from those areas of the northern Mediterranean: Spain, Italy, Greece, and France.

The architects used yellow brick similar to that used for the Cuban Club. Its sweeping staircase, Doric columns, and imposing balustrade accenting the roof line give it somewhat of a Southern elegance. The building contains on its outward façade a specially designed cartouche, which was a unique design created to make public and private buildings somewhat distinctive.

The designs were often symbolic of the buildings initial use, and they also represent features of the beaux art school of architectural design in Paris, which accentuated bold design elements of neoclassical architecture. The massive columns are as imposing as the balustrades at the roof. The building is framed by substantial corner masonry, all elements contributing to its symmetrical design. Today the social club maintains an active membership and its facilities are used for private and public occasions.

**The German-American Club, or Deutsch Amerikanischer Verein, (1909),** like the Asturian Spanish Club faces Nebraska Avenue and is located a few blocks north at 11th Avenue. It was one of the few non-Latin mutual assistance centers.

Most of the German residents employed in the printing of cigar labels and other artistic decorations for the cigar industry as well as construction of cigar boxes left Ybor City, following the discrimination they experienced following the US's entry into World War I.[24]

The building is neoclassical in design as a rejection of the ornamentation of the Renaissance period. It resembles the simpler utilitarian lines of the French Directorate period and the early American Federalist period. The masonry is not ornate or detailed, but it is accented with stone, especially around the windows. There are no elaborate carvings on an arched frieze that appeared on public buildings in ancient Athens or Rome. The elegance of the building is in its symmetry. It is marked by two imposing staircases originating from the north and south ends of the building converging at the entrance under a large expansive portico. The side entrance also includes a columned porch. There is an extensive iron balustrade on three levels of the building, adding a contrast to the masonry but utilitarian in nature. The cornice just below the roof line is imposing due to its symmetry of repetitive design and crowns the building with a distinctive but simple design flair. The focus of the design is geared to its social function rather than the decoration of previous art periods.

*The German-American Center.*

**El Pasaje (The Cherokee Club) (1886)** stands for the "passageway" in Spanish and refers to the passage that surrounds the building. The two-story structure was the office building for Vicente Martinez Ybor and was one of the first brick buildings in Ybor City, constructed in 1886. See photo on page 124.

It has been contended that Vicente Martinez Ybor wanted marble columns to line the walkway of El Pasaje but was told that to order and have the marble cut to specifications would take a couple of years. He opted for a design that utilized rounded brick to form the columns with a marble base and a marble impost block before the arch. The rounded brick design instituted a unique architectural element to the construction of columns.[25]

From this building, Ybor ran his cigar business as well as the many infrastructure projects he initiated to make Ybor City a comfortable and livable community. Its design falls into the Italian Renaissance category with the outward rounded archways common to villas in Italy. Following Ybor's death in 1896, the building has been used for many purposes. The name Cherokee Club refers to a gentleman's club, and the building has also been a hotel that served famous people. It later became a restaurant, then a clinic. It is currently occupied by an energy company.[26]

**The Union Temple** (1930) or The Castle as it is called today, was built in the medieval style of a castle. When constructed in the early 20th century, it served as a union hall where the various unions serving the cigar industry and their members could meet, hold rallies, and socialize. The building has

*The Castle, formerly The Union Temple.*

a Norman Tower somewhat modified by Renaissance features. Today it is a popular nightclub.[27] 

## *Architects Malachi Leo Elliott and Bayard Clayton Bonfoey*

M. Leo Elliott and B. C. Bonfoey collaborated on many buildings in Tampa. Their names are associated with the architectural design of four club buildings in Ybor City: The German-American Club (1908), Centro Asturiano (1913), El Circulo Cubano (1913), and L'Unione Italiana (1917). Bonfoey was possibly involved in the Cuban Club's design, but historically Elliott is credited with its design.

Their architectural firm was formed in 1907 as Bonfoey and Elliott, and it existed until the outbreak of World War I. Elliott started his own firm in 1920. The men had the unenviable task of presenting designs to club clients who wanted their community center to eclipse all others.[28]

## *Casitas*

While unions had been a challenge for Vicente Martinez Ybor even when in Cuba, NYC, and Key West (before being in Tampa), he still felt that he could create the proper industrial environment whereby workers could be satisfied enough with their working and living conditions that they would not seek to join unions. His move to Tampa was a chance to test that theory.

Casita construction was an integral part of Vicente Martinez Ybor's strategy. No other cigar owner had taken sufficient interest in the lives of their workers to consider their plight in obtaining affordable housing. When Ybor secured the property for his factory, he along with some of his colleagues contracted with local builders to construct casitas, "little houses," for the cigar workers. They had hundreds of houses built that were sold initially just above cost with no interest loans. He had hundreds of houses built, sold them just above his cost for between $700 and $900 and provided no-interest loans for the

*Casitas sketch by Nancy Henderson. Used with permission.*

 workers. In many respects their design and construction would assist the workers in surviving as pioneers in the hostile new environment of Tampa despite mosquitos, alligators, and snakes being the creatures that survived best. The casitas were designed with the following elements:

- A hallway that either ran down the middle of the structure, or to one side of the building, going from the front door to the back door. This provided air flow and ventilation in the hot tropical summers. Residents could sleep with the doors open at night. The design was called a shotgun house as a fired firearm could be discharged from the front of the house which would exit the rear of the building.
- The house entrance elevated from the ground by five steps made it difficult for alligators and snakes to reach the front porch.
- A bread holder, which was made by placing a large nail to the right of the front door upon which a delivered loaf of Cuban bread could be hung. This was high enough so that animals would not be able to reach it before the fresh bread was retrieved by the owner.
- Roofs allowed rainwater to run off into a culvert and into the house. The system was designed to be closed to avoid mosquitos contaminating the water.
- Screens on the windows and netting over the beds gave protection against mosquitos.[29]

Be sure to take the Casita Tour referenced in Section 5 (when available) through admission to the Ybor City State Museum.

## ARTIST DR. FERNANDO (FERDIE) PACHECO (1927–2017)

Another important figure in Ybor City was Fernando (Ferdie) Pacheco. He was a physician, artist, author, and boxing commentator and is often referred to as "The Fight Doctor" for Cassius Clay, later known as Muhammad Ali.

### *His Early Years*

Pacheco was born in Ybor City to Cuban parents with ancestral roots in Spain. He worked in his father's drug store located across the street from the Regensburg Cigar Factory (now J. C. Newman), which gave him an interest in medicine.[30]

While growing up, Pacheco became interested in boxing for which Ybor City was a center. Boxing matches took place at the Circulo Cubano de Tampa. He also developed an early interest in art being introduced to the Ringling Museum of Art in Sarasota. He graduated from Tampa Jefferson High School, received a bachelor's degree from the University of Florida and obtained his medical degree from the University of Miami.[31]

## *A Physician and the Boxing World*

Following medical school, Dr. Pacheco opened a medical practice in the Overton community of Miami and continued to attend boxing matches. He came to be introduced to Angelo Dundee, the famous boxing promoter and trainer at the Miami Fifth Avenue Gym. Dundee offered him tickets to boxing matches if Pacheco would sew up his fighters' cuts. This initiated a long-term relationship with the trainer, his boxers, and all facets of the sport of boxing. Pacheco would travel to boxing events all over the world. At Dundee's gym, he met Cassius Clay, and he became the boxer's fight doctor and cornerman at ring side from 1962 to 1977.[32]

## *From Doctor to Commentator to Artist*

In September 1977, Dr. Pacheco advised Ali to retire from boxing due to the impact that the sport was having on his health. When his advice was not followed, he resigned from working with Ali who eventually retired in 1981. The two continued to remain friends as Pacheco moved on to become a boxing analyst and commentator covering matches in both English and Spanish. He retired from broadcasting in the late 1990s.[33]

Pacheco also authored books, plays, screenplays, and short stories. Among the most notable works are "Ybor City Chronicles" (a memoir), "Blood in My Coffee" (an autobiography), the "Columbia Restaurant Cookbook," coauthored with Adela Gonzmart, and two books featuring art.[34]

## *Pacheco, the Painter*

Pacheco's medical training and experience in boxing contributed greatly in his ability to adeptly portray human form in his paintings. According to Pacheco, he was influenced by such historical artists as Vincent Van Gogh, Norman Rockwell, Diego Rivera, and other Hispanic artists.

Pacheco described himself as a self-taught artist, developing his style and technique by duplicating works of painters he admired.[35] His paintings mimicked their use of color transitioning between realism, caricature, and the abstract, all of which were inspirational to him. His colorful portraits of famous people that he admired were particularly abstract.[36]

In Ybor, Pacheco is best known for the vividness of projecting its life and time through street scenes and community settings, which are featured in his book, *Art of Ybor City*. Published in 1997, the book is a must-have for those who love Ybor City, its cultural history, and heritage. Pacheco's depictions of life in Ybor document settings in cafes, inside and outside of factories, in restaurants, and in the streets at times of celebration. They depict life and community drama in simple everyday scenes from cooking and eating, to partying, to working in the cigar industry, to individual portraits.

Pacheco created the individual portraits in various styles including realism, caricature, and the abstract. He received numerous awards for his paintings and their use of color, and his art has been exhibited in galleries and museums throughout the world, especially in Europe and the US. Pacheco becomes more than an artist by documenting a unique cultural society and community far beyond the mere recitation of dates and events—he became an historian with the instrument of the brush.

In addition to Ferdie Pacheco, other Hispanic artists have reflected on Ybor City in their art, including painter Arnold Martinez (1931-2021) and wood sculptor Mario Sanchez (1908–2005).

## *Pacheco Tobacco Leaves*

Between 15th and 22nd Streets on 7th Avenue in Ybor City, there are 132 tobacco shaped leaves on the sidewalks that display excerpts from the book ***The Ybor City Chronicles*** written by Ferdie Pacheco. The book is autobiographical of his early life in Ybor City.

*Dr. Ferdie Pacheco's art books and memorabilia in the Ybor City Visitor Information Center.*

## SATURDAY MARKET

The Saturday Market occurs in Centennial Park every Saturday:
October thru April, 9am-3pm and May thru September, 9am-1pm
This community event is the largest and continually operating outdoor market in the Tampa area. It features an extensive variety of locally produced items for sale:

- Locally grown produce
- Locally prepared gourmet foods
- Arts and crafts booths present unique creations and allow for interaction with local artists
- Other products unique to Tampa and Hillsborough County
- SIDE NOTE: Don't mind the chickens, which are not for sale and may be distraught from being temporarily displaced from their park. They'll take to the streets surrounding the park to let their displeasure be known.

Centennial Park's Saturday Market, has as its mission to:
". . .stimulate entrepreneurial activity among local residents and create a venue for local artists, [artisans], and specialty product producers."[37]
*Website:* ybormarketonline.com

*Centennial Park on a Saturday Market day.*

## COLUMBIA RESTAURANT

An Ybor landmark, the Columbia Restaurant is a must-visit for lunch or dinner, its cultural and artistic surroundings express the heritage of Ybor City and its deeply Spanish influence.

## *Decor*

While the Columbia Restaurant's dining rooms take you back to the bygone era of early 20$^{th}$ century Ybor, its furnishings, including paintings, sculpture, tiled floors and walls, as well as its chandeliers, stained glass, and other antiques are a timeless representation of the heyday of the Cigar Capital of the World.

*El Patio Dining Room, Columbia Restaurant, Ybor City. Photo courtesy of the Columbia Restaurant.*

Five generations of the Hernandez-Gonzmart family have carefully made their mark on the premises located on historic 7$^{th}$ Avenue without impinging on what had gone before. On the Ybor section of the restaurant's website,

*The Front of the Columbia Restaurant on 7$^{th}$ Avenue.*

 one can experience virtually the ambiance of most of the eleven dining rooms which contributes to the understanding of the golden age in which the city thrived.[38]

The dining rooms have their own themes and design crafted to enhance the dining experience with global artifacts obtained throughout the family's history. There is the **Don Quixote Room** with its brilliant tiles creating a mural that recalls the Spanish classical novel by Miguel de Cervantes. Don Quixote de la Mancha represents the path that the restaurant's family has taken in challenging the decline of a historical community by envisioning a future even though it was uncertain. The literary-inspired design pulls the community along to remember a noble past which in subsequent decades of the 20$^{th}$ century largely lost its reason for being.

The murals of Don Quixote themed tiles tell the story of an insensible quest to restore the dignity and honor of the chivalric past in Spain, a clear parallel with the story of the restaurant and its dedication to a future which honors the past of Ybor City. This spectacular room opened in 1935 was the creation of Casimiro Hernandez Jr., of the family's second generation, on whose watch the Great Depression and its impact on the cigar industry was setting in. Into the Don Quixote room, he introduced music and dancing, initiating the entertainment element to the dining experience.[39]

The **Patio Room** is a breathtaking place to dine. From its skylight and mezzanine balconies overlooking the patio floor, every seating location is awe-inspiring. The soft natural lighting and airiness creates an uplifting ambiance that the glories of the past and hopefulness for the future become merged together in this timeless space. Cesar Gonzmart (from the third generation) is responsible for bringing this room to life in 1937.
The room features a statue of a human and a dolphin uncovered in the ruins of Pompeii which he had reproduced for the Columbia. In the days before air conditioning, the skylight would retract at night. The soft light, the airy open feel, and the gentle murmur of the fountain reassures the diner of the peace of the moment and the continuity of time.[40]

In 1956, the **Siboney Room** was added by Adela and Cesar Gonzmart which added to the entertainment experience. The Siboney Room would be renovated to provide space for entertaining from major Latin entertainers but came to provide the backdrop for the flamenco dancers that are the room's regular entertainment today. This artistic group brings alive the heritage of Spanish dancing of shoes hitting a wooden floor to the rhythm of castanets and Spanish dance music, further illustrating the Spanish heritage of this gem of restaurants. (Performed evenings Monday through Saturday.) The timeliness of the room's addition to dining through its art, paintings, stained glass, and tile contrast with the temporary loss of vision that the community experienced in the post-war decades.[41]

Each dining room has its unique scheme of decor, merging art, color, and design in dramatic ways that enhance the dining experience. Other noteworthy rooms include the more recent **Andalucía** and **Familia de Casimira**, created from the old kitchen when Richard and Casey Gonzmart built a state-of-the-art kitchen in 2001 to meet the needs of a restaurant approaching a seating capacity of 1700 in fifteen dining rooms. **La Fonda Dining Room** with its decorative cigar bar and the **King's Room** are also distinctive in their color, tiles, art, antiques, and paintings.[42]

## *Exterior Spanish Tiles*

All the superlatives used to describe the Columbia—the oldest restaurant in Florida, the largest Spanish restaurant in the country, one of the highest awarded eating places in the US—cannot discount the brilliance of its exterior tile. The tiles not only adorn the four entrances to the block-long establishment but also cover the exterior walls shaded by an Italianesque sheltered loggia surrounding three sides of the building. The tile was installed under the stewardship of Cesar and Adela Gonzmart (of the family's third generation) with the first hand-painted tiles affixed in 1973. Moved by a trip to Seville where they discovered local hand decorated tiles, Cesar and Adela contracted for tile to be designed, imported, shipped, and installed for most of the exterior in 1978. Tiles inside and on the exterior of the restaurant also display settings, which can be categorized as murals including the scenes of Don Quixote in the dining room of that name.[43]

*A front tiled entrance of the Columbia Restaurant.*

## VINTAGE SHOPPING

There are plenty of vintage shopping experiences for Ybor City visitors. Read on to learn which stores might be of interest during your tour.

### *Agora,* 1517 E. 7th Ave.

*Merchandise:* Agora is an established Ybor City home decor and gift shop. Its products are marked by an Old World flavor including Asia and the Middle East, fitting right in with the multiethnic flavor of Ybor. The store has a wide range of fabric products, jewelry, furnishings, crystals from around the world, candles, cultural lamps and lighting, mobiles, figurines, beaded products, and stuffed animals. These products represent many cultures and include many one-of-a-kind items. It also sells sweets and ice cream.
*Hours:* Daily, 12pm-8pm;
*Phone:* (305) 609-5650
*Website*: https://www.facebook.com/yboragora/

### *La France,* 1612 E. 7th Ave.

*Merchandise:* This business has been a presence in Ybor City since 1974, and provides vintage classical and retro clothing for men and women including hats, shoes, and other accessories. The store presents styling for everyday wear, and for special occasions with a wide range of price and sizes. Check out the store windows just east of Vincente Ybor's bronze statue in Centro Ybor.
*Hours:* Daily, 12pm-7pm
*Phone:* (813) 248-1381
*Website:* https://www.facebook.com/lafranceybor/

### *Ybor City Chamber of Commerce Visitor Information Gift Shop,* 1600 E. 8th Ave., Suite B104

*Merchandise:* One-of-a-kind souvenirs, a large selection of books on Ybor City including cookbooks, a large assortment of T-shirts, magnets, decals, mugs, vintage cigar labels (framed and unframed), and resources for guided tours.
*Hours:* Mon-Sat: 10am-4pm; Sun: 12pm-4pm
*Phone:* (813) 241-8838
*Website:* https://www.ybor.org/vic, https://www.facebook.com/YborVisitorInformation/



### *Columbia Restaurant Gift Shop,* 2103 E. 7th Ave., at the corner of 21st St.

*Merchandise:* The restaurant gift shop provides cookbooks of its signature dishes as well as food and cooking products used by the restaurant. It sells gift baskets in various arrangements that feature its popular items. The gift shop

also has an assortment of Spanish pottery and sells cigars. And gift cards are also available along with some items being available online.
*Hours:* Sun: 11am-6pm; Mon-Sat: 11am-8pm
*Phone:* (813) 247-2469
*Website:* https://shop.columbiarestaurant.com/

*Entrance to the Columbia Gift Shop on 7th Avenue.*

### *Vintage Roost,* 2326 E. 7th Ave.

*Merchandise:* The Roost is a three-day, twice-a-month market utilizing five thousand square feet. The market features creations of numerous vendors, which tend to be one-of-a-kind works including remodeled furniture, handmade items including clocks and glassware, abstract art, and repurposed clothing. The vintage items complement many environments from the outdoors to country decor, to a Bohemian pad or an upscale avant-garde interior.
*Hours:* 2nd and 4th weekends, Fri-Sun, 9am-5pm
*Phone:* (813) 304-2134
*Website:* https://www.globuya.com/US/Tampa/Vintage-Roost
https://www.facebook.com/vintageroostybor/

### ***Stained Market*, 2106 E. 15th Ave.**

*Merchandise*: A warehouse marketplace with a broad selection of collectible items described as modern, vintage, and antique in nature. The market supports local artists for their unique goods and creations offered at affordable prices. New items are added seasonally.
*Hours*: Mon-Wed, 11am-4pm; Thu, 11am-3pm; Fri, 11am-4pm; Sat-Sun, 10am-4pm
*Phone*: (813) 501-3238
*Website:* www.eventseeker.com

### ***Indie Flea Market***

*Location and Dates*: The Cuban Club, 2010 Avenida Republica de Cuba, indoor and outdoor. First Sundays of the month December 2024 – November 2025.
*Merchandise*: showcases a wide range of selected vendor products featuring handcrafted goods, handmade items, jewelry, hand crafts, gifts, vintage housewares, décor, vintage clothing, mid-century furniture, collectibles, food, music, and art. Food and drink served in the covered atrium.
*Hours*: 12pm to 4pm, Open to the public.
*Email*: info@theindiflea.com
*Website*: http://theindieflea.com/ybor-indie-flea-info

## SPECIAL MONTHLY EVENTS

Every month throughout the year special events occur in the Ybor City community to which the public is encouraged to participate. These events can be accessed through the Ybor City Chamber of Commerce website: https://www.ybor.org

## *Endnotes Section 15*

1 Joe Howden (aka Joe King Carter), artist, historian, and civic leader, provided the Introduction to this Arts and Culture section, June 2021.

2 Joe Harless, "The Rooster Funeral, Giving Ybor Something to Crow About," *Cigar City Magazine*, November-December 2008, paraphrased in the Ybor City Chamber of Commerce Visitor Information Center exhibit display entitled "What's the Deal with the Roosters?"

3 Joe Howden (aka Joe King Carter), artist, historian and civic leader provided this update on the diorama mural to the Ybor Guide, October 2025.

4 "An American Journey: The Legacy of Ybor City and Tampa," The Ybor Art Project, accessed February 2022, http://www.yborartproject.com/.

5 "An American Journey," The Ybor Art Project, http://www.yborartproject.com/.

6 "Our History," Columbia Restaurant, accessed February 2022, https://www.columbiarestaurant.com/The-Columbia-Experience/History.

7 Paul Guzzo, "Tampa Mural Honors 5,000 Women Who Protested Fascism in 1937," Tampa Bay Times, updated April 5, 2023, https://www.tampabay.com/lifeculture/history/2023/03/31/fascismybor-citywomwomens-history-monthspanishcivil-wardolores-ibrrurifrancisco-franco/.

8 James W. Covington, "The Rough Riders in Tampa," Sunland Tribune , vol. 3, article 2 (1977), available at Digital Commons @ University of South Florida, accessed June 2023, https://digitalcommons.usf.edu/cgi/viewcontent.cgi?article=1018&context=sunlandtribune; Plaque adjacent to The Charge of the Yellow Rice Brigade mural, Roosevelt Reading Room and Library, Hotel Haya.

9 Jay Giroux and Edgar Sanchez Cumbas, Living Shades, 2021, mural, east side of the Hillsborough College, Ybor Campus, https://www.hccfl.edu/campuslife/arts/hcc-art-galleries/grounds4art/past-grounds4art-projects, accessed August2023.

10 Trinity Rivard, Generations, 2023, mural, between the Ybor Building and Faculty Building of the Hillsborough College, Ybor Campus, accessed August 2023, https://www.hccfledu/campus-life/arts/arts/galeries-hcc/grounds4art.

11 "Roland Manteiga," *La Gaceta Newspaper*, accessed February 2022, http://lagacetanewspaper.com/our-history/roland-manteiga/.

12 "Nick Nuccio," Wikipedia, last edited December 25, 2021, CC BY-SA3.0, https://en.wikipedia.org/wiki/Nick_Nuccio; Frank T. Lastra, *Ybor City: The Making of a Landmark Town* (Tampa, FL: The University of Tampa Press, 2006), 208.

13 Lastra, Ybor City, *The Making of a Landmark Town*, 307-309; "Tony Pizzo," Wikipedia, last modified January 26,2022, CC BY-SA3.0, https://en.wikipedia.org/wiki/Tony_Pizzo.

14"Immigrant Statue – Ybor City, Tampa, Florida, U.S.A.," Waymarking, accessed February 2022, https://www.waymarking.com/waymarks/WMQ06Y_Immigrant_Statue_Ybor_City_Tampa_Florida_USA

15 Philip Morgan, "Sculptor Steve Dickey adds to Tampa

Bay's Bronze Citizenry," *Tampa Bay Times*, June 16, 2012, https://www.tampabay.com/news/humaninterest/sculptor-steve-dickey-adds-to-tampa-bays-bronze-citizenry/1235549/.

16 Philip Morgan, "Sculptor Steve Dickey," *Tampa Bay Times*, June 16, 2012.

17 "Lost Wax Process," Dickey Studios, access February 2022, http://dickeystudios.com/index.htm.

18 "911 Fallen Heroes Memorial" (titled "Fearless Champions"), Ybor City, Florida, USA, Waymarking, accessed February 2022, https://www.waymarking.com/waymarks/WMQ0F5_9_11_Fallen_Heroes_Memorial_Ybor_City_Florida_USA; Yoselis Ramos, News report (September 11, 2014), WUSF Public Media News.

19 "The Cuban Club," History, accessed February 2022, http://cubanclubybor.com/history/.

20 "El Centro Español de Tampa," History/Architecture, accessed February 2022, last edited October 13, 2021, https://en.wikipedia.org/wiki/El_Centro_Espa%C3%B1ol_de_Tampa.

21 Joanna Lucarino, "L'Union Italiana," *La Gazzetta Italiana*, June 2020 issue, https://www.lagazzettaitaliana.com/history-culture/9447-1-unione-italiana.

22 E. J. Salcines, "L'Union Italiana History," article in the Italian Club website commemorating the Centennial of the Italian Club Building, April 2018, accessed February 2022, https://italian-club.org/.

23 E. J. Salcines, "La Union Italiana History," https://www.italian-club.org/

24 Paul Guzzo, "Tampa's German Club, once a Symbol of Exclusion, Now Symbolizes Inclusion," *Tampa Bay Times*, April 10, 2019, https://www.tampabay.com/hillsborough/tampas-german-club-once-a-symbol-of-exclusion-now-symbolizes-inclusion-20190411/; Reyes, *Cigar City Architecture and Legacy*, 349.

25 Joe Howden (aka Joe King Carter), interview at his residence by author, June 2021.

26 "El Pasaje – Tampa, FL," Waymarking, accessed February 2022, https://www.waymarking.com/waymarks/WM6ZTB_el_Pasaje_Tampa_FL.

27 Steve Rajtar, *A Guide to Historic Tampa Florida* (Charleston, SC: The History Press, 2007), 175.

28 "Malachi Leo Elliott Biography," Wikipedia, last edited December 5, 2021, CC BY-SA3.0, https://en.wikipedia.org/wiki/Malachi_Leo_Elliott.

29 Ybor City Museum Casita Tours, Information provided by Ybor City Museum Florida State Park Employee Tour Guides, Casita tour April 2016. Wallace Reyes, *Cigar City* Architecture and Legacy (Coppell, TX: CreateSpace Independent Publishing Platform, 2015), 297-298.

30 Fernando Pacheco, *Pacheco's Art of Ybor City* (Gainesville, FL: University Press of Florida, 1997), xv.

31 Pacheco, *Pacheco's Art of Ybor City*, xv.

32 Pacheco, *Pacheco's Art of Ybor City*, xviii

33 Pacheco, *Pacheco's Art of Ybor City*, xviii.

34 Pacheco, *Pacheco's Art of Ybor City*, xix.

35 Pacheco, *Pacheco's Art of Ybor City*, xv-xvii, xix.

36 Pacheco, *Pacheco's Art of Ybor City*, xv-xvii, xix.

37 "Shop, Eat, and Explore Safely," Ybor City Saturday Market, accessed March 2022, https://ybormarket.com/.

38 "Our History," Columbia Restaurant, accessed February 2022, https://www.columbiarestaurant.com/The-Columbia-Experience/History; "Ybor City Historic District Location Details," Columbia Restaurant, accessed February 2022, https://www.columbiarestaurant.com/Menus-By-Location/Locations/Ybor-City-Historic-District.

39 "Our History," Columbia Restaurant; "Ybor City Location Details," Columbia Restaurant, www.columbiarestaurant.com.

40 "Our History," Columbia Restaurant; "Ybor City Location Details," Columbia Restaurant, www.columbiarestaurant.com.

41 "Our History," Columbia Restaurant; "Ybor City Location Details," Columbia Restaurant, www.columbiarestaurant.com.

42 "Our History," Columbia Restaurant; "Ybor City Location Details," Columbia Restaurant, www.columbiarestaurant.com.

43 "Our History," Columbia Restaurant; www.columbiarestaurant.com.

# 16

# SELECTED HISTORICAL MARKERS (34)

**(Grouped by subject)**

## VICENTE MARTINEZ YBOR AND THE CIGAR INDUSTRY

1. Historic Emilio Pons Cigar Factory
   On N. 17th St., north of E. 5th Ave.
2. Founding of the Cigar Industry in Tampa
   In front of Vicente Martinez Ybor's Cigar Factory, N. Avenida Republica de Cuba (14th Street) and E. 9th Ave.
3. Vicente Martinez Ybor statue and bronze plaque
   In Centro Ybor, north side of 7th Ave. near 16th Ave.
4. The Birth of Ybor City
   On N. 15th St. just north of E. 7th Ave.
5. Ybor City Historic District
   E. 7th Ave., east of Nuccio Pkwy, left side of entry archway into Ybor City traveling east.
6. Cherokee Club and El Pasaje
   On 9th Ave. at the corner of Avenida Republica de Cuba (14th St.) in front of the building.
7. La Quinta, Ybor's Home, Out in the Country
   North side of E. 12th Ave. at N. 17th St.
8. Tampa's First Cigar Factory
   South side of E. 7th Ave. and N. 15th St.

## MUTUAL AID SOCIETIES, CULTURAL CLUBS

9. Centro Español de Tampa
   On E. 7th Ave. in front of building at N. 16th St.
10. Sociedad La Union Martí-Maceo
    North side of 7th Ave. between 13th St. & Nuccio Pkwy in front of the building, 1226 E. 7th Ave.
11. El Centro Asturiano de Tampa
    At 1913 N. Nebraska Ave. at E. Palm Ave. in front of club building. This location is not on the map.
12. German-American Club
    At 2105 N. Nebraska Ave. on the corner of E. 11th Ave. in front of club building. This location is not on the map.

13. El Circulo Cubano
    On the south side of Palm Ave. near its intersection with N. Avenida Republica de Cuba (14th St.).
14. L'Unione Italiana
    In front of the Italian Club at 1731 E. 7th Ave. near the corner of Angel Oliva Senior St. (18th St.).
15. Italian Club Life in Tampa
    Across the street from the Italian Club on the north side of 7th Ave. near the corner of Angel Oliva Senior St. (18th St.).
16. The Coming of the Italians
    E. 7th Ave. near N. 21st St., north side of 7th Ave.
17. The Krewe of the Knights of Sant' Yago
    On E. 7th Ave., south side, west of N. 22nd St., midblock in front of the Columbia Restaurant.
18. The Birth of Mutual Aide Societies in America
    Centro Ybor, 8th Ave., south side, E. of Centro Español.

## JOSÉ MARTÍ AND THE INDEPENDENCE MOVEMENT

19. Attempt on the Life of José Martí
    In front of the Cuban Club, near the corner of 9th Ave. and Avenida Republica de Cuba (14th St.).
20. José Martí granite marker (in Spanish)
    In front of Ybor's Cigar Factory entrance on 14th St.
21. Cradle of Cuban Liberty
    E. 7th Ave. near N. 14th St.
22. José Martí – Apostle of Cuban Freedom
    Plaque at the base of the Martí statue in Martí Park at E. 8th Ave. and N. 13th St.
23. Antonio Maceo Grajalas
    Bust and Plaque in Martí Park at E. 8th Ave. and N. 13th St.
24. La Casa de Pedroso
    Just inside the entrance to the Martí Park at E. 8th Ave. and N. 13th St.

## YBOR CITY MUSEUM AND CENTENNIAL PARK

25. La Joven Francesca Bakery
    In front of the Ybor City Museum at 1818 E. 9th Ave. across the street from Centennial Park.
26. Immigrant Statue
    Bronze statue in Centennial Park facing E. 9th Ave. between 18 and 19th Streets across from the Ybor City Museum.

27. Mayor Nick C. Nuccio
    Bronze statue and plaque located in Centennial Park facing E. 8th Ave. between Angel Oliva Senior St. (18th Street) and 19th St.
28. Anthony "Tony" P. Pizzo, 1912–1994
    Bronze statue in Centennial Park facing E. 8th Ave. near Angel Oliva Senior St. (18th St.).
29. Anthony P. Pizzo, 1912–1994
    Marker on East 8th Ave. at the corner of N. 18th St.

## MISCELLANEOUS HISTORIC MARKERS

30. Columbia Restaurant Founded 1905
    In front of the building at 2117 E. 7th Ave.
31. Rough Riders – Granite Marker and Plaque
    At E. 7th Ave. in Rough Riders Park, south side of 7th Ave. and east of Nuccio Parkway.
    Top metal plate: "You triumphed Over Obstacles Which Would Have Overcome Men Less Brave and Determined." President McKinley / Plaque displays image of a "Hiker" as the Rough Riders were called.
    Rear Face: This memorial monument honors President Theodore Roosevelt and members of the 1st US Volunteer Cavalry Regiment, known as the "Rough Riders." The City of Tampa was selected as the assembly and embarkation site of the US military in the 1898 Spanish-American War. The bronze plaque honors all the Spanish-American War veterans.
32. Site of First Ybor City Railroad Station 1887
    N. 16th St. just north of E. 6th Ave. on the north side of the railroad tracks.
33. The Rough Riders Rode by Here
    On E. 7th Ave., west of N. 22nd St. in front of Columbia Restaurant.
34. Roland M. Manteiga
    Bronze statue and plaque in Centro Ybor at E. 7th Ave. near N. 16th St.

NOTE: From time to time markers may be removed for replacement or refurbishment or due to construction.

To read the actual marker online, go to https://www.hmdb/search.asp?SearchFor=Marker/. Scroll to Keyword Search or Title Search or Search for Person and input the relevant information.
https://www.hmdb/search.asp?SearchFor=marker/

# MAP OF HISTORIC MARKERS WEST AND EAST

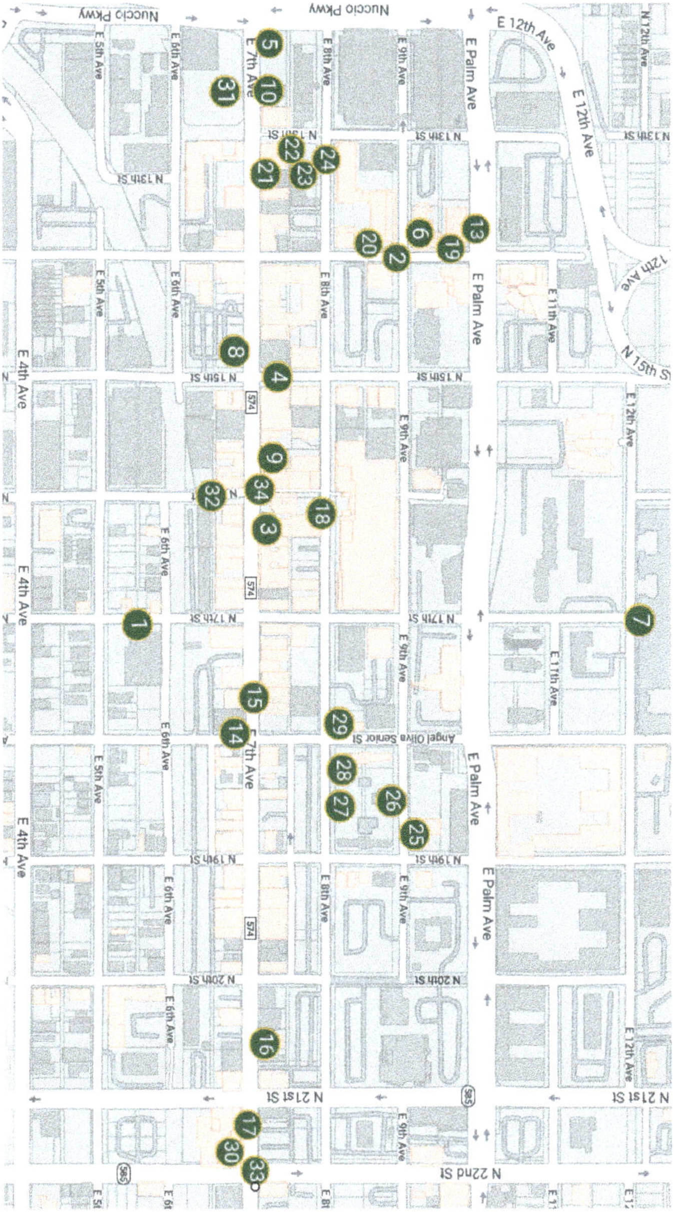

*Map data ©2023 Google/Maptive*

| WORD | EXPLANATION |
|---|---|
| 14th Street | Also known as Avenida de Cuba |
| 18th Street | Also known as Angel Oliva Senior Street |
| Afro Cubans | Black residents of Cuba who were brought to Cuba as slaves beginning in the 16th century and who began to be granted freedom with the end of the Ten Years' War in 1878. |
| Asturians | Spanish immigrants that came from the province of Asturias in northern Spain. |
| binder | Tobacco leaves that are wrapped around the core tobacco leaf bunch filler. |
| blender | A cigar worker who creates the blend of various tobaccos used in a brand of cigars. |
| bolita | Spanish term for "little ball"—a lottery form of gambling popular in Ybor City in which 100 numbered balls are placed in a bag and bets are made on which number will be drawn. |
| buckeye | Small storefront shop in Ybor City typically having the store on the first floor with living quarters and a balcony of the second floor with a wrought iron railing, adopted from New Orleans. |
| buncher | The cigar worker that creates the long filler bunch and rolls it in a binder to hold the bunch together. The bunch is then placed in a mold. |
| café con leche | A coffee beverage originating in Spain consisting of strong coffee, usually espresso, and heated milk in roughly equal amounts. |
| casita | The shotgun homes that Vicente Martinez Ybor and other factory owners built for the cigar workers. |
| cigars | See cigar terminology at the end of Section 7. |
| cigar box art | Cigar box art refers to the colorful artwork created over the decades, which identified the various cigar brands and the maker. |
| Cigar Capital of the World | From the mid 1890s to the early 1930s, the cigar production in Ybor City of more than 100 million high quality cigars annually earned it this moniker. |

| | |
|---|---|
| Cigar City | The name applied to Ybor City and to Tampa in the first decade of the 20th century as it was the largest business in town. |
| cigar workers' payroll deduction | While money was being raised for the Cuban independence movement, cigar workers had deductions from their pay amounting to one day's work per month. It was referred to as "one day for the homeland," or "el diapa la patria." |
| company town | The industrial arrangement whereby a town could be owned and run by one company that prohibited union activity. Ybor City was not a company town in that Vicente Martinez Ybor invited all his competitors to come to Ybor City. |
| craft brewery | Vicente Martinez Ybor and his son began the first brewery in Ybor to supply the needs for the residents of Ybor City, and that tradition lives on today. |
| Cuban bread | A white bread containing no preservatives, developed in Ybor City. It is made into 3-foot loaves which are rectangular in shape and can include three different kinds of flour. It has a hard thin crust, and a moistened palmetto frond is placed on top of the loaves before baking. It is the essential ingredient in a Cuban sandwich. |
| Cuban sandwich | A sandwich designed in Ybor City, which was contributed to by the different cultural and ethnic groups working in the cigar industry with ingredients that are Spanish, Cuban, Italian, and German. |
| deviled crab or devil crab | Is a crab meat croquette which was developed in the Spanish, Cuban, and Italian communities of Ybor City, consisting of crab meat and sautéed ingredients in a seasoning sauce, then rolled in breadcrumbs in the shape of small potato and deep fried until brown. Meant to be eaten by hand. |
| Era of Blood | The period between 1925 and 1959 when there were turf wars in Tampa between Mafia factions in which over 20 individuals involved in Mafia leadership were hit among many others. |
| filler | Long leaves of tobacco (long fillers) or scraps of long filler tobacco (short fillers) which comprise the core of the cigar. |
| Fourth Ward | At the time of its annexation by Tampa in 1887, Ybor City was also known as Tampa's fourth ward. |

| | |
|---|---|
| *La Gaceta* | A weekly newspaper found in 1922 in Tampa, Florida and the only trilingual newspaper in the US. Founded by Victoriano Manteiga, it was headed currently by his son, Roland, and now by the grandson, Patrick. Its famous "As We Heard It" column focused on immigrant issues that were political, social, economic, and individual rights in nature. |
| Golden Age of Ybor | For Ybor City, the Golden Age was from the late 1890s to the mid 1930s, before the effects of the Great Depression. |
| Gonzmart, Cesar | Cesar was the third generation family leader of the Columbia Restaurant. A talented musician, Cesar (and his wife Adela) brought entertainment into the Columbia Restaurant at the same time expanding its operations during a period of Ybor City decline. They were visionaries for the revival of Ybor City. |
| guava | An edible tropical fruit grown in the tropics especially the Caribbean and Central America but also in Florida. It is yellow or light green in color with a deep read or vibrant pink interior with a peachlike consistency. Used in Cuban pastries and found in jams, jellies, and marmalades. |
| Gutierrez, Gavino (1849–1919) | A friend of Vicente Martinez Ybor when Ybor had a cigar factory in New York. After visiting the Tampa area, he met with Ybor and Ignacio Haya in Key West on his return to New York and persuaded them to look at Tampa as a location to develop for their cigar business. Ybor asked Gutierrez, a civil engineer, to survey and lay out the Ybor City community, northeast of Tampa. |
| Havana Clear | The type of tobacco prized by Vicente Martinez Ybor and heavily imported to Tampa prior to the embargo was this light-colored leaf tobacco. |
| Haya, Ignacio (1842-1906) | Vicente Martinez Ybor and Ignacio Haya purchased the first property in Tampa for the purpose of bringing their cigar production to Ybor City. Mr. Haya scouted out the region with Mr. Ybor, and Haya is credited with producing the first factory cigar. |
| immigrate/ emigrate | To immigrate is to settle in a new country, to emigrate is to leave the country of origin. Immigrating refers to arrive or immigrate to America. Emigrating refers to leave or emigrate from Spain. |

| | |
|---|---|
| J. C. Newman Cigar Factory | The last remaining cigar factory in the United States located on 16th Street and E. Columbus Drive. |
| Jim Crow laws | Laws in the US requiring separation of the races, which compelled the Afro Cuban community to create its own community center. |
| Krewes | Organizations formed by the various community centers to recognize, promote, and celebrate the cultural heritage of their center. They participate in parades, cultural events, and celebrations. |
| Lector | Factory readers who read to the cigar workers as they hand rolled cigars. Highly educated, usually from Spain, and paid by the workers. |
| Little Havana | A reference made to Ybor City by the Anglo population of Tampa when immigrants from Cuban and Key West began to arrive. |
| Little Italy | The eastern and southern neighborhoods of Ybor City where a majority of immigrants of Italian descent lived. |
| Lopez, Al (1908–2005) | A Tampa-born American professional baseball catcher, manager of Spanish ancestry, and member of the Baseball Hall of Fame. His home was moved into the historic district of Ybor City to serve as the Tampa Baseball Museum which opened in 2021. |
| Martí, José (1853–1885) | The revolutionary leader who made more than 20 visits to Tampa in the 1890s to raise money and awareness for the independence of Cuba from Spain. He was a great contributor to poetry and political thought, and he unified Latin America in supporting Cuban independence. He was killed in action in 1895 shortly after invasion forces landed in Cuba in the 1895 War of Cuban Independence. |
| mechanization | Cigar machines were introduced in the 1920s, and their use increased as a result of the Great Depression. They added a new element to production in hopes of making cigars cheaper, less labor intensive for consumer purchase, but the quality of the cigar lost some of its artistry. |
| mutual aid society | Community support center which six of the cultural groups formed. They were a place for social gatherings and provided medical (cradle-to-grave) services and assisted new arrivals. Members paid a monthly fee to join and enjoy the benefits. The centers also provided education, recreation, and cultural activities and included eating facilities frequently referred to as cantinas. |

| | |
|---|---|
| Nuccio, Nick (1901–1989) | The first Latin mayor of Tampa serving two terms in the 1950s and 1960s. He was raised by Italian immigrant parents in Ybor City. Known for his public works projects to develop Tampa neighborhoods. |
| organized crime | Ybor City and Tampa were centers of organized crime from the 1920s extending into the 21st century. Illegal activities involved bribery, extortion, bootlegging, prostitution, gambling and other illegal activities which also infiltrated the operation of local government. |
| El Pasaje | The building known as *El Pasaje* (pah-sah-hey) means the "passageway" and was Vicente Martinez Ybor's office complex located next to his factory. It was later used as a men's club, restaurant, clinic, hotel, and recruitment center. |
| patrone | Factory owners. |
| Plant, Henry (1819–1899) | The industrialist who extended the railroad from Sanford to Tampa and built a large luxury hotel envisioning the future of the struggling little town of Tampa. |
| Prince of Wales | Vicente Martinez Ybor's most well-known brand of cigars (El Principe de Gales). |
| regentrification | After failures to redevelop Ybor, regentrification began in the 1980s as artists moved in and created an art colony followed by bars, night clubs, and entertainment in which many old buildings were renovated. Since then, more businesses and residents have moved in as well as restaurants. |
| roller | The work of a buncher who assembles the filler tobacco and rolls it in a binder leaf is passed on to the roller who applies the outside wrapper to the cigar and applies the cap to the cigar. |
| Roosters | According to historian Wallace Reyes, the Roosters were brought to America by the Spanish arriving in Cuba in the late 1400s. From there cigar workers brought them to Key West, then to Tampa. In the days before refrigeration, they were an important food source for the early settlers. When Ybor went into decline, the chickens stayed and became feral. They are protected by law. |

| | |
|---|---|
| Rough Riders | The nickname given to the US voluntary cavalry which was engaged in action in Cuba under the leadership of Theodore Roosevelt in the Spanish-American War; they participated in the famous charge up San Juan Hill in 1898. |
| Santo Stefano Quisquina | The town in Sicily from which many of the Italian immigrants came. |
| La Segunda | The historic Bakery of Ybor City has been run by the same family since it's founding in 1915. The Bakery makes its legendary Cuban for Tampa and beyond and is noted for its many Cuban delicacies.. |
| Setima/ Septima | 7$^{th}$ Ave, the main street in Ybor City, also referred to as "Broadway." Septima is the formal Spanish spelling. The Ybor colloquial expression, the result of various immigrant groups, led to its pronunciation without the "p" sound and the spelling Setima. |
| Spanish-American War | The US intervention into the Cuban War of Independence occurred when the battleship USS Maine sent by the US to protect its interests was blown up in Havana harbor. Tampa became the staging point for troops to be sent to Cuba who were called the Rough Riders and led by Theodore Roosevelt. |
| streetcar | The original streetcar developed by Vicente Martinez Ybor for use between Ybor City and Tampa bears a resemblance to the one used today. While his streetcar was pulled by a locomotive, both the old and new reside on a rail car chassis. |
| strippers | Cigar workers responsible for removing the stem that runs down the middle of the tobacco leaf and which is not usable in the making of cigars. They use cutters or a machine to cut the stem on each side in order to remove it. |
| tabaquero | Cigar worker. |
| Ten Years' War | The name designated to identify the first War of Cuban Independence. It began in the year 1868 and continued until 1878 and accomplished little in the way of allowing Cubans to become more involved in their government. Spanish colonial rule continued. |
| torcedore | Cigar workers who rolled the finished cigar product. |

| | |
|---|---|
| urban renewal | With many abandoned buildings in Ybor City with the decline of the cigar industry, urban renewal became the reason for tearing down large sections of Ybor City and the creation of two expressways that ran east and west through Ybor City, Interstate 4 and the Selmon Expressway. |
| War of Cuban Independence | The third and final attempt to overthrow the Spanish control of Cuba took place from 1895 to 1898 at which time the US intervened and the conflict is referred to as the Spanish-American War. |
| wrapper | Tobacco leaves that are the most pristine and blemish free are wrapped/rolled around the filler and binder blend of tobacco. |
| Ybor Avenues | Run east and west. |
| Ybor Streets | Run north and south. |

Allen, Esther, ed./trans. *José Martí: Selected Writings*. New York: Penguin Books, 2002.

Barbie, Rose Tambuzzo and Rosalie Guarino Simms. *Ybor City . . . a quick peek into its history*. Tampa, FL: Printed by the authors, 2014.

Cinchett, John V. Vintage *Tampa Signs and Scenes*. Images of America series. Charleston, SC: Arcadia Publishing, 2009.

Cinchett, John V. Vintage *Tampa Storefronts and Scenes*. Images of America series. Charleston, SC: Arcadia Publishing, 2012.

Deitche, Scott M. *Cigar City Mafia: A Complete History of the Tampa Underworld*. Fort Lee, NJ: Barricade Books, 2005.

De Quesada, A. M. *Ybor City*. Images of America series. Charleston, SC: Arcadia Publishing, 1999.

Dunn, John M. *José Martí: Cuba's Greatest Hero*. Sarasota, FL: Pineapple Press, 2015.

Gannon, Michael, ed. *The History of Florida*. Gainesville: University Press of Florida, 2013.

Huse, Andrew T. *The Cuban Sandwich: A History in Layers*. Gainesville: University Press of Florida, 2022.

Ingalls, Robert P. and Louis A. Perez, Jr. *Tampa Cigar Workers*. Gainesville: University Press of Florida, 2003.

Kaiser, Robert J. *Tampa: The Early Years*. Images of America series. Charleston, SC: Arcadia Publishing, 2014.

Lastra, Frank T. *Ybor City: The Making of a Landmark Town*. Tampa: University of Tampa Press, 2006.

Lopez, Alfred J. *José Martí, A Revolutionary Life*. Austin: University of Texas Press, 2014.

Mormino, Gary R. and George E. Pozzetta. *The Immigrant World of Ybor City: Italians and Their Latin Neighbors in Tampa,* 1885-1985. Gainesville: University of Florida Press, 2017.

Norman, Robert and Lisa Coleman. *Tampa*. Images of America series. Charleston, SC: Arcadia Publishing, 2001.

Odom, Ersula Knox. *African Americans of Tampa*. Images of America series. Charleston, SC: Arcadia Publishing, 2014.

Norman, Rob and Marcia Jo Zerivitz. *Jews of Tampa*. Images of America series. Charleston, SC: Arcadia Publishing, 2013.

Pacheco, Ferdie. *Blood in My Coffee: The Life of the Fight Doctor*. New York: Sports Publishing, 2012.

Pacheco, Ferdie. *Pacheco's Art of Ybor City*. Gainesville, FL: University Press of Florida, 1997.

Rajtar, Steve. *A Guide to Historic Tampa Florida*. Charleston, SC: History Press, 2007.

Reyes, Wallace, PhD. *Once Upon a Time in Tampa: The Rise and Fall of the Cigar Industry*. Scotts Valley, CA: Create Space Publishing Platform, 2013.

Reyes, Wallace. *Cigar City Architecture and Legacy*. Coppell, TX: CreateSpace Independent Publishing Platform, 2015.

Ripoll, Carolos, ed. José Martí, *Thoughts/Pensamientos: A Bilingual Anthology.* New York: Eliseo Torres & Sons – Las Américas Publishing, 1980.

Sterngass, Jon. *José Martí*. New York: Chelsea House / Infobase Publishing, 2007.

Tinajero, Araceli. *El Lector: A History of the Cigar Factory Reader*. Austin: University Press of Texas, 2010.

U.S. National Archives, *Records of Immigration and Naturalization Services, 1891-1957: Immigration Records, Passenger Arrival Records by Port of Entry.* https://www.archives.gov/research/immigration/ports/.

The Gjenvick-Gjonvik Immigration Archives. U.S. Immigration through Primary and Other Sources, Immigrant Passage Archives 1880s-1920, Immigrant Passenger Information By Port of Call, By Region, By Port of Entry, By Year. https://www.gjenvick.com/Immigration/index.html.

Westfall, L. Glenn. *Don Vicente Martinez Ybor: The Man and His Empire*. New York: Garland Publishing Inc., 1987.

# INDEX

INDEX

INDEX

## MAP OF WEST SIDE OF YBOR HISTORIC DISTRICT (NUCCIO PARKWAY TO 17TH STREET)

E Palm Ave
E Palm Ave
HCC Ybor City Child Development Center
The Castle
Hillsborough Community College Public Service...
N 15th St
E 9th Ave
E 9th Ave
Tampa Bay Brewing Company
GameTime Tampa
Centro Ybor Station (#2)
E 8th Ave
Cider & Mead
Barterhouse Ybor
Funny Bone Comedy Club
The Florida Museum of Photographic Arts
Exhibit of historic & contemporary works
New York New York Pizza
Pizza · $
La France
Vintage clothing store
King Corona Cigars Bar And Cafe
Cigar shop
N 17th St
E 7th Ave
Showbar Ybor
The Ritz Ybor
N 16th St
Club Prana
Relevant Church
E 6th Ave
E 6th Ave
Centro Ybor Garage
Jimmy's Tacos
Tacos · $
PMS Parking Lot
ChargePoint Charging Station
E 5th Ave
E 5th Ave
El Puerto Restaurant & Grill
Latin American · $$

## MAP OF EAST SIDE OF YBOR HISTORIC DISTRICT (17TH STREET TO 23RD STREET)

E Palm Ave
E Palm Ave
E 10th Ave
Chateau Cellars
Wine store
Entrepreneur
Collaborative Center
Rosenheim
Middle Eastern
N 20th St
N 21st St
E 9th Ave
585
Hillsborough County
Sheriff's Office (HCSO)
FedEx Drop Box
9/11 Fallen
Heroes Memorial
E 8th Ave
E 8th Ave
717 Parking L44
Valley Bank
Shrimp & Co.
Seafood · $$
Southern · $$
E 7th Ave
Columbia
Centennial Museum
Columbia
Spanish · $$$
N 20th St
Casa Santo Stefano
AnswerFirst
585
Fairy Hair by
Nataly India
Fashion accessories store
N 21st St
E 5th Ave
Cohen Violins
Violin shop
Gasparilla Distillery
& Cocktail Bar

WAS THIS GUIDE HELPFUL?

If this book was helpful to you in learning about Ybor City, its history, background, culture, and what to see and do while you are there, please consider going on line to leave a short sentence or two review of this guide so that the word may go out about this gem of a national historic landmark district.

Go to the Amazon site, input the title under "Search" (Ybor City Pocket Guide) to be taken to the book's paperback and ebook page.

www.ingramcontent.com/pod-product-compliance
Lightning Source LLC
Chambersburg PA
CBHW051145120626
46547CB00012B/950

* 9 7 9 8 9 8 6 7 1 3 2 4 3 *